D1507740

Leadership Change and Work-Group Dynamics

An Experiment

Leadership Change and Work-Group Dynamics

An Experiment

BY NED A. ROSEN

NEW YORK STATE SCHOOL OF
INDUSTRIAL AND LABOR RELATIONS
CORNELL UNIVERSITY

Cornell University Press

ITHACA, NEW YORK

189050

First published 1969

Library of Congress Catalog Card Number: 69–11690

PRINTED IN THE UNITED STATES OF AMERICA
BY THE COLONIAL PRESS, INC.

To my family, who all helped

Preface

This book contains an account of an extensive longitudinal research project conducted in a furniture factory over a span of more than four years. The study, involving an important organizational change in an entire department, was conducted during normal operations on the factory floor with minimal researcher intervention.

The objective of this research was to ascertain whether formal work-group leaders—the foremen—have a causal impact on the productivity of their work groups under highly structured technological conditions. This nagging question has remained unanswered for years despite the proliferation of correlational attitude research evidence suggesting such an impact.

In the course of the research, attention was given to such variables as group cohesion, or morale, and the attitudes of workers toward supervision and various aspects of their jobs. The treatment given these variables and the research strategy used were greatly influenced by the work of Robert Bales, Bernard Bass, Rensis Likert, Martin Orne, Stanley Seashore, and Ross Stagner. Addressed primarily to professional and academic audiences, the study assumes that the reader has, or is in the process of acquiring, a command of basic behavioral science research techniques, of statistics, and of the research literature bearing on leadership and industrial supervision.

My purpose was to present research material of substantive importance and relevance in the fields of organizational behavior and social psychology in a way that would interest students of the research process. Thus the project is presented largely in chronological form, so that the reader may examine the dynamics of the experimental field research itself. The methodological commentary is incorporated in the text wherever possible but is relegated to footnotes in places where it might disturb the reader's train of thought. One point should be made here, however, regarding the matter of statistical hypothesis testing. Many of the analyses reported produced statistics that reached or exceeded customary significance levels while others did not. I have reported the raw statistics, for example, correlations regardless of significance level, because the patterns and trends of the data appear to be sensible and instructional. In fact, given the small N for many analyses, coupled with control difficulties in most field experiments including this one, a case might be made for omitting significance levels altogether. The reader will have to draw his own conclusions upon examining the data, especially in Chapters 4–6.

It should be noted that the study has been written in the first person. While this style is unorthodox for psychological research reports, the narrative account herein seems to flow more naturally this way.

I am indebted to several colleagues, particularly Isadore Blumen, Paul Breer, Felician Foltman, William Friedland, Leopold Gruenfeld, Henry Landsberger, and Lawrence K. Williams, for their suggestions and encouragement in connection with either this study or the preparation of the manuscript. Professor William Foote Whyte deserves special thanks for his valuable suggestions in the planning, implementation, and reporting of this research. The experiment was enriched as a result. I am also indebted to Professor Ross Stagner for his constructive review of an early draft of the manuscript.

Thanks are also extended to Walter Nord, Stephen Sales, Allan Schwartzbaum, Joseph Alutto, Ted Edgecomb, and other former graduate students who assisted in data collection or analysis. Walter Nord in particular helped to organize the early phases of this work. His field notes were especially useful in the preparation of Chapter 2. Nicholas Yarmoshuk's work on the production scheduling data and operations described in Chapters 6 and 7 was quite extensive. Janice Lodahl and Alan Hundert made numerous useful suggestions upon reading an early draft of the study.

Several individuals who work in the research site and who participated in the study deserve recognition. The enlightened commitment to research of the plant manager, J. R., and his patient cooperation made this study possible. Thanks are also due the eight foremen—George, Larry, Woody, Willard, Warren, Bill, Ben, and Dick—who unwittingly were submitted to what must have been an uncomfortable experience, at least in the short run. The patience of Chris, Dick, and Red, other officials in the management, is also appreciated. The union officials and rank-and-file membership who participated in this study also deserve special acknowledgment. The friendly relations of the foremen, union officers, and workers with the researcher and his students even after they had discovered the true nature of the research work is a tribute to their fairmindedness and good sportsmanship. The anonymity of all these people is of course protected throughout the book.

I am also indebted to my two former secretaries, Jo Richards and Ann Vandemark, without whose patience, skill, loyalty, and strong motivation the manuscript could not have been prepared.

It should be noted that the New York State School of Industrial and Labor Relations, at Cornell University, through its former Research Director, Professor Leonard Adams, absorbed all the costs of this research study. Professor Adams' patient cooperation is greatly appreciated.

Finally, I wish to thank the American Psychological Association for its permission to reproduce or quote extensively from other published materials.

N. A. R.

London, England
May 1968

Contents

Plates

Figures

Tables

Leadership Change and Work-Group Dynamics

An Experiment

CHAPTER 1

Introduction

A number of industrial survey research studies have been reported in recent years showing substantial relationships between supervisory "behavior" as perceived by subordinates, on the one hand, and various measures of employee job satisfaction, productivity, labor turnover, or absenteeism, on the other. (Several of these have been summarized by Likert [1961], Krech *et al.* [1962], and others.) Many of these extensive cross-sectional research studies support the interpretation that participative, democratic, considerate, and other humane forms of supervisory behavior cause higher productivity and job satisfaction and lower absenteeism and labor turnover than is caused by undemocratic, inconsiderate treatment.

This causal interpretation, which appears in a wide variety of publications, indeed is comforting and satisfying to all of us whose personal preferences and values lie in this direction. It is doubtful, however, whether there is an industrial psychologist anywhere in the United States who has not encountered, in one setting or another, situations where individuals or entire work groups, through behavior that was inefficient, recalcitrant, or generally difficult to deal with, have caused their otherwise democratic or considerate supervisors to adopt an authoritarian or inconsiderate style in dealing with them. Management folklore is replete with incidents of new managers being appointed to "straighten out" certain groups that are in trouble. Frequently, such groups are in trouble because of unfortunate selection decisions, incompatible personalities, the development of personal problems at home carrying over to clashes at the work place, and unfavorable technological or other environmental influences. These factors lead to poor performance or negative attitudes to which the supervisor frequently responds by changing his behavior ("getting tough"), thereby often compounding his problems. (Exact parallels can be found in many families where considerate, permissive parents have been converted into autocrats by the behavior of their offspring. The same phenomenon also occurs in the university classroom.)

Inasmuch as the great majority of the above-mentioned studies present only correlational evidence regarding the interrelations among productivity, supervisory behavior, labor turnover, absenteeism, and job satisfaction variables, two major, although not new, logical-methodological issues must be resolved before this evidence can be interpreted unequivocally. One of these issues, sometimes referred to as the "chicken-egg" question, which is present in all cross-sectional research, concerns the direction of causality: Is the supervisory behavior dimension the independent variable or are employee productivity, the employees' general job satisfaction, turnover, and absenteeism the independent variables that influence supervisory behavior? [1] The other issue, closely intertwined with the first, concerns the measurement ap-

[1] It also is possible that some additional variable(s), as yet unspecified, simultaneously accounts for variation in productivity and perceived supervisory behavior. It is recognized, moreover, that "causality" is a potentially treacherous concept. Despite the tendency of modern scientists to avoid using it, we still must ascertain whether supervisory behavior in intact work groups has an impact on behavioral criteria which justifies all the attention given the supervisory problem in training courses and through elaborate selection procedures.

proach to the supervisory "behavior" dimensions involved.[2]
Supervisory "behavior" has been measured through four
different techniques in various cross-sectional studies of the
relationship of such behavior to the kinds of organizational
criteria mentioned above: supervisory behavior as viewed by
subordinates; supervisory behavior as viewed by social scientists who have made direct on-the-job observations; supervisory behavior as viewed by higher level managers or peers;
and supervisory behavior as measured by self-report techniques—through tests, questionnaires, and interviews. Any
of these measurement strategies, and these four seem to exhaust the possibilities, especially when employed in a cross-
sectional study design, can lead to substantial but misleading
correlations between leadership behavior and one or another
organizational criterion. It is unsafe to conclude, even on
the basis of extensive replication, that data obtained through
any of these strategies produce unequivocal inferences with
regard to causal direction. In fact, the technique used to
measure supervisory behavior in cross-sectional studies may
invite interpretation difficulties regarding the "cause" question. For example, let us examine the typically used "subordinate perceptions" approach to supervisory behavior as
a measurement strategy. It seems quite plausible, where this
strategy is employed, that productive or highly satisfied work
groups that know (or think) they are productive or highly
satisfied relative to others will quite sincerely ascribe certain
behaviors (for instance, consideration) to their supervisors
because of implicit leadership theories common in our culture, even when such behaviors are not objectively present.
Thus, a group that knows it is successful is likely to generate
a warm glow toward its supervisor and ascribe to him a

---

[2] The conceptual issues vis-à-vis the meanings of the many dimensions
of supervisory behavior (e.g., consideration, authoritarianism, general
supervision) also are important, of course, and may still be in need of
clarification. See Argyle *et al.* (1957).

variety of socially desirable characteristics and behaviors. Groups with low productivity may employ a similar mechanism in reverse. In other words, conditions in the work group—low pay, for example, or unpleasant work—which conceivably have nothing to do with the immediate supervisor, may very well "cause" the worker to perceive his supervisor in certain ways.[3] If we rely mainly on the opinions of subordinates to measure supervisory "behavior," we must entertain this possible interpretation of correlational data in the literature.[4] A similar "contamination" or halo effect argument can be made in relation to studies employing perceptions reported by superiors.

Self-reports coming from the supervisors themselves, or observations reported by on-the-scene social scientists, in cross-sectional studies also can be misleading even when such reports are accurate. This is so because one does not know whether the supervisor behaves the way he reports (or is observed to behave) as a result of having a viable group, or whether the group is viable because of the way he behaves. Thus, cross-sectional research evidence of correlations between productivity and such variables as initiation of structure, consideration, and A_sO or LPC (Fiedler, 1964), even when these variables are measured through self-reports from the leaders themselves, does not necessarily provide an accu-

[3] Excellent examples may be found in Richardson (1961). Richardson describes in great anthropological depth events in a factory assembly department over an extended time period during which several supervisory replacements were made. He dedicates his monograph to "Teddy, the expendable leader; another *scapegoat* in the struggle to overcome our ignorance of why groups fail" (*emphasis mine*).

[4] Subordinate perceptions of supervisory behavior are relied upon heavily in such research for several reasons. The most important stems from the fact that this measurement approach is consistent with certain theoretical approaches to psychology in general and group behavior in particular. Many social psychologists, for example, probably would maintain that "objective" (independently observed) leadership behaviors (how the supervisor appears to impartial observers) are less important than how he is perceived by his followers.

rate picture of causality. A foreman or a tank commander, for example, may reveal himself as a highly structure-oriented, low A_8O person when responding to a questionnaire. This does not necessarily indicate a stable personality or style syndrome. Rather, he may have become this way because of conditions in his group. Thus, a sloppy, poorly motivated crew or work group which does not accept the formal goals of the organization may reject almost any leader appointed over it by the formal organization. Under such circumstances, a previously considerate, high A_8O leader may well become a more structure-oriented, lower A_8O leader to maintain order and get something done. In short, while the pre-occupation of behavioral scientists with cross-sectional designs has been quite understandable given the difficulties we have in setting up "real-life" experiments in ongoing organizations, there is, nonetheless, no substitute for predictive, experimental designs.

Awareness of these methodological difficulties and the attendant causality question, especially in survey studies, has led some writers to support the "leader as cause" interpretation by citing Feldman's narrative account (1937) of a field experiment in an insurance company which, on its face, seems to justify such an interpretation. It is hazardous to rely on the Feldman study in this way because no data are presented in the original source to substantiate the author's claim, among others, that "high producing" supervisors when transferred experimentally to "low producing" sections raised productivity while low producing supervisors had a reverse effect on the high producing sections to which they were transferred. In addition to the absence of data in this early study, the operational definition of productivity that was employed—cost reduction during a special campaign— leaves something to be desired. It is even more hazardous to conclude that the supervisor "causes" *productivity* variance (as some writers, but not Jackson himself, mistakenly have done) on the basis of Jackson's valuable experiment

(1953) showing that workers respond attitudinally to super-visory reassignments. No productivity criterion was employed in Jackson's study!

There are, however, certain admissible experimental studies in the literature that are relevant to the question involved here. Coch and French (1948) and Morse and Reimer (1956) conducted research on an experimental basis in industry, where the independent variable revolved around the issue of participative management. Although the managerial behaviors that the researchers instigated certainly are closely allied with the general problem under consideration, neither study employed a supervisory reassignment procedure. Moreover, the Coch and French study, whose results seem to favor worker participation in decision-making, may very well have been influenced by demand characteristics because the researchers themselves actively intervened at the work place, especially in one of the experimental treatment conditions. Viteles (1953) elucidates this argument quite nicely. The important and ambitious Morse and Reimer experiment, although producing evidence suggesting that employee participation in decision-making leads to certain kinds of favorable results, did not reveal any conclusive productivity advantage for this approach to management.

A very provocative experiment by Schachter *et al.* (1961) also bears on the supervisory issue as stated here, although like the studies cited above, this experiment also was conducted without benefit of an actual supervisory reassignment procedure. The researchers arranged for a series of harassments on the part of time-study personnel and various other managers so that certain groups of employees were harassed for a specified period of time while others received normal treatment prior to the introduction of a technological change in both sets of groups. Those groups that were harassed tended to have greater difficulties in reaching reasonable production levels after the introduction of technological change; the unharassed groups adjusted to the same change with little difficulty.

On balance, the above three experiments, plus the original Hawthorne research by Roethlisberger and Dickson (1947), indirectly suggest that supervisory behavior may bear a causal relation to work-group behavior. The evidence, however, is far from convincing. Moreover, while the extensive survey research evidence cited earlier suggests specific kinds of supervisory behaviors that are of potential importance, it seems likely that different leadership styles and personalities can be equally efficacious, at least as far as productivity is concerned.[5] Of course, specific environmental circumstances may exert strong moderating influences in favor of one or another supervisory approach, as Katzell (1962) and Fiedler (1964) have nicely articulated.

It also seems likely that under some highly technologically or otherwise structured circumstances the supervisor's behavior may have no impact at all on group productivity. Dubin (1965) elaborates this line of reasoning quite convincingly. He compares unit-manufacturing operations with continuous-process operations and shows clear-cut qualitative differences in their supervisory demands and potential supervisory impact. Dubin also resurrects the always embarrassing question of supervisory power; many supervisors in American organizations have extremely limited control over rewards and punishments that can be used to influence their subordinates. Consequently, he argues, they are merely figureheads who are unlikely to affect work-group productivity, at least on a motivational basis. The contingency model of leadership employed by Fiedler (1964) also takes this matter into account.

[5] It is worth noting that in a recent review of research on teacher effectiveness in the classroom, McKeachie (1963) points out that variations in teaching style (e.g., democratic vs. autocratic) have not led to conclusive or consistent results as far as student achievement (production) is concerned.

The study described in the following pages, although of modest proportions, was designed to contribute some insight into this general problem. A fortuitous combination of stable technological arrangements, a very stable labor force, and a remarkably progressive plant manager made possible a field experiment in which supervisors were reassigned in accordance with a plan designed by the experimenter. *The design of the experiment enables a specific test on the hypothesis that foreman behavior, as perceived by subordinates, is an independent variable that influences employee productivity and certain employee attitudes in a highly structured manufacturing setting. The experimental design also enables a test on the reverse hypothesis: that productivity influences supervisory behavior, as perceived by subordinates, and group attraction.* It should be emphasized that the study is concerned with only one of the several possible strategies for measuring leadership behavior, namely, leadership behavior *as perceived by subordinates.* Additional field experiments are required to test similar causal direction hypotheses where supervisory behavior is measured by self-reports and ratings by superiors, peers, and independent observers.

I admit to setting up something of a straw man in the causality question. Most students of the problem seem to think that the leadership–group dynamics process is best conceived of as a social system within which several variables mutually influence each other and upon which many variables can create chain reactions. While this no doubt is true, experiments testing the cross-sectional survey research evidence on a longitudinal basis are still needed, particularly in highly structured settings where the formal leader may indeed have low impact on the system. In any event, the two deliberately over-simplified hypotheses were formulated for experimental purposes. The data should facilitate tests on both. In addition, the experimental design should permit an evaluation of leadership impact within the context of systems theory, which is discussed in more detail in Chapter 7.

HOW IT ALL BEGAN

The study was conducted in one plant of a multiplant organization manufacturing living-room furniture. The company accounts for a very sizable percentage of all the living-room furniture manufactured in this country. Although there is a vigorous corporate headquarters staff, the various plants in the firm enjoy considerable local autonomy. A furniture-workers' union has represented the entire company's hourly workers for a number of years. When the contracts come up for negotiation, each local associated with the respective decentralized plants takes a strike vote at the direction of the international union. The vote can authorize a corporate-wide strike, however, only if a majority of the entire corporate bargaining unit votes in favor of a strike. During contract negotiations in the several years immediately preceding the researcher's introduction to this plant, the only local union group that consistently voted in favor of a strike was that local representing the employees of the research site. The top management of this plant (which we will call hereafter the Northeast Plant) and the corporate management were understandably concerned over these periodic strike votes. Their concern was magnified by the fact that the Northeast Plant was (and still is) the corporation's most efficient and highest-producing component.

As a result of their concern, the plant manager and the corporation's labor relations director contacted the New York State School of Industrial and Labor Relations requesting a meeting with faculty members who might be interested in a small consulting project. Specifically, they requested two faculty members[6] to conduct a small-scale attitude survey at the Northeast Plant by means of personal interviews with a stratified random sample of employees and supervisors. The specific objective was to ascertain the reasons

[6] F. F. Foltman and the author.

behind the "no confidence" strike votes. It should be emphasized that since the local was consistently outvoted by the
combined strength of the several other locals in the corporate
bargaining unit, no strikes had actually occurred.

During the subsequent three-day interviewing program, I
became acquainted with the union officers and stewards and
with a cross section of managers and rank-and-file employees.
A tour of the plant during that period revealed that eight
manually paced production lines were operating simultaneously in a particular department. Each line was staffed by
a group of from eight to ten men including a foreman. The
apparent technological comparability of the groups, all of
which were engaged in upholstering, coupled with the fact
that each group had its own supervisor, suggested immediately the broad outline of the experiment described in
this book. A few guarded inquiries put to some of the office
staff during that three days revealed that these particular
groups were characterized by extremely low turnover rates,
which helped to cinch the case for an experiment. Stable
group membership would be needed if the experimental
effects of leadership changes on productivity were to be
assessed without being confounded by extraneous effects of
membership changes.

When our report was presented at a meeting several weeks
later, I commented upon the Upholstering Department research prospects in general terms (without mention of an
experiment as such) to J. R., the plant manager. He responded that I must be a "would-be Hawthorne research
type." Obviously, J. R., a high-school graduate who had
risen from the furniture workers' ranks to the top position
in this plant, was acquainted with the Western Electric
studies. He stated that at any time in the future when I
might be interested in doing research in his plant he would
be happy to discuss the matter with me. The issue rested
for almost two years until a graduate student became available for field research in connection with his thesis plans.

The consulting nature of my early relationship to this organization cannot be overemphasized;[7] it undoubtedly accounts for some of the findings in our early experimental work to be described in Chapter 2.

THE EXPERIMENTAL SETTING

The Plant. The Northeast Plant, which employs approximately 450 men and women, is located in a predominantly rural community. While the surrounding community is largely rural, there has been very rapid and substantial economic growth during the last fifteen to twenty years. Several other manufacturing organizations, some of them affiliates of large corporations, are also located in the same community.

The organization of the plant at the time this research was initiated is suggested in Figure 1. The reader will note a fairly standard set of functional specialities not very different from those in most manufacturing organizations. The people of primary concern to us in this study are those directly below the plant manager in the chart, including the manufacturing superintendent and the lines foremen.

Figure 2 is a layout of the factory showing the approximate location of the more significant operations. The arrows indicate the flow of materials and final products. The Frame Department manufactures wooden frames for couches and chairs on an assembly line basis; the workers use a variety of hand and power tools in the process. The frames are stored in the designated storage area and subsequently are dispatched to the various production lines in the Upholster-

---

[7] The consulting project itself revealed well-founded complaints regarding the parking lot, the lunch room, and similar matters. However, the concern of the men at various organization levels was focused on pay. Their pay satisfaction levels were being increasingly affected by the influx of new industries and the growth of others in the community. They also focused on certain communications and supervisory problems growing out of middle-management levels. These had a serious bearing on union-management relations and also affected administrative strategy in the research described in this book.

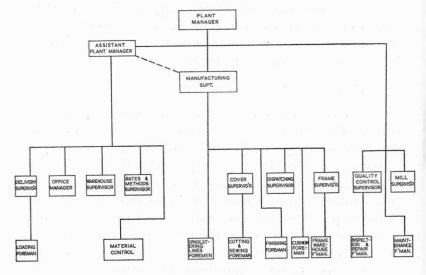

Figure 1. Organization chart of the Northeast Plant

ing Department. At the appropriate times in each production schedule, cushions are moved into the Upholstering Department from the Cushion Department and covering material is brought in from the Cutting and Sewing Department. The lines or work groups in the Upholstering Department then produce the final product, which passes through Inspection and Repair or is sent directly to the Shipping Department.

It is worth noting that the Upholstering Department is acknowledged to have the highest status of any department in the plant. The skill levels required are high and the wages are distinctly greater than those paid in other areas of the plant. The upholsterers' position in the organization is somewhat analogous to the flyers' position in an air force. Just as flyers have a number of support units backing them up on the ground, the Upholstering Department has its support units elsewhere in the factory.

The Upholstering Department Layout. Figure 3 shows

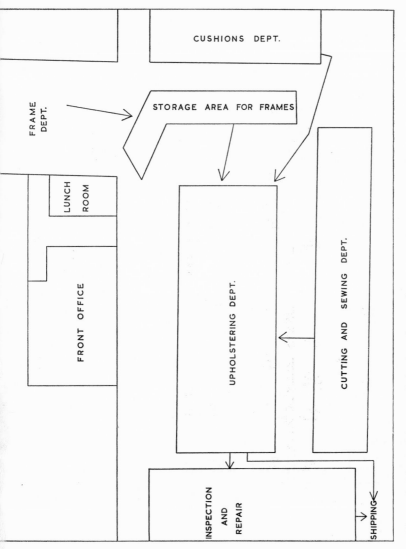

Figure 2. Physical layout of the Northeast Plant

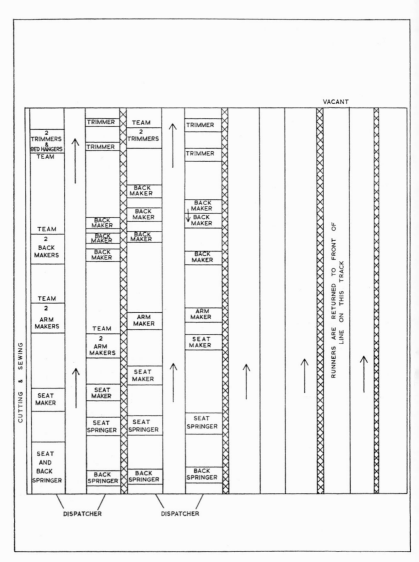

Figure 3. Physical layout of the Upholstering Department

the way the lines are laid out within the Upholstery Department. The arrows indicate the direction of the product flow. The job titles of the various workers are indicated on each of four lines and would be the same on the other lines although the spacing between men on the lines varies somewhat. Each line has back- and seat-springing operators, armmakers, seat-makers, back-makers, and final-trimmers, who install fancy decorative materials and skirts of various kinds on the furniture before it comes off the line. As the reader can see from Figure 3, the lines are parallel to each other, the distance between them being approximately fifteen to twenty feet. The physical arrangements permit a fair amount of interpersonal interaction among the workers not only within lines but also between adjacent lines. For a view of the department as one looks down one of the lines, see Plate I.

The Workers. The experiment concentrated on the seventy-three men working in the upholstering operations, plus eight foremen. Because of the lengthy time period required to achieve proficiency in this type of work, the workers can be considered to be at least semiskilled. The long tenure of these men, however, suggests that their work might be called "stereotyped" in the same sense implied by Schachter *et al.* (1961). Except for those slight modifications in the assembly routine necessitated by minor changes in style and raw materials, the men work almost automatically. Most of the men are high-school graduates. At the time of the study, their average length of service was ten years; only five or six men had been with the company for less than two years. This long seniority, coupled with the small size of the community and the prevalence of car pools and personal interaction on the job, all contributed to the research methodology employed in the study. These factors made it possible to ask certain kinds of sociometric questions of the workers and foremen which were useful later in developing the experimental manipulations.

Several additional factors should be pointed out here. First of all, work-group membership on these lines is highly stable; few transfers or terminations occur in any given year. During the twenty-eight weeks of the supervisory reassignment experiment, including the pre-experimental base line period and the post-experimental change period, only five manpower changes were made in the eight groups. Three of these occurred in one group, which was eliminated from certain analyses for this and other reasons to be discussed in later chapters. Absenteeism during this extensive time period also was extremely limited.

The Foremen. All eight foremen in the department are paid on a straight salary basis. Seven of them had been promoted from the ranks after many years' service as upholstering workers. Their ages and educational characteristics are quite similar to those of the workers. The eighth foreman, who also is a high-school graduate and was about fifty years old at the time, had joined the department only a few years prior to the experiment when Northeast purchased his former employer's factory.

Krech *et al.* (1962), on the basis of numerous studies reported in a variety of social settings, indicate that group leaders generally serve the following primary functions in their groups: (1) executive (coordinator of group activities); (2) planner (deciding ways and means by which the group can achieve its ends); (3) policy-maker (primarily establishing goals); (4) expert (source of information and skills); (5) external group representative; (6) controller of internal relations (among members); (7) purveyor of rewards and punishments; and (8) arbitrator and mediator. The Northeast foremen are expected to perform all these role functions (although they are circumscribed considerably in roles 2 and 3—planning and policy-making). In other words, these foremen are more than mere figureheads. In Fiedler's terms (1964), they have at least moderately high "position power." Much of this stems from their expertise and long experience with the various products made at Northeast and the attendant operating problems. Each foreman, then, is an integrated member of his group because of his task knowledge and the many functions he is expected to perform during the production process. It is important that this point be kept in mind by the reader as he considers later chapters. The experiment to be described essentially involved the removal of more or less well-integrated group members (foremen) and their transfer to new surroundings where integration had to be achieved all over again.

Technological Matters. There are no mechanized conveyors in the Upholstering Department. Each line is set up along a single metal track inserted in the factory floor. Each piece of furniture is placed upon a small truck at the head of the line, where the springers begin work on the frame (*see* Plate II). This truck has two flanged wheels which ride down the track while its other two wheels ride on the concrete floor. The trucks are pushed from one work station to the next by the upholstering operators. Since there is only limited space to accumulate partially finished work between the work stations, each worker's pace is influenced considerably by the pace of his neighbor on either side of him. An individual financial incentive system, MTM,[8] is applied to the workers despite the highly interdependent nature of their work.

As was indicated earlier, the work of each group is thoroughly rationalized—one man installs seat springs, another stuffs and covers arms, another does backs, and so on. A variety of hand tools and pneumatic staple guns are used in the process. The pneumatic staple gun, like those being used in Plates III and IV, represents the only major technological change these groups have experienced in several years; they formerly used tacks and tack hammers exclusively. The foreman assists the line in keeping the flow steady and fast. The

[8] MTM is a standardized work measurement procedure based upon time study techniques. It serves as the basis for establishing incentive rates on each operation that the workers perform. See Strauss and Sales (1960) for fuller details.

expediters provide the necessary raw materials from other departments, although the foremen frequently must leave their groups when necessary to correct errors in raw materials or seek relevant information. The union contract provisions officially do not permit the foremen to work alongside their men. The foremen, however, do instruct workers and demonstrate various operations as necessary.

Coupled with the rationalization of the work, the individual incentive system creates certain kinds of difficulties in the production of furniture on these lines. Because the men work predominately on certain operations—for example, arms, backs, and seats—they acquire their greatest skill at these operations. They tend to maximize their earnings accordingly. However, bottlenecks frequently occur on the lines for a variety of reasons. Such circumstances demand that a worker leave his regular work station and move to another, where he performs operations that are somewhat different than his usual ones. He moves to the station immediately in front or in back of him on the line as the occasion requires. Thus, an arm-maker may have to work on seats or a back-maker may have to help the final-trimmer. Although the men receive incentive credit for all work they do at all work stations, the foremen often have difficulties in persuading the men to move, because the individual incentive system rewards them maximally for working at their regular stations, where they have acquired great skill. There is considerable feeling among managerial personnel that group cohesion in certain of the work groups has helped overcome this particular problem. A group incentive system, it should be added, was discarded in the plant a few years ago, allegedly because it produced too much friction among the workers.

There is a considerable amount of product specialization among the groups. Thus, one line concentrates on sleeper couches, two others concentrate on sectional couches, two others concentrate on suites (chair and couch combinations), two others do a large proportion of the plant's chair production, and one line works primarily on the company's high-quality furniture. Although the products differ from group to group, the operations performed by the workers are quite similar and all the lines are called upon to do at least some work outside their usual product specialty. Moreover, the time-study system theoretically smooths out differences in difficulty among the tasks of the lines in relation to their performance.

THE EXPERIMENTAL PLAN AND TIMETABLE:
AN OVERVIEW

The experimental plan and timetable, described quite briefly, had essentially five different phases. The first phase incorporated the collection of base line data, the development of measuring instruments, the conditioning of the plant and the department for research operations, and the conducting of certain preliminary experimentation to be described later. Phase 1 lasted a total of six weeks. A little more than a year later, Phase 2 was begun. During the intervening one-year period, various data analyses were conducted to assess the reliability and utility of several potentially important measurements. Equally important, the foreman experiment was planned during this period and "sold" to the plant manager. Phase 2 included the actual introduction of the foreman reassignments and the collection of productivity data to assess the results of the change. The third phase involved the collection of repeated measurements on certain attitudinal variables. These measurements were taken ten weeks after the introduction of the supervisory reassignments. Approximately one year later, Phase 4 occurred. This included a series of feedback meetings during which the plant manager and the upholstering supervisors were informed regarding the results of the study. The fifth and final phase occurred about six months later, when an intensive study of the production scheduling and control function was made because of certain matters learned about through the feedback process in Phase 4.

Although the methodological and substantive details of each phase will be specified in the appropriate chapters, several factors should be noted here. When Phase 1 of this project was entered, the plant manager was unaware of my long-range hope for an experiment that would require the reassignment of his upholstering formen to different groups. The feasibility of such an experiment had not yet been established, and it did not seem wise to raise the question before his inevitable doubts about the project could be satisfactorily answered. Thus, Phase 1 research activities were relatively innocuous—including the presence of observers for two weeks and the adminstration of a fairly extensive questionnaire. The occasion also was used to acquire considerable quantities of the plant's productivity and quality data on the experimental groups. At this stage, we had no idea of what to expect regarding variance within and between groups on relevant dimensions. The potentially relevant dimensions included productivity (for which data were available through the company's incentive records on the respective individuals and groups), quality (measured through data on rejects), attitudes toward authoritarianism of workers and foremen as measured by the California F-scale, the workers' and their foremen's attitudes on Fleishman's initiation of structure and consideration dimensions (as measured by his Leadership Opinion Questionnaire), and a variety of tailor-made sociometric and work-attitude items designed in part to measure group attraction or cohesion.

The small size of this department and the high degree of personal interaction among the workers precluded the possibility of any instrument pretesting. All homemade attitude questions and personal-history items had to be developed without benefit of dry runs. Pre-testing, even on a small number of the workers, would have led to communication among them that could have influenced the outcome of later research. Moreover, the period of time available to us between the date that the management gave us permission to enter and the date by which time we had to begin our Phase 1 field work was brief.

At this point the stage was set for an experiment on supervisory effects on work groups by virtue of the fact that eight "comparable" work groups had been identified accidentally in a stable technological environment. Further progress required answers to several questions: Could a reasonable basis for reassigning the foremen be found without contaminating the results by our presence as researchers? Could reliable and relevant criterion measures be developed by which to assess the effects of an experiment? Finally, could the plant management be convinced that such an experiment in fact should be done at its own risk? The next two chapters provide the answers.

CHAPTER 2

Feasibility Research and Tooling Up[1]

As was indicated toward the end of Chapter 1, the mere
locating of several apparently comparable groups each having
its own leader is only the first step in developing a field experiment. Before such an experiment can be devised it is
essential that preliminary research be conducted to ascertain
answers to many questions. For example, how comparable
are the groups? What explains productivity differences, if
any, that typically exist among them? How reliable a criterion measure is available on these groups? What administrative arrangements will be necessary to conduct a leadership
experiment? All of these, and more, require the collection
and analysis of preliminary data. A major purpose of Phase 1,
then, was to pursue these matters.

Another important objective of this phase of the research
program was to determine whether a social-science research
process itself, in a field study of this industrial organization,
would have an influence on employee productivity which
might conceivably become confounded with the influence of
other, more legitimate, independent variables. This was a
critical question because the research strategy in later phases

[1] Parts of this chapter are based on a paper read at the 1964 meeting
of the International Congress of Applied Psychology in Ljubljana,
Yugoslavia, a revised version of which was published by Rosen and
Sales (1966) in the *Journal of Applied Psychology*. Much of the text
and most of the tables in the chapter are therefore reproduced with
the kind permission of the American Psychological Association. This
chapter also rests heavily on Nord (1963), from which I have borrowed
freely.

of this project—the foreman reassignments—could be affected by our findings in Phase 1. Thus, if Phase 1 were to show that the upholstery workers would be likely to distort their behavior because of the presence of research operations and research personnel, the hoped-for foreman reassignments at a later date would have to be made without the presence of researchers on the scene.

The problem of research process effects is not new, although its dynamics are not fully understood. It often is referred to in social research by the term "Hawthorne effect," based on the classical industrial research conducted at the Western Electric Company in the 1930's (Roethlisberger and Dickson, 1947).[2] Orne (1959, 1962) has published perhaps the most thorough analyses of the problem as it relates to experimental social psychology. He makes a strong case for the existence of "demand characteristics" in the social psychological experiment. According to Orne, the perceived cues in an experimental setting "demand" that the subject act (consciously or unconsciously) in accordance with the overall impression he forms regarding the experiment from these cues. The result is that at least some subjects may assume that certain role behaviors are proper, thus affecting the experimental results in ways not intended by the experimenter.

There can be no doubt that many cues exist in all research settings that interact with subjects' needs and personalities so as to produce hunches among subjects regarding the experimenter's purpose and hypothesis. Moreover, the evidence suggests that the researcher often may "get what he is looking

[2] The problem under consideration here is not restricted to the social sciences. Heisenberg pointed out long ago that the measurement process can affect matter under study even in the physical sciences; a simple thermometer, if its own temperature is different from that of a vessel of water, may not accurately measure the water's temperature. For an interesting fictional treatment of the traditional "Hawthorne effect," see *Mike Mulligan and His Steamshovel,* a children's story by Virginia Burton (1939) in which Mike and his steamshovel, Mary Ann, always work faster when people are interested enough in them to watch.

for" as a result of perceived cues. Examples from a wide variety of behavioral research studies can be found in Viteles (1953), Dunette and Heneman (1956), Selltiz *et al.* (1961), Rosenthal (1963), Cook (1962), Cantor (1951), Hovland *et al.* (in Selltiz *et al.*, 1961), and Remmers (1954).

In some cases, however, a researcher may find that subjects sometimes act *contrary* to the perceived research purposes. Examples are described by Argyris (1952), Scott (1963) and Vidich and Bensman (1960), all on the basis of industrial experiences. Block and Block (1955) provide additional support from an experiment using college students as subjects. Their experiment, which closely parallels the field research to be described here, also demonstrates the potential influence of moderator variables on research effects.

No evidence is reported in the literature on the ways environmental cues and individual characteristics may interact to produce contaminated research results with respect to a productivity criterion in formal organizations. The experiment described below was designed in part to clarify our knowledge in this regard. Moderator variables (personality and demographic variables, for example), which may lead to individual differences in subjects' reactions to research stimuli, were included because of the growing tendency in industrial research to relate the effects of independent variables to such moderating characteristics.

It should be emphasized that the "non-experiment" described below was designed to serve multiple purposes. While it afforded a golden opportunity to test "Hawthorne effect" and "demand characteristics" hypotheses, at the same time it was used as a vehicle to collect base line data for the hoped-for leadership experiment to be conducted later. Thus, a number of group and leadership variables were included which went far beyond our needs in the immediate "non-experiment." For example, while we wanted to test in the "non-experiment" on research process effects the moderating influences of authoritarianism and age among the workers, we expected to need for the later foreman experiment measures of group cohesion and group attitudes toward foremen. Therefore, all these variables were included in the preliminary "non-experiment" questionnaire (to be described later) so that we could accomplish both objectives simultaneously.

PLANNING A NON-EXPERIMENT

Experimental Design. The study was conducted over a six-week period during the spring of 1963. The six weeks were divided into three periods of two weeks each, called the "before," "during," and "after" periods.[3] The research, the independent variable of this study, was conducted in the middle period, labeled "during." The before and after periods were used to provide data we could compare with those obtained during the actual research period when research operations were conducted.

The experimental design takes into account three distinctly different sampling units: the overall 73-man department treated as one unit; the eight separate production groups (lines), each treated as one unit; and the 73 individuals, each treated as one unit. Thus, analyses were designed to test for research effects at all three levels; total department, work groups, and individuals. The relative importance of the three units, of course, depends upon the purposes of a particular investigator.

Independent Variable. The independent variable in this phase was merely the presence or absence of behavioral research operations in this plant. The research operations in-

[3] The experimenters attempted to use the upholstering department in one of the company's other plants, eight hundred miles away, for certain control purposes. During the six-week period in question, however, we found that the other "comparable" department was operating on a reduced work week that had a decided effect on productivity and team composition in that plant. We therefore restricted ourselves to a repeated-measurements design in one plant. No other departments in this plant could have been used for control purposes because of technological and group differences (for example, machines, sex mix, and skill levels).

cluded preliminary research meetings with top management and local union officers. Because of my earlier work at the plant as a management consultant two and a half years before, we sought to overcome any view of us as "management spies." Immediately after the plant manager had agreed to cooperate with the project,[4] attempts were made to present ourselves to other managers and local union officers as social scientists who, being from a state-sponsored school, of necessity were impartial in union-management relations. About three months before the actual study in the plant the local union president, who worked in the Upholstering Department, was invited into the plant manager's office along with the plant superintendent. There, Walter Nord, my research assistant, and I explained briefly our purposes and emphasized that management had no financial sponsorship role in the project. This, of course, was true. We assured the workers' anonymity and agreed to return to allow union and company representatives to read our questionnaire, with the implication that we would omit any items to which either party objected strongly.

Shortly before the Phase 1 study began, Nord and another graduate student, Allan Schwartzbaum, went to the plant to discuss final plans with the plant manager, the plant superintendent, and a union official. Since the president of the union had taken a leave of absence, at the suggestion of the plant manager Nord and Schwartzbaum spoke with the shop steward from the Upholstering Department. All three men read our proposed questionnaire and raised no objections. The only comment came from the steward, who said that there were "wise guys" in the plant and he did not know if he could get them to cooperate. It was explained that he would not have to "sell" our study but that we merely wanted his

---

[4] The plant manager knew, at this point, that we wanted to do a "Hawthorne effect" experiment simply to find out how the workers would react to being goldfish in a bowl. He also knew that we were going to analyze his productivity records in some detail. Although we promised him no specific items of practical information, he probably assumed that something practical would come of all this.

approval. Some minor wording revisions were made in the questionnaire after this meeting, but no substantial changes were made. The final questionnaire appears in Appendix A.

The plant superintendent was included in our early contacts because the foremen of the upholstering lines report to him. Since the research plans included a separate questionnaire for the foremen, a copy of which appears in Appendix C, we wanted his approval and aid. Also, it seemed desirable to work at as low a level in the organization as possible to reduce the risk that we would be indentified with management. Whether we were successful or not in this attempt will be reserved for later discussion.

Rather general descriptions of the proposed research were provided the plant superintendent and union officials. No mention was made of our real intent except to the plant manager. All other parties (including the workers) were told that we wished to compare the attitudes and working conditions of furniture workers with those in other industries.

The meetings were followed by letters, on university letterhead (Appendix E) to the workers' and foremen's homes. These letters, signed by Nord, described the proposed research, including mention that a thesis would grow out of the study. A few days later, the two graduate students entered the department and spent two full work weeks (ten working days) observing and informally interviewing the upholsterers and their supervisors. Two "planned" interviews were conducted with each worker in addition to the spontaneous interviews that were initiated by workers. The emphasis in most interviews during the first week was on technological considerations. Notes were recorded openly. Both researchers appeared on all lines and also ate lunch and took coffee breaks with the workers. The nature of the questions asked gradually shifted to the areas of leadership and group preferences, the topics of additional research conducted a year later. A questionnaire, which included a number of attitudinal and personal-history items, was administered on the ninth day during the one and a half hours of company time for which the workers were paid their average hourly earnings. A team of six additional graduate students "invaded" the Upholstery Department on this occasion to help Nord and Schwartzbaum administer the questionnaire. The workers knew that their responses were *not* anonymous, although assurances were given to them that no one in the company or union would ever see their individual questionnaires. Their names were needed so that we could link their questionnaire data to individual productivity records for correlational purposes.[5] By administering the questionnaire on the ninth day rather than the tenth, the researchers avoided Friday absenteeism. They also gained qualitative insights into the workers' reactions to the questionnaire by returning for a full day of observational-informal interviewing on the following day.

Dependent Variable. The primary dependent variable of this study was productivity as measured by percentage of base rate achieved by each worker during each of the three two-week periods in question. Percentage of base rate is calculated on the basis of time-study data. Thus, if a worker produces 110 units during a period in which time-study standards say he should produce a base of 100 units, he produces at 110 per cent of base rate. Data were collected without the workers' knowledge from the company records and were treated statistically in several different ways. The range of percentage of base rate varied, on a weekly basis, anywhere from 60 per cent to 200 per cent among the seventy-three production workers involved. This index varies on a *work group* basis (means) from about 110 per cent to 160 per cent weekly. The differences between groups are statistically

[5] The writer prefers to be straightforward about the anonymity issue rather than engage in deceptions which might be discovered. The evidence suggests that distortion effects in several studies of questionnaire administrative procedures are not worrisome. See Pelz (1959), Rosen (1960), Klein *et al.* (1967), and Dunnette and Heneman (1956), for empirical studies and discussion.

significant on the basis of an overall *F*-test. Reliability studies of this criterion, conducted on the same workers during several time periods prior to this experiment, demonstrated that this measure is highly reliable; Pearson correlation coefficients, for percentage of base rate achieved, between one- and two-week contiguous time periods, consistently fell in the range of .88 to .95 for individual workers *and* for the work groups.[6]

It might be pointed out here that since the percentage of base rate index turned out to be highly reliable in a statistical sense, and since group differences occurred, one of the crucial questions raised at the end of Chapter 1 has been answered. We did, in fact, find a relevant and reliable criterion measure for potential use in an experimental assessment of the foremen's impact on worker productivity.

Moderator Variables. Four moderator variables were employed in the experiment. These were selected to facilitate tests on specific hypotheses to be described later.

1. Authoritarianism. The workers' attitudes toward authoritarianism were measured by thirteen items selected, on the basis of high item-total correlations, from the California *F-Scale*. The thirteen items were buried deep in the questionnaire to reduce the possibility that they would provide a clue to the workers as to the experiment's purpose.[7]

---

[6] Data also were collected on quality as a possible criterion measure. The amount of variance, however, was extremely limited, thereby precluding useful analyses.

[7] Originally, we planned to use the California *F*-Scale items having the highest correlation with total score (the best half) in the original research done by Adorno and his associates. This would have given us thirteen items. We had to substitute for one of these items, however, because it dealt with deviant sexual behavior. The substitution was necessary because after plant-wide discussion and debate a sexually deviant worker had been "voted" back into the plant after receiving extensive psychological assistance following a morals offense in the community. It is possible that had the original, heavily weighted *F*-scale item been included in the questionnaire we might have jeopardized the entire project. We learned about this man, incidentally, during the initial consulting project by Professor Foltman and myself.

2. Rural-urban background. This nominal variable, which may also measure acceptance of authority, was measured by means of a personal-history item in the questionnaire.

3. Age. The age of the workers, which ranged from eighteen to sixty, was also obtained from self-reports.

4. The union activity level of the workers. This variable was measured by summing each worker's response to two items regarding the extent of his participation in the business and social affairs of the local union. Five-point *ad hoc* scales were employed with each question, using answer continua ranging from "always" to "never" for each item. The analysis based on these items that eventually was employed included only the five most active unionists and the five least active. The "active" group said they *always* attend union business meetings and social affairs while the "inactive" group said they *never* attend either type of function. Only two items in the questionnaire were related, on their face, to this issue. (Additional items could not have been included without doing far more ground work with the union local and international than we had time for.) Men registering on the extremes of the scale were used for this analysis because of the measure's crudity. All the workers in the sample are union members by virtue of a union-shop contract clause. The active group, as defined above, includes all the major local officers.[8]

Hypotheses. Several hypotheses were tested in this phase of the study. It should be emphasized that three levels of analysis were considered: overall department, eight groups, and 73 individuals. While the leadership experiment to be described later was to be conducted at the group level of

[8] Sociometric status also was tried as a moderator variable on the hypothesis that isolates would show a traditional "Hawthorne effect." The sociometric data were not analyzed, however, because of certain problems workers had with the instructions. Specifically, they used different psychological sets, inserted names of ineligible people, and omitted first names which were necessary for the identification of numerous people having the same last name.

analysis, we believed that "demand characteristics" should be studied at all possible levels to maximize our insight into the problem. Our hypotheses were:

1. The research operations will have no effect on the overall average productivity for the 73 workers analyzed as a total group. This hypothesis is based on the premise that the effects of research will be demonstrated differentially among individuals and that, in a heterogeneous group, they will cancel out. (In the absence of evidence in one direction or the other, it was assumed here that those wishing to cooperate with the management-supported researchers would cancel out those who would be hostile or suspicious. It might be noted, incidentally, that even in the Hawthorne studies there were individual differences in the reactions of the workers.) The hypothesis was tested by applying repeated measurements analysis of variance methods to differences among the three time periods, before, during, and after, using the total group of 73 men as the sampling unit.

2. The research operations will have no differential effect on the eight production-line groups in this study. The logic here is identical to that suggested above regarding the entire department. This hypothesis was tested by comparing correlations among the eight lines' productivity means for the three time periods in question and between the two halves of the pre-experimental reliability control period mentioned earlier. We reasoned that if the hypothesis were true, these four correlation coefficients should be essentially the same; the reliability-period coefficient was .91.

3. There will be individual differences among the workers in reaction to the independent variable. This hypothesis was studied by examining the correlations among the workers' productivity levels for the three time periods in the study and the reliability control period. (Again four correlation coefficients were computed.) The statistical reasoning was similar to that described for hypothesis 2, above, except that now individual rather than group measures become the focal

point. For this analysis, however, appropriate differences, rather than equality, were expected among the correlations.

4. Those workers characterized by high (above the median) authoritarianism scores on the California *F*-Scale will show increased productivity in the face of the experimental variable, while those characterized by low (below median) scores will show a decrease. This effect was hypothesized because of observations and data reported by others—for example, Argyris (1952) and Block and Block (1955)—indicating that researchers are perceived as authority figures, at least by some subjects. We expected the low *F*-scale scorers to behave as many workers do when a time-study man observes them. Authoritarians were expected to respond differently.

5. Workers raised on farms will show an increase in productivity when compared to the other workers. This hypothesis was based on observations of factory "rate-busters" made by Dalton, as reported in Whyte (1955), and more recent observations by Edith Lentz suggesting that farm-reared nurses make better adjustments to the authoritarian organizational practices of hospitals than their city-bred peers (see Strauss and Sayles, 1960). These observations may be a reflection of the often-discussed protestant work ethic that is supposedly stronger among farmers than among city dwellers.

6. Older (above median) workers will show an increase in productivity relative to the younger (below median) workers. This hypothesis was based on insights gained from the earlier consulting done in this firm. At that time, older employees seemed to feel that they were "poor stepchildren" in this organization, which, like most others, has no systematic policy to transfer older workers into less physically demanding work. Thus, we expected an increase from them either because of the extra attention they were going to receive or because they might perceive a threat in this situation.

7. The productivity of workers reporting high activity levels in the union either will decrease, since they are anti-management, relative to that of men reporting low levels of

union activity, who are anti-union or pro-management, or will remain the same while the productivity of the others increases.

In general we expected a certain pattern of productivity to occur for the three time periods (before, during, and after) in the high F-scale, farm-reared, older, and inactive unionist groups; an increase followed by a decrease. We expected a decrease followed by an increase in the low F-scale, non-farm-reared, younger, and active unionist groups. The effects were tested for statistical significance by repeated measurements ANOV procedures for a $p \times q$ experimental design (Winer, 1962). The interaction effects were tested by the F-statistic computed as follows:

$$ F = \frac{MS_{AB}}{MS_{BXSs \text{ within groups}}}, $$

$$ df = q - 1 \text{ and } p(n - 1)(q - 1). $$

The interaction test is on the statistical hypothesis that profiles, over time, for the moderator groups (for example, older versus younger workers) are not different. Simple main effects also were tested, regardless of the interaction-test results, because they were hypothesized in advance of the experiment (See Winer, 1962, page 208).

QUANTITATIVE FINDINGS IN A NON-EXPERIMENT

Hypothesis 1: Department Productivity $(N = 73)$. The hypothesis that there would be no significant research effect on the total upholstering department is not fully supported by Table 1. An overall F-test on the three means is significant beyond the .01 level $(F = 8.55)$. Application of the Neuman-Keouls procedure, described in Winer (1962), testing the difference between ordered pairs of means, reveals that the before and during periods differ from one another just below the .05 level. The during-after difference is significant beyond the .05 level. Although some of the differences in the

Table 1. Productivity means (per cent of base rate)
and standard deviations for the before, during,
and after time periods, for 73 workers

Time period	$\bar{X}$	s
Before	134.6	28.3
During	133.8	28.9
After	138.3	30.8

table are statistically significant, they are quite small in a practical sense.

Hypothesis 2: Group (Line) Productivity. The left-hand portion of Table 2 shows the Pearson product-moment cor-

Table 2. Pearson product-moment correlations among eight upholstering lines and among 73 workers on productivity (per cent of base rate) for the three experimental periods and a reliability period

	r	
Time period	8 lines*	73 workers†
Before-during	.98‡	.95‡
Before-after	.97‡	.92‡
During-after	.95‡	.93‡
Reliability§	.91‡	.94‡

* Based on pairs of group means for the eight lines in each period.

† Based on 73 individual pairs of observations.

‡ $p < .01$.

§ Based on an analysis of contiguous time periods prior to the before period.

relations among the eight production lines for the various time periods in question and for the two halves of a pre-experimental reliability control period. All the correlations are in the .90's and are statistically significant beyond the .01 level. Thus, the hypothesis of no differential research effects on the eight intact employee groups is supported. The groups did not change their productivity levels relative to one another at any phase of the experiment.

Hypothesis 3: Individual Productivity. As in the case of the group data reported above, the between time-period correlations for individuals, in the right-hand column of Table 2 are almost uniformly high, ranging from .93 to .95. This seems to contradict our hypothesis that different individuals would react differently to the experimental treatment. Findings 4 through 7, however, suggest that this correlational analysis may hide the effects rather than reveal them.

Hypotheses 4–7: Authoritarianism, Rural-Urban Background, Age, and Union Activity Level Moderators. Figure 4 summarizes the several moderator variables.[9] The shapes of the profiles for the low *F*-scale scorers, urban, younger, and active union worker groups are all very similar and show the expected decline during the research period followed by an increase afterward. The high *F*-scale scorers, rural, older, and inactive union worker groups show the expected increase during the experimental period. These increases were followed by further increases, however, rather than by decreases.[10]

---

[9] The low and high *F*-scale groups contain equal proportions of rural and urban-reared workers. They also are equivalent on age. The rural and urban-reared groups, in the second portion of the table, are equivalent on *F*-scale means and age. The age groups are equivalent on proportions of rural and urban background workers and on *F*-scale means. The active and inactive unionist groups do not differ significantly on any of the three moderator variables. Age, incidentally, correlated only .32 with length of service.

[10] Three of the moderator variable profiles (rural-urban background, age, and union activity level) differ significantly (beyond the .05 or .01 level) according to the results of interaction effect *F* tests ($F = 3.57$, 5.51, and 10.29 respectively). The authoritarianism interaction effect is significant only between the .25 and .10 levels ($F = 1.55$). Simple main-effect results, however, show that the three production means (before, during, and after) for the high *F-scale* scorers differ beyond the .01 level ($F = 6.56$) as do the three means for the low *F*-scale workers ($F = 5.34$), thus supporting the moderator hypothesis on this variable. The other simple main-effect tests provide further suggestive data. It

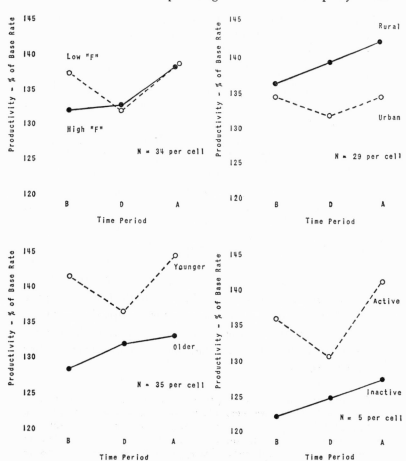

Figure 4. Productivity interaction profiles for authoritarianism, rural-urban background, age, and union activity level in relation to the before (*B*), during (*D*), and after (*A*) time periods

Given the equivalence of the various comparison groups, the data in Figure 4 generally support the moderator-variable

seems that the major effects of the experimental treatment were felt by the rural ($F = 5.78$, $p < .01$), younger ($F = 12.19$, $p < .01$) and active union workers ($F = 2.90$, $p < .10$ but $> .05$). Smaller effects occurred for the urban ($F = 1.88$, $p < .25$) older workers ($F = 2.44$, $p < .10$ but $> .05$). The simple main effect for inactive unionists did not even approach significance ($F = 1.37$).

hypotheses. Thus, characteristics of individuals in this non-experiment did influence different people to react in different ways to the research process. The significance levels in some cases are marginal by customary standards, however, and the practical magnitudes are not large.

It is worth noting in passing that the four moderator variables were not related at all to productivity changes in time periods several months before the non-experiment was conducted. This adds credence to the interpretation that they occurred as a result of the experimental intervention in the factory.

The quantitative findings, in general, support most of the hypotheses of this phase of the study. The research effect on average productivity for the total group of 73 workers was statistically significant. Contrary to expectations, however, individual workers' relative productivity positions were not strongly affected, as indicated by the before, during, and after period intercorrelations in the .90's. Nonetheless, statistically significant moderator influences were demonstrated for age, authoritarianism, rural-urban background, and union activity levels.

While the data reveal statistically significant results, the practical magnitudes of some of the differences do not seem alarming at first glance. However, the data nevertheless are somewhat scary if one considers the mildness of the experimental treatment.

The moderator-variable influences also suggest generalized patterns of either authority-dependent reactions or anti-authoritarianism on the part of the subjects.[11] The quantita-

---

[11] Some readers may prefer to think of the *F*-scale as a measure of acquiescence in line with fairly recent research on response sets associated with this instrument. Such an interpretation would be consistent with the findings reported herein; high scorers acquiesced with the perceived management representatives, while those with low scores not only failed to acquiesce, but sandbagged as well. The phenomenon seems identical to the one observed by Block and Block (1955) in a laboratory experiment on college students. If the reader prefers still

tive data are supported strongly, in this regard, by the un-
solicited comments made by many of the workers to the
researchers. The comments in fact shed considerable light on
these and other reactions to the research process. Walter
Nord's editorially abbreviated field notes should help to
flesh out the statistical skeleton provided by Tables 1 and 2
and by Figure 4.

QUALITATIVE REACTIONS OF GOLDFISH IN A BOWL

Why Are You Really Here? Frequent comments made
by the upholstering workers to the field researchers reflected
clear attempts by the workers to define the graduate students'
effective institutional identification or loyalty, and to establish their real purpose in being present. One man said,
for example, "I think you're a company man," despite the
Cornell University letterhead on the letter he had received
prior to the observers' arrival. The researchers frequently
were asked how they had come to select the Northeast Plant
for study and whom they knew to "open the door." As Nord
puts it, "Our research was perceived as management-initiated,
despite our efforts to avoid any such cues. It seems likely that
those who perceived us in this light would have done so even
if the earlier study [the Foltman-Rosen consulting interviews]
had not occurred, since they could not understand how a company which 'could . . . not afford to give us a Christmas
turkey this year (a long-standing practice in past years) could
afford to spend $450 on your thesis if it isn't getting some-
thing out of it.'

---

another conceptualization of the *F*-scale, namely that it is a measure
of general intelligence, the data again are reasonable. Thus, high
F-scorers, being of relatively low intelligence, failed to see the researchers as being a potential threat and showed a classical "Hawthorne effect." Meanwhile, their low *F*-score counterparts, being more
intelligent, were sensitive to the possible threat to their welfare and
slowed down. In any event, whatever the original 26-item scale measures,
the 13-item form used herein seems to measure it more reliably because
of the items' high internal consistency.

"After our questionnaire had been administered, several of the workers still thought that we had been hired by management. This feeling had created some dissonance in their minds, since we felt that they basically liked us and trusted us as individuals. The result of such an incongruent relationship was the view that *we* were on the level but that they did not know what kind of deal our professor had made with the Plant Manager. These suspicions became stronger after we administered our questionnaire.

"Attempts to guess the purpose of our study were the most widely attempted adjustments that we observed. First of all, one worker asked if we were timing the jobs. This response was uncommon, but showed that some men thought that our purposes were involved with management time studies. Other questions which sought our purpose included: 'Did the company give you those questions?' 'Are you working for the company? If you are, I hope that you don't write down all the names we call the company.' Other people stated that we had to be working for the company. They reasoned, 'If you weren't, why would he (the Plant Manager) pay for the time (during which we were to administer our questionnaire)? He must be getting something out of it or he wouldn't do it. I wouldn't if I were him.' We responded to these queries by stating that we had agreed to give him a copy of my thesis the same as we had the union.

"Attempts to determine our purpose were far more varied than just to see if we were company men, and reflected very pointed guesses. Thus, some perceived our purpose in terms of what they thought psychology was like as applied to an industrial setting. One worker said: 'I hear you wrote down that X had an inferiority complex. Wait until you talk to him (pointing), he's a nonconformist.' This individual continued to use psychological jargon when referring to what we were doing. Some other workers, however, saw us more as interviewers, probably because of the earlier study at this site. One asked, after I had spoken to him for the first round of questioning, 'Is this my interview? I want to hear you interview him.' Judging by the information that I obtained from this individual later, he had a lot which he wanted to be sure I found out. Another worker, while inquiring about our questionnaires asked, 'What are they about, how happy we are?' Another asked, 'Is your report going to include the bad things as well as the good?' All these comments reflect the significant amount of thinking that had taken place about what we were doing. Also, they reflect the fact that they had formed an impression about what research is and what researchers do, probably from the earlier study at this site, and tried to fit us into these preceptions. All these attempts were not successful as demonstrated by the number of times we were asked, *'What are you really doing?'* by both workers and foremen.

"Other people imputed different purposes to our study. One asked, 'How many different styles have you counted?' After I told him that I had not kept count, he replied, 'Oh, I thought maybe you were counting the styles.' Other people thought we were primarily interested in technology. Many spent long periods of time explaining exactly what they were doing, even though we had not sought such a response. Further, many people said after they filled out the questionnaire that they had answered them thinking that we were interested in technology, indicating that they would have answered the sociometric items differently had they known that technology was not our primary or only concern."

It is clear from Nord's account that the quantitative data on productivity reported earlier reflect individual differences among workers relevant to the extent to which the researchers were trusted or perceived as management agents. In this case, the traditional "Hawthorne effect" looks more like a "time-study man" effect.

When Do We Take the Test? According to Nord, "The Questionnaire, both before and after its administration, aroused by far the most curiosity and anxiety. Before they completed the questionnaire, thoughts were expressed by a large percentage of workers in some form or other concerning what the items were like. 'When are the *tests*?' 'What are they about?' 'Will the union get a copy of the report?' 'It's a wonder the company would pay for something like that, isn't it?' Nearly everyone referred to the questionnaire as a 'test.' Every time this word was used, we made an effort to correct the term. The use of 'test' was so widespread that it is quite likely that the participants expected some measure of intelligence. In any case, 'test' aroused different thoughts in the minds of different people. Some workers thought it necessary to tell us that they had not done well in school. Despite our efforts to have our questionnaires taken as a 'Gallup Poll,' the idea of 'tests' persisted among the participants. Every day a barrage of questions arose about the 'tests,' up until the day they were administered.

"The day following the administration of the items, curiosity about the reasons for our questions and our overall purpose seemed to reach an all-time high. Since it was difficult directly to relate many of the questions to the work situation, many of the comments were of a suspicious nature. The comments became numerous and intense.

"Some of the respondents apparently dismissed us as just plain stupid. 'Your questions were a lot of bullshit. One contradicts the other.' Another commented that we were probably company men and that we asked very stupid questions. 'My mother-in-law is an educated college woman. She used to teach school. She said you never ask kids who they don't like. No one in their right mind would ask you who you don't like.' [This refers to one of our sociometric items.] Others still could not understand the company's motives. 'The biggest gift the company ever gave us before was an afternoon off for voting out the union. We figured out how much it [the time required to fill out our questionnaires, which the company paid for] cost. I can't imagine the company paying out $800 for nothing.' One worker from another line corrected this figure saying that it had not cost that much. We figured it out together in rough terms and found the true cost was closer to $400. What this gross overstatement of the cost means is uncertain. It was quite obvious from the number of comments that were made by a large number of people in this department that much thought had been given about the cost to the company. In this context, suspicion was almost an inevitable result.

"Other people had perceived our instrument as an intelligence test or some kind of trick device. One worker said, 'I couldn't see the point to some of the questions. You had to be careful or you'd contradict yourself. I see you had a carbon copy in one.' This statement showed that some amount of guessing had taken place about the questionnaire even during the administration. The 'carbon copy' refers to the Leadership Opinion Questionnaire, which is a self-scoring device requiring a carbon insert. Other workers emphasized the word 'contradicts' with respect to our items. This word suggests the situation existed where the subject was looking for some purpose or pattern while in the process of completing his questionnaire. Other people perceived our instrument as if we were some type of management consultants, or a sounding board for complaints."

It is clear from Dr. Nord's account that the questionnaire was a threatening stimulus to these workers, even before they saw it, let alone afterward. The workers' apparent perception of the questionnaire as a "test," moreover, suggests that they probably thought there were "right" and "wrong" answers, despite the researcher's standard admonitions to the contrary.

Defense against the Outsider. Argyris (1952), on the basis of his extensive field-research experiences, has mentioned that people in an industrial situation often feel defensive when they are dealing with people from universities. They may seek to defend themselves by talking of things they believe will impress the observer or at least be an acceptable topic of conversation to him. This phenomenon was quite obvious during our study. According to Nord, "One worker volunteered information on competition in the furniture industry and the American market. He named the chief foreign competitors with United States furniture companies, and spoke of the copying of styles between American companies. He stated also that he could not understand why people in the space age wanted early American furniture. The reader may wish to place another interpretation on this incident, but since it came on my first talk with the individual, it appeared to this observer that the individual was attempting to make what he thought would be a good impression of himself in the eyes of a university affiliate.

"Other persons responded to the presence of university people by saying: 'The work here isn't as easy as it looks.' Another remarked: 'Would you like to switch jobs?' Another commented, 'Go to school so you don't have to work here.' Other workers frequently spoke of people they had known who went to college, or associations they had had with university life and people. In addition, several workers commented on their regret that they had not gone to college while others stated their intentions of having their children go to advanced schools. Some of these statements seemed to reflect envy of us as well as defensiveness. For example, several workers made such comments as, 'It must be nice to have a rich daddy to send you to college.' Still others said, 'Don't write down that bad English,' or 'We're not really smart, but we're not going to give you stupid answers.' " Another commented, 'I hated school.' "

It appears that individuals made attempts during this phase of the study to adjust to, and defend themselves from, the perceived or expected sophistication of college-trained researchers. In all probability this attitude helps explain the productivity decline among the *younger* workers during the researchers' presence in the department (see Figure 4). The younger men were the most likely to be resentful of Nord and Schwartzbaum, who were both twenty-three years old at the time.

Defense against the outsider also appeared at another level. Thus, when asked, "What do you think an ideal foreman on your line would be like?" many people answered immediately that they had never thought of it, or they had never had one. Probing into the matter Nord found that these people did not want to answer such a question, often because "I don't want to hurt ours." A closely related example of such denial was an apparent attempt to appear cooperative by answering but yet to remain noncommittal. For instance, several subjects said, "Well, ours is pretty good," or "It's hard to be perfect." These statements perhaps could be best included under Argyris' heading of surface collaboration or talking around the point.

It is likely that some of this denial or related behavior carried over to the questionnaire. Approximately 30 per cent of the workers chose their own foreman as their first choice when they completed the questionnaire. Moreover, the distribution of these ranks was quite skewed in most groups; they became even more skewed when we returned to the plant for our follow-up study some time later.

Are You Getting What You Wanted? The final category of worker behavior that was observed is perhaps the most interesting in terms of the recent literature on "demand characteristics" and this phase of the study as a whole. Under this heading Nord observed widespread behavior which demonstrated that the respondents were concerned with how well they were playing their role of research subject. A large number of the people in the plant asked the observers at one time or another "Are you getting what you want?" "What can we do for you today?" "What did you learn today?" or some similar question. After an observer talked with a worker, a common response was "Did I give you what you wanted?" From the above description of the search for the purpose the respondents made, it is quite evident that serious

I. View of the Northeast Upholstering Department as one looks down an assembly line

II. A back-springer at work on a couch

III. A seat-maker stapling padding to the frame of a chair

IV. A back-maker applying covering material to the back of a chair

efforts were made to find out what we wanted. This factor, in conjunction with the extreme interest in whether they were helpful or not, indicates that many of the workers were quite interested in helping to make the project a success. No evidence was collected on the extent to which they would have gone to support any hypothesis we might have had. More careful studies of the field situation similar to those conducted in the laboratory by Orne and others will be required to measure this factor.

DISCUSSION

The quantitative and qualitative data reported in this chapter should be considered from two points of view. First, how generalizable are the results of this "non-experiment" likely to be? Second, how seriously should we take these results in relation to planning the subsequent experiment on foreman effectiveness in this plant?

The findings in this chapter seem to reflect *weaker* research effects on production than might be found in many other research settings. Several conditions that might have attenuated the statistical productivity results herein are: the use of graduate-student researchers rather than professors or consultants (although their youth may have led to the age effect described earlier); the technological interdependence of the tasks performed by the subjects; the financial incentive system; the long tenure of the workers and high stability of their work groups' membership; the high pay and status of these workers relative to others in the plant; the size of the community, which caused range restriction on the rural-urban variable—very few came from large-city backgrounds; and the sex of the workers (all male). Other kinds of technological arrangements (for instance, noninterdependent batch-work, which characterizes what Fiedler (1964) calls a "co-acting group," may well produce more dramatic effects because individual differences in reaction to the research process would have a freer rein. The growing body of literature on this general problem and the evidence herein suggests that further attention should be given this matter. It is likely that most research workers, despite their university affiliations, will be perceived to some extent by rank-and-file employees (and even by many managers) as agents of the management.[12]

This line of reasoning (with special emphasis on the fact that a faculty member, not students, would be the future field worker), coupled with the quantitative and qualitative results of the non-experiment, suggested that any further experimental work done in the Upholstery Department of the Northeast Plant should be done *without* the potentially contaminating presence of research workers. The next phase, an experimental reassignment of foremen, if carried out, could enhance our knowledge all the more if research observers could be present. If they were present, however, the upholstery workers again probably would engage in a guessing game as to the reasons behind such an experiment, which would be a far more dramatic event than the research operations used in Phase 1. Rather than obtain misleading results either from well-meaning workers who would try to be "good subjects" by trying to help us verify what they perceive as our experimental hypothesis or from anti-management types, it was decided to sacrifice the potential gain from on-the-spot observations. Subsequent events, to be described in Chapter 5, turned this conservative decision into one of great sagacity.

The "non-experiment" described in this chapter was designed to assess the potential seriousness of so-called "Haw-

[12] In all fairness, however, it is possible that my consulting work in this plant prior to the "non-experiment" was at least partly responsible for the pattern of results. Thus, if the workers' first contact with Cornell people had been with the students, the thesis rationale might have been more believable and the traditional "Hawthorne effect" might have occurred instead of the "time-study man" effect that did occur.

thorne effects" and "demand characteristics" in the research site prior to conducting a later experiment on foreman effectiveness. The data revealed individual differences in worker reactions to being observed for two weeks and interrogated by questionnaire for one and a half hours. Younger, urban, low F-scale workers and active unionists tended to restrict output during the two-week research period, whereas their older, rural, high F-scale counterparts showed increased productivity, although these statistically significant results did not appear to be of practical magnitude. Qualitative remarks made by the workers, however, supported the general trend of the data and strongly supported the observations of such people as Argyris (1952), Block and Block (1955), Scott (1963), Vidich and Bensman (1960), and Orne (1959, 1962). On balance, I concluded that if a foremen effectiveness experiment were to be run subsequently in the Upholstery Department, it would have to be run without benefit of on-the-spot observers. In fact, the research nature of that experiment, I decided, should be hidden altogether from the workers and their foremen.

The data presented in this chapter also revealed that a relevant *and* reliable productivity criterion (per cent of base rate) for assessing the potential effects of a foreman experiment was available. Stability reliability coefficients were in the .88 to .95 range.

It now remains to be seen whether a reasonable scientific basis for the foreman experiment can be established and whether such an experiment will be acceptable to the plant manager.

CHAPTER 3

Building an Experimental Plan

WHAT SHOULD THE INDEPENDENT VARIABLE BE?

F-Scale, Initiation of Structure, and Consideration Scores. The search for an independent variable to guide the potential foreman reassignments was facilitated by the analysis of the questionnaire data collected during the "non-experiment." The following is a list of the measurements available, based on individual workers, groups of workers, or individual foremen; all these, before the data were collected, were considered to have potential value in establishing an experimental plan that would articulate with the large body of cross-sectional research literature referred to in Chapter 1:

Individual workers	*Work groups (lines)*
Score on California F-Scale	$\bar{X}$ score–California F-Scale
Initiation of structure score*	$\bar{X}$ score–initiation of structure*
Consideration score*	$\bar{X}$ score–consideration*
Preference rank assigned to each foreman	$\bar{X}$ preference rank assigned to each foreman

Individual foremen
Score on California F-Scale
Initiation of structure score
Consideration score
Preference rank assigned to each group

Those indexes marked by an asterisk were obtained from Fleishman's Leadership Opinion Questionnaire; however, the workers were instructed to indicate by their answers how they thought the "ideal line foreman *should* act" with respect to each question. The various preference ranks in the list were taken from item 3a in the worker booklet (Appendix A) and item 2a in the foreman booklet, (Appendix C).

These variables offered some intriguing possibilities for experimental manipulations from which we eventually would have to make a single choice. One possible strategy would have been to build upon the cross-sectional work of Vroom (1959) and Vroom and Mann (1960) by reassigning foremen to groups in such a way as to *maximize* the fit between foreman and worker values as measured by the F-scale for half the groups while *minimizing* the fit in the other half. A similar strategy of minimizing or maximizing value conflict between supervisors and their subordinates also could have been employed on the basis of Fleishman's initiation of structure and consideration dimensions. Thus, half of those groups desiring high structure from supervision would receive supervisors expressing high structure as their preferred style while the other half of the groups demanding high structure would receive foremen who prefer to give low structure. The groups preferring low structure would receive similar treatment.

Although this general strategy had great appeal conceptually, the empirical evidence in this case ruled it out. There were *no statistically significant differences among the work groups' (lines) mean scores* on any of the three dimensions— consideration, structure, or F-scale—although there was considerable individual variance within groups. Moreover, there was no significant relationship between the foremen's scores on any of these dimensions, on the one had, and work-group productivity, on the other, during the base-line study period. These variables, then, showed no promise for our experimental purposes and accordingly were discarded.

Pre-experimental Productivity Levels as an Independent Variable. Before examining the empirical prospects for the preference rankings as independent variables, let us examine one other strategy that was entertained, namely, a replication of the one reported by Feldman that was described in Chapter 1. Feldman, it may be recalled, reported circumstances where supervisors of high-producing groups were transferred to low-producing groups while the supervisors of the low-producing groups took over the high-producing groups. I decided against this strategy because, in addition to regression-effect problems, it did not seem to offer a full opportunity to test the causality question growing out of the cross-sectional survey research evidence appearing in recent years. I believed, therefore, that a foreman-effect experiment must stem directly either from attitudes toward authoritarianism, consideration and initiation of structure among workers and foremen or from more general worker perceptions—in this case, preference ranks. Of course, had the worker perception data (preference ranks) shown no empirical promise (a matter we shall examine below), the Feldman strategy would have been better than nothing.

Preference Rankings and Related Attitudes. The workers, as noted earlier, ranked the eight groups in the Upholstery Department and the eight foremen, indicating their personal preferences in both instances. (See items 2a and 3a in the worker booklet, Appendix A, for the ranking instructions they were given.) Thus, they were asked which line they would most like to work on, which one they would next most like to work on, and so on until all the lines were ranked. Similar instructions guided their ranking of the foremen.[1] Additional questionnaire items were administered to ascer-

[1] The respondents were asked to *rank* the groups and foremen rather than rate them on continuous scales because we were worried about ties. On the basis of past experience with rating scales among blue-collar workers I had learned that many workers and foremen resist the whole idea of discriminating among people; they will often say, "They are all doing a good job," or, "One is as good (or as bad) as the next." Ranking procedures sharply reduce this problem. It must be conceded, however, that the perceived discrepancies among some of the foremen may not have been large; thus, the independent variable may have suffered from some amount of range restriction.

tain the workers' reasons for their first, second, and last choices of lines and for their first and last choices of foremen.[2] (See the worker booklet, items 2b, 2c, 2d, 3b, and 3c, in Appendix A.) Table 3 summarizes the analyses of the

Table 3. Intercorrelations (Rho) among foreman preference, group cohesion, status consensus on foreman, and productivity, for eight groups*

Variable	X_1	X_2	X_3	X_0
(X_1) foreman preference (mean rank) within each group	1.00	.83	.93	.62
(X_2) group cohesion (mean rank) within each group			.79	.69
(X_3) status consensus on foreman (standard deviation) within each group				.68
(X_0) productivity of each work group†				

* These are group-based data. All means and standard deviations within each group were converted to ranks for this analysis. Critical value of Rho, $N = 8$, .05 level, one-tail test = .64.

† Mean percentage of base rate for a four-week period *prior to* the "non-experiment" was used for this analysis.

ranking data based upon groups, not individuals, as the unit of analysis. That is, the individual ranks were converted to group measurements—means and standard deviations—to facilitate this analysis. For example, X_1 in Table 3 represents the average (mean) rank assigned each foreman by his own subordinates. Several points may be made about this table: (1) the more favorably disposed the group is toward its fore-

[2] The men were asked to describe their second-choice line in addition to their first choice because we thought their first choice might be made as an automatic response to protect their own group's image; that is, we expected many to pick their own group as first choice because "it's the thing to do" when an outsider asks. Many workers, however, failed to respond to item 2c altogether. Most others filled it out exactly as they did for 2b. Therefore, we dropped their descriptions of their second-choice lines from our analysis plans.

man (X_1), the higher its productivity (X_0) is likely to be (Rho = .62); (2) the more favorably disposed the group is toward itself (X_2), the higher its productivity (Rho = .69); (3) the more favorably disposed the group is toward itself, the more favorably disposed it is toward its own foreman (Rho = .83); (4) the more internal agreement within the work group about its foreman (X_3), the greater its productivity (Rho = .68) and the more favorably disposed it is toward itself (Rho = .79) and its foreman (Rho = .93).

In addition to Table 3, it also is worth noting that the more internal agreement within each group on its foreman, the more attractive its foreman is to outsiders in the department (Rho = .72).

The magnitudes and conceptual consistency of these rank-order correlations are impressive indeed. (The reader should note, however, that with an N of only eight groups the Rho's must be quite large [.64] to achieve statistical significance at the .05 level for a one-tail test.) The data in Table 3 and the two paragraphs immediately preceding this one provide strong support for the findings of other cross-sectional studies where technological differences among groups were not as small.

The evidence herein and elsewhere—see Seashore (1954), and Krech *et al.* (1962)—also argues strongly for a group approach to the supervisory-influence phenomenon. The group, rather than the individual, is the proper unit of analysis in this study because in general the process of leadership involves an entire group, including its role structure, behavioral norms, and shared attitudes. Moreover, in this case specifically, the tasks within each group are highly interdependent, and therefore the study deals with group operations requiring teamwork. The foreman has to perform within prescribed limits if his team is to function effectively. It also is likely that he, like leaders in similar small groups, must be a follower as well as a leader, despite the fact that he is appointed by top management. The correlational data seem to support this view. While leadership effects in the experiment described below can be looked for at the level of individual group members, none are likely to appear because of the task interdependence in these groups. The long-established norms and shared attitudes in these groups also are likely to mitigate against individual effects because of the potent influence such group variables have on individual members. Although small individual effects did occur in the previously described "non-experiment," they are not inconsistent with the present line of reasoning. The operations in the non-experiment were ambiguous stimuli for the workers. Relevant group norms and shared frames of reference had not previously developed. Consequently, individuals were somewhat free to vary, within the limits imposed by task interdependence. In the foreman experiment to be described below, however, there can be no question that group norms and shared frames of reference clearly existed prior to the experimental manipulation. The data in Table 3 and the correlations between group indices, on the one hand, and the department-wide indices, on the other, support this view. Thus, individuals probably had less freedom to vary in the foreman experiment than in the "non-experiment."

It also is worth emphasizing that the conceptually consistent correlational evidence discussed above still does not answer the question of time order, which, in turn, relates to the causal-interpretation problem. Thus, high cohesion (for reasons of agreement on group objectives or compatible group-member personalities) may have led to high productivity through willing, cooperative effort among group members doing this highly interdependent work on the upholstering lines. (The workers' agreement on objectives may be related to a common interest in money.) On the other hand, high productivity (for reasons of favorable combination of group-member skills, physical endurance, and, perhaps, product mix) may have led to feelings of achievement that were rewarded (reinforced) by the financial incentive system. These phenomena, in turn, could have led to satisfaction with the group and high internal agreement-cohesion.[3]

A few words are in order regarding X_3, the extent of agreement within each group about its foreman as determined by the size of the standard deviation of the ranks assigned to the foreman by the individual group members. This index reflects a conceptual dimension of small groups, called "status consensus," that is employed by Bales and others (as described by Heslin and Dunphy, 1964). Status consensus on the leader is the degree of agreement among the rankings by group members of their leader. Laboratory and field-study evidence reviewed by Heslin and Dunphy shows a significant correlation between status consensus on the leader and both productivity and satisfaction measures, using groups as the unit of analysis. Group consensus in rankings apparently reflects agreement among the group members as to the criteria for a status continuum, as well as agreement on the relation of the leader to the criteria. Fiedler (1964) presumably is working with a similar dimension when he measures "leader-member relations" by sociometric methods.

It is clear that the above research work has direct relevance to conditions in the Upholstering Department. The "agreement index" used here is a type of "status consensus" index that probably reflects the extent of agreement within each group on what constitutes an appropriate criterion of foreman performance. This index (status consensus on foreman)

---

[3] The large magnitudes of the correlations between supervisory and group rankings on the one hand and productivity on the other may well have occurred because of the data collection schedule and operations used. Thus, the productivity criterion included four weeks of data *immediately preceding* the beginning of the non-experiment. In other words, the workers may have been influenced by their very *recent* accomplishments when performing the ranking tasks. Their rankings did not correlate significantly with productivity levels at later times.

also probably reflects the extent that group members agree on how well these criteria are being met by their foreman. The data in Tables 4 and 5 should explicate this point. In any event, the "consensus" index appears to be of paramount importance and will be discussed again in later chapters.

Before we leave Table 3 in general and the agreement index specifically, a few more conceptual-operational points need to be made. The following terminology will be used in the balance of this book when referring to variables X_1 through X_3, which were discussed above: (1) group perception of, or preference for, foreman, as measured by the mean preference rank assigned by all the group members to a particular foreman; (2) status consensus on foreman, as measured by the standard deviation, within each group, of the above rankings; (3) group attraction, as measured by the mean preference rank assigned by all the group members to their own group. Thus, "group foreman preference" is a within-group popularity index, while "status consensus on foreman" reflects the extent to which the various group members have a shared frame of reference about the foreman's popularity. "Group attraction" reflects the extent to which the group members wish to remain in the group. While group preference for foreman and status consensus on foreman appear to be highly correlated (see Table 3), conceptually they are not identical. It is theoretically possible for a leader to have a high average popularity index in his constituent group, but there may be a range of possible follower consensus levels; that is, the standard deviation may range from small to large. Therefore, all three of these group dimensions were retained for further study.

Worker Ratings of First- and Last-Choice Groups. Table 4 offers perceptual evidence, based on the workers' opinions, which bears on the above discussion. (See items 2b and 2d in the worker booklet, Appendix A.) The table presents mean ratings provided by the workers on selected characteristics of

Table 4. Mean descriptions by workers ($N = 72$) of their
first- and last-choice work groups (lines) and *t*-tests*
on the differences, by scale† and group choice

Rating-scale item	$\bar{X}$		t
	First-choice line	Last-choice line	
Amount of money you can make	5.7	4.0	6.8‡
Speed of work pace	5.7	4.4	5.3‡
Amount of cooperation among the workers	5.1	4.1	3.9‡
Opportunity to use your head	5.4	4.6	3.7‡
Friendliness of workers	5.7	4.9	3.3‡
Amount of self-pacing	5.5	4.7	2.7‡
Fairness of rates	4.3	3.9	1.7‡
Amount of physical effort required	5.8	5.5	1.4‡
Amount of skill required	5.6	5.4	0.9§
Opportunity to talk	5.1	4.9	0.1§
Amount of variety in the work	5.4	5.3	0.0§

* For correlated measures.

† Seven-point numerical scales were used, anchored at each end. For example:

"Amount of money you can make on this line"—A lot 7 6 5 4 3 2 1 A little

‡ Significant beyond .05 level by both one and two-tail test standards. (Critical values = 1.29 and 1.66, respectively.)

§ Not significant.

their most (first-choice) and least (last-choice) preferred work groups.[4] The characteristics are arranged in the table in

[4] The seven-point scales on which the workers described their first- and last-choice lines probably reflect a combination of objective reality and projected characteristics that exist only in the minds of the respondents. The scales used were selected largely on the basis of the job satisfaction literature plus our desire to determine the groups' shared attitudes relative to management objectives in general and the motive to produce in particular. Data on the intercorrelations of these scales will be presented in Chapter 4.

descending order in terms of the extent to which each characteristic discriminates between first- and last-choice groups. The extent of discrimination is determined by the magnitude of the *t*-test results. It is easily seen that *money* and *speed of work pace* are the most discriminating items in the table, although others are also statistically significant. As the reader will see in Chapter 5, the extent to which the separate groups discriminate between their first- and last-choice lines on the basis of money-making potential can be operationalized as a crucial motivational variable. Conceptually, this variable is analogous to what Seashore (1954) refers to as group "acceptance or rejection of company goals." A systems analysis of leadership effects will require us to include this variable in our eventual analytical scheme.

Given the correlational data reported in Table 3, the *t*-test results in Table 4 suggest that group attraction is based largely on incentive earnings in this department. This interpretation is further supported by a rank-order correlation of .81 between the workers' job-title preference rankings (e.g., springer, seat-maker, trimmer) and their rankings of the same job titles with respect to their incentive-pay potential. Thus, they prefer those *jobs* and *lines* where income potential is perceived to be high; they rank low the less remunerative lines and jobs.

These data, then, reveal a strong departmental production ethic based largely on a shared positive attitude toward money. It would seem reasonable to conclude, on the basis of this finding plus the intercorrelations in Table 3 involving attitudes toward foremen, that the workers' rankings of foremen will be influenced primarily by their perceptions of the foreman's technical and administrative skills, his job knowledge and planning and organizing ability. In fact, Walter Nord reported one upholsterer as saying to him during the non-experiment that "the right kind of foreman is worth 30 cents an hour to the worker" if he stays on top of his job. Let us see what the data reveal.

Worker Ratings on First- and Last-Choice Foremen. Table 5 presents data representing the workers' descriptions of their first- and last-choice foremen in terms of eight different

Table 5. Mean descriptions by workers ($N = 74$) of their first- and last-choice foremen and t-tests* on the differences, by scale† and foreman choice

	$\overline{X}$		
Rating-scale item	First-choice foreman	Last-choice foreman	t
Personality (pleasant-unpleasant)	6.3	3.8	10.7‡
His ability to get things for his men from management	5.1	3.4	7.1‡
His ability to plan and organize the work	5.5	4.1	6.4‡
His ability to get along with the union	5.4	4.1	6.1‡
The extent of his job knowledge	6.1	5.0	5.2‡
The way he treats his men (easy-strict)	5.0	3.6	3.9‡
His skill as an upholsterer	5.9	5.2	2.5‡
Amount of seniority he has	5.8	5.5	1.2§

* For correlated measures.

† Seven-point numerical scales were used, anchored at each end. For example:

"Personality of this foreman"—Pleasant 7 6 5 4 3 2 1 Unpleasant.

‡ Significant beyond .05 level by both one- and two-tail test standards. (Critical values = 1.29 and 1.66, respectively.)

§ Not significant.

characteristics. Like Table 4, it is arranged in descending order on the basis of t-test results. The many statistically significant discriminators are very reminiscent of the data reported by a variety of other researchers in this field.[5] Inter-

---

[5] Most of the eight dimensions used were chosen directly on the basis of extensive survey research evidence reported by Likert, his many coworkers and other researchers in this field. The intercorrelations of these dimensions and others will be examined in Chapter 4.

estingly enough, "personality" is by far the most discriminating item, not those items which on their face reflect the more obvious technologically related skills.[6]

The Question of Personality. Given the enormous t (10.7) in Table 5 on the personality dimension, one must become concerned about the prognosis of an experimental manipulation based upon the workers' preference rankings. Specifically, how can the foreman's agreeable or disagreeable personality, as perceived by the workers, have any theoretical link to group productivity? In the case of these upholstery lines, it seems reasonable to expect that a foreman's perceived personality will affect his relations with, and therefore his influence over, a variety of people who in turn can affect the group's output. Thus, when the need arises because of a production bottleneck, some foremen may have a much easier time than others in persuading the appropriate upholsterers to change positions in the line on a timely basis. Moreover, the foreman's lateral relations with the supervisors of the Cushion Department, and the Cutting and Sewing Department are extremely important in maintaining a timely flow of component materials to the upholstery lines. There can be little question that a disagreeable personality can be a distinct handicap to a foreman in these instances. Moreover, if he is really disagreeable, his own men may fail to inform him, at least occasionally, about such impending emergencies as material or staple shortages. Of course, they will be sacrifying personal income when doing this. Such behavior, however, is not at all uncommon either inside or outside the work place.

Some data collected at a much later date further illuminate the question of a foreman's personality. The data reflect the answers given by the workers when they were asked to describe the personalities of the first- and last-choice foremen

[6] It should be noted that different workers were describing different foremen when filling out these scales. For example, the first-choice foreman for any given worker was a lower choice for many other workers.

after the reassignments were made. The questionnaire included thirty-three items, many of which in one form or another appear in a variety of personality inventories. Wording and format were altered so that they would fit my instrument, again using seven-point scales like those described in Tables 4 and 5. The purpose, of course, was to find out what constitutes a "disagreeable personality," which was identified in the preliminary study as the single most discriminating variable in the workers' minds when describing their first- and last-choice foremen. The items showing the largest *t*-test results on the perceived personality differences between first- and last-choice foremen include, in descending order of *t*-magnitude: (1) moody, temperamental; (2) hard to talk to; (3) grouchy, grumpy; (4) bossy; (5) has a chip on his shoulder; (6) unfriendly; (7) flies off the handle; (8) gets upset; (9) acts too quickly without thinking; (10) likes to criticize. The obtained *t* for each of these items exceeded 10.0, significant beyond the .001 level. The thirty-three personality items plus others were subjected to a factor analysis that will be presented in Chapter 4. For present purposes, the above descriptions certainly seem to describe the difference between agreeable and disagreeable foremen. It also seems clear that a supervisor who is perceived as having all the above characteristics is very likely to have low influence over others, and, therefore, he also may have low productivity. Such an individual will not only be disliked, but he also may be seen as unpredictable, which might be even more disadvantageous from the standpoint of running a production organization under pressure.

Foremen's and Workers' Views Compared. Table 6 summarizes the worker ratings that appear in Table 5 and also presents the comparable ratings provided by the foremen themselves. That is, the foremen also were asked to rank the same list of foremen's names, including their own. (Their composite rankings, incidentally, correlated only .22 with the workers' composite preference rankings.) They, too, were

Table 6. Mean descriptions by workers (N = 74) and foremen (N = 8) of their first- and last-choice foremen and t-tests* on the differences, by scale† and foreman choice

Rating-scale item	Worker data $\bar{X}$				Foreman data $\bar{X}$			
	First-choice foreman	Last-choice foreman	t	Rank of t	First-choice foreman	Last-choice foreman	t	Rank of t
Personality (pleasant–unpleasant)	6.3	3.8	10.7‡	1	5.8	4.8	3.8‡	4
His ability to get things for his men from management	5.1	3.4	7.1‡	2	5.5	3.2	4.0‡	2
His ability to plan and organize the work	5.5	4.1	6.4‡	3	6.4	3.5	8.0‡	1
His ability to get along with the union	5.4	4.1	6.1‡	4	5.4	4.4	1.8‡	6
The extent of his job knowledge	6.1	5.0	5.2‡	5	6.8	5.0	3.0‡	5
The way he treats his men (easy-strict)	5.0	3.6	3.9‡	6	4.2	4.8	.4§	8
His skill as an upholsterer	5.9	5.2	2.5‡	7	6.9	4.8	3.9‡	3
Amount of seniority he has	5.8	5.5	1.2§	8	6.2	4.8	1.5‡	7

* For correlated measures.
† Seven-point numerical scales were used, anchored at each end. For example: "Personality of this foreman"—Pleasant 7 6 5 4 3 2 1 Unpleasant
‡ Significant at or beyond the .05 level, one-tailed test.
§ Not significant.

then asked to rate their first- and last-choice foremen on the same eight dimensions provided the workers. (See items 3a, 3b, and 3c in the foremen's booklet, Appendix C). An examination of the *t*-test columns in the table, and the rank orders on their magnitudes, shows that while "personality" was by far the most significant discriminator for workers, "ability to plan and organize the work" was by far the most significant discriminator in the foremen's eyes. The foreman's "skill as an upholsterer," moreover, ranks third in importance (*t*-test magnitude) for the foremen but runs a weak seventh for the workers. The table also shows that supervisory style—"The way he treats his men"—is regarded much differently by the workers than by the foremen. For the latter the difference between their first and last choice, while not statistically significant, suggests that strictness is desirable. The workers see it the other way around. Interestingly enough, both foremen and workers see "ability to get things for his men from management" as highly important.[7] This, of course, is another way in which the foreman's personality can affect his group's performance, through the extent to which he can influence his superiors to give him prompt action on operating problems.

It seems clear that to some extent the foremen, as a group, employ different standards in defining their jobs than do the workers when they define the same job. The foremen generally seem to place emphasis on technical and administrative competence, while the workers place more emphasis on "personality." The workers by no means ignore technical and administrative competence, however, as is observable from the substantial *t*-test results in Tables 5 and 6. The difference between the two populations appears to be a matter more of relative emphasis than of kind.

---

[7] These findings blend nicely with the evidence reported by Pelz (1951) on the general issue of supervisors' influence on their own superiors in the chain of command.

DO WE HAVE AN INDEPENDENT VARIABLE?

The answer to the question "Do we have an independent variable?" appears to be a resounding "Yes." The relationship of the groups' mean foreman preference rankings to their productivity levels, and the workers' apparent reasons for their preferences (which correspond nicely with many other cross-sectional research study results), should enable us to test a causal-direction hypothesis experimentally by reassigning foremen in accordance with work-group preferences. If the typical causal-direction interpretation, discussed in Chapter 1, is correct, a group whose foreman is replaced by one it ranked higher should increase its productivity, because the new foreman, as perceived by his subordinates, will have some combination of a more agreeable personality, better planning and organizing skills, more influence with management and the union, more job knowledge and upholstering skill, and a more easy-going manner in dealing with his men. A group receiving a new foreman it ranked lower than its original foreman should show a decline in productivity accordingly. Of course, for the reasons discussed in Chapter 1, such hypotheses may not be supported.

THE PROPOSED EXPERIMENTAL PLAN

On the basis of these empirical and conceptual considerations, I developed a tentative experimental plan for the plant manager's consideration. The plan and the productivity hypotheses for each work group are summarized in Table 7. The seven work groups are designated by capital letters *B* through *H* so that their identity will not be known to any readers who happen to work in the Northeast Plant. For each work group the table indicates the mean preference rank assigned to that group's initial foreman, before the experimental change was made, and the mean preference rank assigned by that group to the foreman provided in the

Table 7. The experimental plan and productivity
change hypothesis for each group

Work group	Mean worker preference rank for initial foreman*	Mean worker preference rank for experimental foreman*	Hypothesized productivity change
B	1.7	6.0	decrease
C	2.0	5.3	decrease
D	1.4	5.8	decrease
E	2.8	3.8	decrease
F	6.5	2.9	increase
G	5.1	2.7	increase
H	3.1	5.2	decrease

* Measured *before* experimental change, during the preliminary phase of the study. A rank of 1 is favorable.

experiment. The experimental plan called for reassignments of the foremen so as to maximize the discrepancies (either positive or negative) between the mean preference ranks for the two foremen involved for each group. Since most of the foremen were relatively popular with their own groups, most of the changes would have to be made in a negative direction. Thus, five groups (lines, B, C, D, E, and H) would lose foremen they considered good (high average rank) and receive foremen they considered not as good (low average rank). Two other groups, F and G, would receive a reverse treatment. One additional group (A), a line that specializes in the production of the company's high-quality furniture products, was used in various attitudinal analyses but was not included in the experimental plan, even as a control group. The technological circumstances of this line are somewhat different from those associated with the other seven lines. For example, it has its own private dispatcher to provide raw materials, while the other lines share dispatchers who deliver frames only. Moreover, since several group-member changes were made in this group between the Phase

1 non-experiment and the time we were prepared to reassign the foremen, we questioned the potential validity of including the group in the experimental plan. As it turned out, the plant manager strongly agreed with this decision, because he wanted to keep the incumbent foreman on the line.

Given the plan outlined above, the stage was set for the crucial question—would J. R., the plant manager, approve?

SELLING THE PLAN AND INTRODUCING THE CHANGES

Armed with some of our preliminary data, Nord and I journeyed to the Northeast Plant ostensibly to provide feedback to the plant manager on the results of the non-experiment. J. R. appeared to find our presentation of data quite interesting, and he seemed to feel that he had learned something useful about the social psychology and productivity of his upholstering groups.

About half-way through the meeting, I began to explain the chicken-egg causality question as it related not only to our own preliminary Northeast Plant data, but also as it related to the literature in general. (As yet, no mention had been made about doing further research in this plant, let alone conducting an experiment.) As I unfolded the chicken-egg problem to the plant manager, a broad grin spread across J. R.'s face; obviously he had known for some time exactly what my objectives were. He asked, "What do you have in mind as a next step, Ned? Do you want to run an experiment with my foremen?" After expressing a hopeful affirmative reply, I (Nord was about to complete his degree at that time) awaited J. R.'s decision, which was not long in coming: "I don't see why we couldn't work something like that out here. We occasionally have switched two or three foremen around in past years. However, we haven't done anything like that for several years." It was as simple as that. Except for the administrative details, which were in fact quite significant ones, it appeared that a legitimate social experiment was going to occur in an ongoing, formal work organization.

The discussion then turned to consideration of the basis for the experimental reassignments, that is, the workers' preference rankings, along with the question of a timetable. J. R. wished to put off the actual experiment until after the first of the year, when his usually busy Christmas-rush production season would taper off somewhat. It was now late summer, and this postponement left several months during which to plan the implementation of the experimental arrangement. It also resulted in several months of anxiety as to whether the experiment would in fact occur. After all, one could not know whether J. R. might have a change of heart for any number of reasons, corporate or personal.

During the intervening time period, I met and talked on the telephone clandestinely with J. R. on several occasions. Two of these meetings were in a hotel lobby and coffeeshop part way between Cornell and the plant manager's factory. Once we met at the plant manager's home.[8]

No one in the Northeast Plant other than the plant manager was informed that the University was involved in this experiment, which was to be conducted more than a year after the initial "non-experiment." We (J. R. and I) hoped that the long intervening time period, coupled with the fact that similar foremen reassignments had been made occasionally in the past, would encourage the workers and foremen to accept the experimental reassignment as a legitimate and normal organizational change.

The security problem gave us some difficult moments. Just what should the foremen be told about the experiment in advance? Should the plant superintendent, to whom the

[8] It may amuse the reader to know that one of my "secret" meetings at J. R.'s home was interrupted by a call from the Northeast Plant switchboard operator. She informed J. R. that Professor Rosen's secretary at Cornell University was trying to reach him. The switchboard operator could not have known what our meeting was about, although the potential security problem here ought to be recognized by future field experimenters.

foremen report, have a role in the implementation of the experimental change? Rather than let the plant superintendent in on the entire scheme, an act that I felt could have disastrous repercussions if he should for any reason be in opposition, I convinced J. R. to approach the superintendent on a less than fully open basis. J. R. informed the superintendent that he had been thinking for some time of reshuffling the upholstering line foremen (there was, in fact, a certain amount of truth in this position)—that the department would benefit from a bit of a "shaking up" and that the experience would be good for the foremen and the workers. He made the specific point that it would be useful from the organization's point of view if the foremen were to acquire some breadth of experience on product problems somewhat different from the ones they were accustomed to. In other words, the plant superintendent was sold a bill of goods regarding the potential training and management development value of such a change. He was not told of the experimental research element involved. In fact, the plant manager himself looked upon the experimental reassignment as a major organizational change with which he would have to live for a considerable period of time before he could even think about making any further foreman reassignments.

After meeting two or three times with the plant superintendent, J. R. obtained from him his own ideas as to which foreman should be reassigned to the various groups. J. R. "took these under advisement," making no promises, and relayed the information to me. I found it possible to make a minor adjustment in the experimental plan in order to accommodate one of the plant superintendent's wishes. One of the "maximal" preference rank changes differed little from a somewhat smaller discrepancy between an initial foreman and a foreman replacement recommended by the superintendent. It seemed to me that incorporating this change in the experimental design would not particularly affect the results of the experiment. One or two of his other suggestions could not be absorbed, however, so the plant manager had to "make the final judgment."

The change itself was to be implemented by the plant manager at a regular weekly meeting involving him, the plant superintendent, and the upholstering foremen. This meeting was to be held late on a Friday afternoon immediately preceding the change, which was scheduled for the following Monday morning. (According to J. R., this is the "normal" time span he would have employed even if there had been no experimental element involved.) In explaining the reassignments at the meeting, J. R. was to use the same rationale he used when selling the project to his Superintendent. The training and management development aspects of the change were to be stressed.

Two foremen in the group meeting attempted to get the plant manager to change the reassignment plan to accommodate their personal desires. For example, one man resisted the new assignment scheduled for him because one of his brothers worked as an upholsterer on that particular line. We had not anticipated such contingencies, and at this eleventh hour no accommodation could be made. The plant manager was placed in the uncomfortable position of having to stick to his original plan on what must have appeared to be a fairly arbitrary basis. Arbitrariness, however, marks no unusual behavior in this fast-paced manufacturing operation, where many arbitrary decisions are made every week.[9]

On the critical Monday morning when the change was to have been implemented, I was visiting another university in the Midwest and I called J. R. to find out how things were

[9] Even if there had been time to consider the various foremen's preferences, previous examination of the rankings they provided earlier revealed little that could be done about accommodating group and foreman preferences simultaneously. Had there been several more groups to work with this dual approach might have been manageable. Hopefully such an experiment can be conducted in the future.

going. He informed me that nothing at all had happened—due to certain production exigencies, the entire program had been postponed for a week. The foremen had not yet had their meeting with J. R. and consequently were not informed (so he thought) about the impending reassignments. The change did occur at last, however, and the production data began to accumulate through the mails.

SOME RANDOM COMMENTS

The reader having industrial experience undoubtedly recognizes that the wholesale reshuffling of work-group supervisors in this experiment, on two days' official notice to the foremen and even less to the upholsterers themselves, had to be viewed as a serious matter by the participants. One of my colleagues even suggested the possibility of a wildcat strike. The experiment had to be brought off simultaneously for all the groups, however, because of potential complications that might have arisen from summer vacations and internal communications in the department. Even if these complications could have been avoided, I would have pushed for simultaneous reassignments if only to forestall the possibility of a change of heart by the plant manager, or, worse yet, a new plant manager.

The ethical implications of the deceptions employed may be disturbing to some readers. The experimenter and J. R. both operated on the sincere assumption that there would be no serious or long-range psychological damage to the supervisors. We expected them to show some anxiety, but we did not think it would last very long. It is true that these men had much more at stake than the usual college-student experimental subject, but on balance the potential gain from the experiment certainly seemed to outweigh the mild appearing risks.

This chapter has traced the conceptual analysis and related empirical data analyses that preceded the formulation of an experimental plan. The data analyses were based on measurements taken during the preliminary "non-experiment" described in Chapter 2. Several possible independent-variable manipulations were examined and found wanting, either for empirical or conceptual reasons. Worker preferences for foremen, however, were found to be highly correlated with group cohesion; both variables were highly correlated with percentage of base rate, a reliable productivity index. These interrelationships made conceptual sense and clearly agree with other researchers' cross-sectional findings. The time-order question, however, is still in doubt. Thus, the stage was set for an experiment. The chapter also points out that the phenomenon being dealt with here should be handled primarily at a group, rather than at an individual, level of analysis.

The data show that on the whole the workers in question are money motivated; they discriminate between work groups and jobs largely on the basis of income potential. As far as their foreman preferences are concerned, the workers place heavy emphasis on personality considerations, although they do not ignore matters of technical and administrative competence.

An experimental strategy, based on maximizing or minimizing the discrepancies between work-group preferences for various foremen, was established and "sold" to the plant manager. All administrative arrangements were made, and the show began on Monday morning, April 7, 1965.

CHAPTER 4

Experimental Findings: A Descriptive Account of Group Change

We must now determine whether the leadership reassign-ments had any impact on the various group indexes we were trying to influence. Specifically, we must ascertain whether group performance levels (productivity), group attraction, or work-group perceptions of leadership behavior (prefer-ences) changed subsequent to the experimental manipula-tion. If nothing changed, we shall have a short book. If changes occurred in any or all of the above group indexes, on the other hand, it will become necessary in a later chapter to manipulate the data in various ways to test alternative explanatory hypotheses. The present chapter includes a de-scriptive account of what happened to several relevant vari-ables following the foremen's reassignments and a detailed analysis of group characteristics and leadership "behavior" as perceived by the workers both before and after the experi-mental change.

GROUP PERFORMANCE LEVELS

Productivity. One of the notable characteristics of the Up-holstering Department prior to the foreman reassignments was the performance consistency of the various work groups. As shown in Chapter 3, the groups' relative productivity levels remained similar from one two-week period to the next; the correlations between adjacent time periods averaged about .90 when eight groups were included in the analysis.

Therefore, a quick way to find out whether the experimental foreman reassignments had any effect on the department would be to examine the consistency of the groups' performance levels after the foreman change.

Table 8 shows the extent to which the groups retained

Table 8. Stability trend of group productivity
levels (means) over time*

Adjacent time periods†	Correlations (Rho)
12-week base vs. weeks 1–2	.26
Weeks 1–2 vs. 3–4	.21
Weeks 3–4 vs. 5–6	.43
Weeks 5–6 vs. 7–8	.71‡
Weeks 7–8 vs. 9–10	.75‡
Weeks 9–10 vs. 11–12	.79‡
Weeks 11–12 vs. 13–14	.75‡
Weeks 13–14 vs. 15–16	.79‡

* The means, whose ranks are reflected in this table, may be found in Appendix G.

† The experimental leadership change occurred on Monday of Week 1, immediately following the pre-experimental base period.

‡ Significant at or beyond .05 level, one-tail test.

their productivity positions relative to each other during the course of the experiment. The low correlations near the top of the table indicate that the stability of the groups' productivity levels relative to each other was clearly disrupted during the first few weeks following the foreman change. Over time, however, a consistent pattern gradually emerged and stabilized.[1]

[1] The reader may recall that the correlations between group productivity levels for adjacent time periods was found to be in the .90's in our earlier work with the "non-experiment." The larger correlations in that phase of our work are explained by the fact that we were working with eight groups rather than seven. The eighth group, the one omitted from the foreman experiment, was always last in the productivity performance lists. Therefore, it contributed to higher

The low correlations between adjacent time periods in the early stages following the foreman change suggest that the department was thrown out of equilibrium as a result of the simultaneous reassignment of seven supervisors; ordinarily the correlations would have been uniformly high. Additional data analyses show that the correlation between the groups' pre-experimental twelve-week base-period productivity levels and their total productivity levels for sixteen weeks after the foreman change is only .46. (For weeks 13–16 the Rho is .55.) For the same time periods during the preceding calendar year (1963) the comparable correlation was .82. During 1965, the calendar year following the experimental year, the comparable correlation was .64. The lower correlation in 1964 presumably was caused by the experimental change.

On balance, it appears that something happened to group productivity levels in the Upholstering Department in 1964. The fact that in time the groups' relative positions stabilized again reflects a homeostatic principle frequently observed in social systems, groups, and individuals. When groups are thrown out of equilibrium, a number of forces begin to operate toward the restoration of balance. In this instance, when the groups stabilized relative to each other, their new productivity levels were considerably different from their pre-experimental ones (Rho $\cong$ .50). While a Rho of .50 is not statistically significant, it is large enough to suggest that the initial forces that helped create the pre-experimental equilibrium state did not lose their potency entirely. In other words, the supervisory change appears to have had an impact on group productivity, but other influential variables, to be described later, also operated on productivity at the same time.

Percentage Change in Productivity Levels. Despite the ho-

---

correlations than we are working with in the current chapter, both because of its consistently low rank and because of the larger N used in calculating Rho.

meostatic tendency of the groups' productivity levels, apparently a good deal of change took place. For two reasons, I believed that these changes, if they could be measured reliably, might represent a more useful productivity variable than productivity levels (averages) alone. First, assuming a systems model (or continuous feedback loop model) for the variables in this study, it seemed likely that work-group members, after what seemed to them a major organizational change, would assess the implications of that change by comparing the new situation to the original. Thus, the workers' motivation to earn money (previously established in Chapter 3) would encourage them to compare their post-foreman change earnings (directly geared to productivity) with their pre-change earnings and form or revise their attitudes about their new foreman and their group accordingly.[2] Second, even if this reasoning were not borne out by data to be presented later, a productivity percentage-change variable would be desirable for another reason. Specifically, the previous section of this chapter showed that group productivity levels (averages) did change relative to each other. It seems only reasonable to ask, "How much?" A percentage change variable will answer this question.

Each group's weekly production mean (production of base rate during that week) was compared with its twelve-week pre-experimental base rate. The appropriate subtraction was made and the balance was divided by the pre-experimental base rate. The quotient was multiplied by 100. The percentages for any given post-experimental time period then were ranked from 1 through 7, a 1 indicating the largest per-

[2] This formulation rests heavily on Thibaut and Kelley's conceptualization (1959) of comparison levels and salience in relation to attitude formation. The pre-experimental base productivity figure for a group is its comparison level, in their terms. Salience is assumed to be high for all the groups because of their interest in money; actually the groups differed somewhat in this respect, a matter which will be explored below. The comparisons were "triggered" by the arbitrary managerial change.

centage increase for that time period and a 7 the smallest percentage increase, or, as the case may be, the largest percentage decrease. The following list is an example of how this calculation was handled for seven work groups during a given post-experimental time period:

Group	Pre-experimental base level	Productivity Week 2	Difference: Week 2 — base	Difference ÷ base	× 100 = % change	Rank
B	123	138	+15	+.12	+12	2
C	156	166	+10	+.07	+ 7	5
D	140	135	− 5	−.04	− 4	6
E	131	141	+10	+.08	+ 8	4
F	130	151	+21	+.16	+16	1
G	136	118	−18	−.13	−13	7
H	140	154	+14	+.10	+10	3

Table 9 summarizes weekly percentage *change* data for all the groups throughout the sixteen-week experimental period. The totals at the bottom of the table show what happened to the entire department. There was a large percentage increase in the first week following the foreman reassignments. In fact, every one of the seven groups increased in productivity over and above its pre-experimental productivity level, despite the fact that five of the groups received a foreman they had previously described as being less desirable than their original foreman. Not only were some of these percentage increases quite large; it is rare for all groups in this department to show an increase during the same one-week period.[3] Some observers might call this a traditional

[3] The reader might be interested in knowing that certain groups began to show large productivity increases during the week *preceding* the reassignment of the foremen. The data were so out of line for these groups that my suspicious nature led me to interrogate certain company officials about this on a much later occasion. An interview with the plant superintendent revealed that he, in fact, had "leaked" a certain amount of advance information on the foreman reassignments before he was supposed to. My interview questions about this made him quite nervous, because he clearly had acted contrary to the in-

Table 9. Summary data, by work group, showing twelve-week pre-experimental productivity levels and percentage changes in each of sixteen weeks following the experimental manipulation

Work group*	Pre-experimental % of base rate†	Post-experimental productivity changes (increases or decreases)‡																16-week total
		Week																
		1	2	3	4	5	6	7	8	9	10	11	12	13	14	15	16	
F	130	11	16	5	−2	6	9	9	14	12	7	23	3	11	18	12	15	11
G	136	16	−13	6	10	−5	−8	4	−6	1	1	25	2	17	−7	5	8	4
E	131	14	8	−6	−5	−5	2	−5	−10	1	−7	5	−8	−5	0	1	1	−2
H	140	6	10	−6	6	−2	−4	−4	−10	−4	2	5	−6	−2	−4	4	12	0
C	156	12	6	6	6	2	5	6	9	4	3	4	4	13	10	−1	−1	6
B	123	24	12	−1	9	−40§ (10)	−50§ (10)	−50§ (10)	12	11	5	17	1	9	6	15	13	9
D	140	10	−4	2	−4	−1	−3	−2	4	−7	0	−11	−10	−1	1	2	2	−1
Total		93	35	6	20	5	11	18	17	18	11	68	−14	42	24	38	50	27

* There are from seven to ten men in each group. The groups are ordered on the experimental variable; Group F received the most favorable foreman change while Group D received the most unfavorable foreman change.

† A twelve-week composite figure representing the percentage of base rate achieved by each group, in incentive system terms, before the experimental change was made.

‡ Expressed as percentage of pre-experimental base figure.

§ Group B was given a different product line than it was accustomed to during these three weeks, which explains the remarkable decreases. For data analysis purposes this group's average percentage change for the other thirteen post-experimental weeks was assigned as a more representative figure—10%.

"Hawthorne effect"—increased effort as the result of a change —analogous to what happened when the lighting was reduced to an illumination level comparable to moonlight in the Western Electric Plant. The data from the Northeast Plant, however, do not support the notion that the workers were reacting *positively* (voluntarily) to having special attention from management-staff experts. On the contrary, there was a high negative correlation (Rho = —.61) between percentage increase in productivity, on the one hand, and pre-experimental *level* of productivity, on the other hand. In other words, the poorest-producing lines before the foreman reassignments showed the largest initial gains after the reassignments. This rather predictable finding suggests that the workers' first reaction to the changed foreman assignments was characterized by threat or pressure. In any event, the effect was temporary.

The bottom row of Table 9 reveals that an unusual productivity increase appeared in week 11. This happened to be the week that several graduate students and I invaded the Upholstering Department on a Monday afternoon to readminister some of the attitude questionnaire items that had been administered to these people more than a year earlier. The table suggests that our activities in the plant for about two hours that Monday afternoon produced a decided impact on the production levels of the various groups; there were some marked percentage increases. The week-12 column once again suggests an equilibrium recovery effect. Following week 12 and before week 13 the entire plant was closed for a two-week vacation. This probably explains the fairly size-

---

structions of the plant manager. He owned up to his actions, however, and explained that he felt the plant manager was not giving sufficient notice (two days) to various foremen about the impending change. As the foremen's superior in the chain of command he probably felt that there were certain individuals who should be tipped off in advance lest they make difficulties for him later. He maintained that he had not revealed which foremen were going to be reassigned to which groups, but only the fact that there were some changes in the wind.

able jump in productivity in the thirteenth week, when the men returned. The increases in weeks 15 and 16, also somewhat large, remain a mystery; I have no knowledge of anything special that happened in the plant at that time.

The reader also might notice the large percentage decreases in productivity shown by Group B during weeks 5, 6, and 7. Group B did not work on its usual kind of furniture during these weeks, but did work exclusively on the high-quality furniture normally produced by the eighth line, not included in our study. It therefore appears that a task change can have a much greater impact on a group's performance than a negative change in supervision. These three weeks, during which Group B was paid its average hourly earnings based on past performance, posed a methodological problem which was handled by substituting an average percentage increase figure for the actual ones. Thus, weeks 1, 2, 3, and 8 through 16 were averaged for line B and that average (a 10 per cent increase in productivity) was substituted in each of three atypical cells of the experimental design.

THE STATISTICAL SIGNIFICANCE OF PERCENTAGE CHANGES
IN GROUP PERFORMANCE

The data presented thus far suggest strongly that production changes occurred among the upholstering groups as a result of the supervisory changes. Before proceeding to an analysis of other variables, let us consider whether these productivity changes are statistically significant rather than being merely chance events. Statistical analysis (see Appendix F) reveals that the changes in weekly production levels, in comparison with each group's twelve-week pre-experimental base rate, were not random over the sixteen-week experimental time period. In other words, the groups differed beyond chance expectations in their propensity to increase or decrease. This, of course, does not mean necessarily that the changes were the direct result of the experimental manipulation. It is always possible that some intervening or spurious events, rather than the experimental reassignment of the foremen, produced the changes. No major changes or unusual events occurred during these sixteen weeks, according to all the managerial people with whom I consulted on this question, which strengthens (but by no means proves) the case for an experimental rather than a spurious effect. The pattern of the data, as outlined in subsequent pages, should add credence to this interpretation.

CHANGES IN GROUP ATTRACTION AND PERCEPTIONS
OF FOREMAN BEHAVIOR

Obtaining a Second Round of Attitude Measurements. The data analyses to be presented in this chapter and the next cannot be understood fully without a brief methodological discussion at this juncture. As indicated earlier, several of the pre-experimental attitude questionnaire items were administered a second time on Monday of the eleventh week following the foreman reassignments. The eleventh week was selected for this purpose because I judged that whatever changes in performance, group cohesion, and foreman preference were going to take place probably would have developed and crystallized by then. This assumption is supported by Table 8, above, which suggests that a new equilibrium state was forming approximately six weeks after the foreman reassignments. Moreover, the factory's vacation shutdown, which was to occur after the twelfth week, coupled with vacation scheduling problems for the graduate students, made it imperative that the data be collected at this time rather than later in the summer. Finally, I wished to analyze productivity data in relation to the *new* attitudes *after* this eleventh-week measurement to determine what effects the new measurements might have on subsequent group performance. This analysis also necessitated a summer measurement date because by early autumn the plant gets quite busy with Christmas production.

As was the case in the earlier research, a letter on University letterhead was mailed to each worker's home announcing that some research people and graduate students were going to pay another visit to the Northeast Plant and indicating that the worker's assistance would be appreciated. (See Appendix E.) The language of the letter suggested that I was aware that "certain changes" had occurred in the factory since the previous research more than a year earlier. Therefore, the letter probably provided a strong clue that the University had had a hand in the foreman reassignments. The mailing of the letters was timed so that they would be delivered on Thursday or Friday of the tenth week, so that they could not influence productivity prior to the eleventh week. The usual matters of protocol were worked out with the local union officers and top management in the plant during the tenth week, at which time the foremen also received a letter from me.

Seven people from Cornell invaded the Upholstery Department at the designated time and requested the workers to rank once again all the foremen and groups in the department. They also were asked to describe on our seven-point scales their first- and last-choice foremen and groups. I included, in connection with the foreman descriptions on this occasion, thirty-three personality items that had not been included in the previous research. The administration of this questionnaire required only a few minutes and was conducted right at the various groups' work locations. (See Appendixes B and D.)

While the questionnaires were being examined by the research team for completeness, one of the graduate students, who knew the men from his previous research work in the plant, hastily interviewed about two-thirds of the men in the department. He attempted to find out from the men, through indirect questions, whether they had suspected the University's role in the change when it had been made initially. Roughly one-third of the respondents indicated that they had suspected University involvement when the foremen first were reassigned, but that they had dismissed this explanation in favor of the one provided through management channels. The management explanation struck them as being more logical in view of the fact that this is a production organization. They had found it difficult to believe that a practical factory manager could initiate such an important organizational change simply to facilitate frivolous university research. The other two-thirds of the respondents indicated that they had never suspected the University's influence.

While all this was going on, I risked entering a room having only one exit to meet with the upholstery foremen. Although some hostility was exhibited by one or two of the foremen, the majority appeared to take the experience extremely well. I explained to them in general terms why such an experiment had to be made and why their particular operation was an excellent one for the study. I did not explain to them at that time the experimental variable involving worker preferences for foremen. I also assured them that they would receive detailed feedback on the overall project when we had finished analyzing our data; as far as they were concerned, the experiment was over that afternoon. They were not told that we were going to watch the productivity data reports for several more weeks.

Upon the conclusion of this meeting with the foremen, I learned from my research assistants that seven workers had not completed that portion of the questionnaire that asked them to rank their work groups. I had to make a personal appeal to each of these men in order to obtain their cooperation. Undoubtedly, the resistance from these men was caused by their fear that they would be the next ones to be reassigned. Actually, the union contract prohibits such an arrangement, which indeed had considerable experimental appeal.

Sample Attrition. It should be pointed out that all but a few of the workers who responded to the initial questionnaire prior to the experiment were present on this second occasion. Three were on different lines than they had been previously and six others either were no longer with the company or were absent on this occasion. More than half of the sample attrition occurred in the work group that was not included in the foremen reassignment experiment. Only four people out of the other seven groups were lost.

Variables. The major attitudinal variables extracted from the eleventh-week questionnaire for use in this chapter are: post-experimental group attraction ($\overline{X}$ preference rank in each group); post-experimental group foreman preference ($\overline{X}$ preference rank in each group); and post-experimental status consensus on new foreman (standard deviation of foreman preference ranks in each group; an agreement index). These variables are the direct counterparts of those used in the preliminary work reported in Chapter 3. Their repeated measurement here permits the assessment of attitudinal and productivity changes concurrently.

Foreman Behavior and Status Consensus on Foremen. The correlation between the work groups' pre-experimental perceptions (average rank) of their new foremen before they got him and their post-experimental perceptions eleven weeks after he had been assigned to them is .71. This rank order correlation reflects the mean preference ranks that each group assigned to its new foreman before and after the experiment. While this correlation reveals that the attitudinal dimension in question apparently did not change a great deal, the correlation is not perfect and suggests that some amount of change did take place, either because of environmental changes or because of unreliability of the measurement.[4]

The pre-experimental status consensus on the new foremen

[4] The author assumes that most of the changes in this attitudinal dimension and others described below occurred *after* the foremen were reassigned, *not* during the one-year interval between the initial measurement of the attitudes and the introduction of the foremen reassignments. This, of course, is a crucial assumption and is supported by data to be presented in Chapter 5.

and the post-experimental status consensus are barely correlated at all (Rho = .24). In other words, the extent of
agreement within the various groups on the new foremen
before they were reassigned as measured by standard deviation within groups, did not correspond to the extent of agreement on them after the groups had been exposed to the
supervisory presence of the foremen. Substantial changes
took place in the extent to which the various groups accepted
and closed ranks around their new foremen. The magnitude
of the apparent change in this dimension, in comparison with
the relatively small amount of change that took place in the
mean foreman preference index, suggests that consensus
may well be the more important variable to examine in this
study.

The last four columns of Table 10 present a more detailed
view of what actually happened to the groups' perceptions
of their foremen and reflect the consensus formation process.
While all the groups except H show more favorable percep-

Table 10. Group attraction, foreman preference, and status
consensus on foreman, by group, before and
after the experimental change

Group*	Group attraction (mean)†		Foreman preference (mean)†		Status consensus (standard deviation)‡	
	Before	After	Before	After	Before	After
F	3.6	1.4	2.9	1.4	2.0	0.5
G	3.4	1.1	2.7	1.0	1.3	0.0
E	2.6	2.7	3.8	2.5	2.7	1.8
H	1.5	2.4	5.2	5.8	1.8	1.7
C	1.0	1.6+	5.3	1.9	1.8	1.7
B	1.4	1.6	6.0	3.0	1.7	1.3
D	1.4	1.6+	5.8	2.6	1.5	1.9

* The groups are ordered on the experimental variable. Group F re-
ceived the most favorable foreman change and Group D the least.
† The smaller the mean, the more favorable the attitude.
‡ The smaller the standard deviation, the closer the consensus.

tions of their new foreman after getting a ten-week look at him than they did before the experiment, it is clear that some groups moved more than others on this dimension. The standard deviations of the foreman rankings are particularly interesting in this regard. The data for groups F and G suggest a "closing of the ranks" phenomenon (consensus formation) and, together with their average preference rankings, suggest favorable effects of the experimental manipulation. Group E, which received a rather mild foreman change as far as magnitude of preference discrepancies is concerned, appears to have achieved consensus around its new foreman to some extent. The other groups, all of which received larger negative foreman changes, show little or no improvement in status consensus around their new foreman. One group (D) shows a decline. Apparently certain members within the various groups, particularly those groups receiving a negative foreman change, were unwilling or unable to change their perceptions sufficiently to permit the development of status consensus. Their strongly negative pre-experimental expectations about their new foremen presumably affected their ability to develop a more positive, shared frame of reference with others in their groups. This is not an unexpected finding in view of the attitudinal consistencies found in this department that were described in Chapter 3.

In short, considerable changing of opinion occurred within groups in relation to the new foremen. Some groups achieved a great deal of internal agreement about their new foreman; other groups did not. Moreover, the *mean* preference ranks also tended to change. It should be clear, therefore, that the independent variable that was manipulated in this experiment apparently changed during the process of consensus formation on the new foreman. This is a critical matter to which we shall return. Meanwhile, suffice it to say that such a rubbery independent variable is not likely to predict very well.

Group Attraction. The changes in the group attraction dimension are even more startling than those characterizing the foreman rankings. The group attraction rankings that prevailed a year before the experimental change was introduced apparently correlate *negatively* (Rho $= -.37$) with the group attraction rankings that prevailed eleven weeks following the experimental manipulation. While this correlation is not significantly greater than zero, it is of opposite algebraic sign and suggests that the group attraction or cohesion dimension changed rather drastically in comparison with the milder changes in perceptions of foreman behavior previously reported.

Table 10 illustrates the dramatic changes in group attraction in some detail. It is easily seen that certain groups changed their "images" markedly. For example, Group F had the lowest level of group attraction ($\overline{X} = 3.6$) *prior* to the foreman reassignment. Ten weeks *after* the foreman reassignments, this group developed one of the most favorable group-attraction scores ($\overline{X} = 1.4$) in the department, according to the data in Table 10. Several of the other groups also shifted around markedly, some in a negative direction.

WORKERS' CRITERIA FOR JUDGING GROUPS AND FOREMEN

The reader may recall that during the pre-experimental collection of base-line data, the workers were asked to describe on nineteen seven-point scales their most- and least-preferred work groups and foremen (see Chapter 3). When we re-entered the plant eleven weeks after the experimental foreman reassignments, we repeated the measurements on these nineteen scales. The following paragraphs present a comparison between the pre- and post-experimental descriptions the workers gave us of their most- and least-preferred work groups (eleven scales) and foremen (eight scales). This analysis will enable us to draw some tentative conclusions about the experimental impact on the criteria employed by workers in evaluating their groups and supervisors. It also should help explain the experimental results.

A later section of the chapter presents a factor analytic treatment of forty-one behavioral descriptions of most- and least-preferred foremen. This factor analysis, which includes the eight foreman scales plus thirty-three additional ones, will provide a parsimonious summary of the dimensions used by the workers to differentiate between effective and ineffective foremen and should explain what the workers had in mind when considering foreman "personalities." It also should help explain the perceived supervisory behaviors that influence consensus formation, a phenomenon reflected in data reported earlier.

The reader should note that the scale ratings provided by the workers when describing their most- and least-preferred groups and foremen are not "pure" measures. To some extent they probably reflect objective reality; that is, a given worker's description of a group or foreman is accurate and valid. On the other hand, the measurements also are likely to be influenced strongly by internal, subjective factors indigenous to the rater. Thus, to some extent the descriptions are projective measuring devices.

Workers' Criteria for Evaluating Groups before and after the Experimental Change. Table 11 summarizes an analysis of the workers' descriptions of their first- and last-choice work groups and the *t*-test results on the differences between these two extremes. The analysis includes only those workers who were present on both measurement occasions and who were in groups directly involved in the foreman reassignment experiment.

Perhaps the most striking finding observable in the table is that seven of the eleven pre-experimental *t*-test results declined when the comparable analysis was made on the post-experimental data. This suggests that, in general, the workers are inclined to discriminate less among groups after experiencing a foreman reassignment than they were before the experiment was made.

The table also reveals that "the amount of money you

Table 11. Mean description by workers $(N = 60)$* of their first- and last-choice work groups and *t*-tests on the differences, by scale and group, before and after experimental change

Rating-scale item	Pre-test			Post-test		
	First-choice line	Last-choice line	*t*	First-choice line	Last-choice line	*t*
Amount of money you can make on this line	5.6	4.0	5.46†	4.8	3.5	4.64†
Speed of work pace	5.6	4.4	3.95†	5.1	4.4	2.94†
Opportunity to use your head	5.4	4.6	3.36†	4.4	4.4	0.00
Amount of cooperation among workers	5.1	4.2	2.84†	4.1	3.7	1.28‡
Friendliness of workers	5.6	4.9	2.58†	4.8	4.3	1.90†
Amount of self-pacing	5.6	4.8	2.45†	4.6	4.6	0.00
Amount of physical effort required	5.8	5.6	1.44†	5.6	5.4	1.64†
Fairness of rates	4.2	3.9	1.40†	3.7	3.4	1.27‡
Amount of skill required	5.7	5.5	0.89‡	5.5	5.2	2.05†
Amount of variety in work	5.5	5.3	0.69‡	5.5	5.4	1.02‡
Opportunity to talk	5.0	5.0	0.00	4.8	4.6	1.24‡

* N includes only those workers present on *both* measurement occasions who were involved in the experiment proper and who provided usable data.

† Significant beyond .05 level. (Critical value = 1.29, one-tail test.)

‡ Not significant.

can make on this line" remains the most discriminating scale. "Speed of work pace" remains second in magnitude. Despite the fact that the *t*'s for these two scales remained fairly high in magnitude relative to the other nine, they did shrink from the magnitudes they exhibited before the experimental change was initiated. Presumably this shrinkage reflects an accurate perception that the lines' productivity levels in fact moved closer together. The important point, however, is that "amount of money you can make" and "speed of work pace" (which are highly correlated) remain the most significant discriminators when workers compare most- and least-preferred lines (groups). In other words, they have clearly indicated both before and after the experiment that group attraction is linked to monetary rewards, which, in turn, are directly geared to productivity. The data presented so far, however, do not enlighten us as to the time sequence of the variables.

Four of the pre-experimental t's increased in magnitude when computed on the basis of post-experimental data. These are the only scales in the questionnaire which, on their face, have anything to do with intrinsic work characteristics: "amount of skill required," "amount of variety in the work on this line," "amount of physical effort required on this line," and "opportunity to talk on this line." On balance, the changing pattern of the t-test results suggests that the workers, as a result of the experiment, became somewhat more conscious of intrinsic work characteristics associated with the technological requirements on the respective lines, without changing their continuing concern about money. The increased emphasis on technological characteristics probably is a direct result of the workers' experiences in coping with the stresses created by the foreman reassignments. (The fact that stress occurred is illustrated by the disequilibrium reflected earlier in Table 8.)

Workers' Criteria for Evaluating Foremen before and after the Experimental Change. Table 12 provides the same kind of analysis described above, but this time focuses on descriptions of first- and last-choice foremen. The pattern of the pre- and post-experimental t-test results in this instance is much different from the pattern shown when the workers were describing their most- and least-preferred work groups. Thus, Table 12 reveals that on seven of the eight scales used, the magnitude of t *increased* after the experimental reassignment, sometimes quite dramatically. The "personality" scale (pleasant-unpleasant) showed a decline in its t value, although it remained the largest on the list. Overall, it appears

Table 12. Mean description by workers ($N = 63$)* of their first- and last-choice foremen and *t*-tests on the differences, by scale and foreman choice, before and after experimental change

Rating-scale item	Pre-test			Post-test		
	First-choice fore-men	Last-choice fore-men	*t*	First-choice fore-men	Last-choice fore-men	*t*
His personality (pleasant–unpleasant)	6.2	3.7	9.77†	6.1	3.4	8.95†
Ability to get things for his men from mgt. (lot–little)	5.2	3.4	6.78†	5.0	3.0	8.05†
His ability to plan and organize the work (lot–little)	5.6	4.0	6.10†	5.6	3.5	8.32†
His ability to get along with the union (lot–little)	5.6	4.1	5.49†	5.3	3.6	6.73†
The extent of his job knowledge (lot–little)	6.1	5.0	4.93†	5.8	4.2	5.63†
The way he treats his men (easy-going–strict)	5.0	3.5	4.34†	4.9	3.3	6.82†
His skill as upholsterer (lot–little)	5.8	5.2	3.02†	5.8	4.2	5.56†
His length of service (lot–little)	5.7	5.6	0.53‡	6.0	4.8	3.75†

* Only the seven groups that had participated in the actual experiment were included in this analysis.

† Significant beyond .05 level. (Critical value = 1.29, one-tail test.)

‡ Not significant.

that the experimental manipulation made the workers more discriminating about the foremen than they had been previously.

Although the workers apparently became more discriminating about their foremen because of the experiment, the relative salience of the eight dimensions appears to remain the same as it was before the experiment began. That is, when one ranks the pre-test t's and the post-test t's, a correlation of .90 occurs between the two sets of ranks. Nevertheless, the substantial increases in the magnitudes of certain t's suggests that technological-administrative skills of the foremen assumed greater importance after the experimental change than they had before. (Notice the large difference between the two largest t's for the pre-experimental data in comparison with the much smaller differences between their post-experimental counterparts.) Thus, "ability to plan and to organize the work," "skill as an upholsterer," and "his length of service" showed substantial increases in their t-test values indicating the extent to which they discriminated between first- and last-choice foremen. In other words, the experimental experience apparently influenced workers to change their foreman-evaluation criteria and perceptions in ways which brought them into closer conformity with the standards applied by the foremen themselves prior to the experiment (see Chapter 3, Table 6). Further, it appears that "strictness" (the way he treats his men) became more salient for the workers when comparing most- and least-preferred foremen.

It also may interest the reader to compare the first-choice foreman means (in Table 12) obtained before the experiment with the first-choice foreman means obtained after the experiment. Relatively small differences appear. On the other hand, there are sharp differences on several of the comparisons between pre-experimental last-choice foreman means and post-experimental last-choice foreman means. All this suggests that "good" foremen are not perceived any differently after the experiment than before; "poor" foremen are seen as being less technically competent. On balance, then, while "personality" still seems to be the overriding consideration in the workers' minds when evaluating foremen, the technological-administrative competencies of the foremen appear to have gained in importance as a result of the experimental exposure. These findings suggest that the new foremen were judged at least partly on their ability to help each group re-establish equilibrium following the foreman reassignments. Hence, we find increased emphasis in Table 12 on their technological-administrative competencies.

THE PSYCHOLOGICAL MEANING OF THE WORKERS' CRITERIA
FOR EVALUATING FOREMEN

The reader will recall that thirty-three personality-scale items were included in the post-experimental data collection phase of this research in order to explicate the "personality" findings that first were observed before the experiment began (and which reappear, above, post-experimentally). Specifically, it seemed desirable to find out what the workers mean when filling out a scale called "personality—pleasant vs. unpleasant." (Appendix H summarizes a repeated-measurements *t*-test analysis on these data.) Accordingly, the seventy-three men present when we re-entered the plant in the eleventh week after the experimental change described their most- and least-preferred foremen on these thirty-three personality dimensions. As was indicated in Chapter 3, the characteristics "moody-temperamental, hard to talk to, grouchy-grumpy, bossy, has a chip on his shoulder, friendly, flies off handle, gets upset, acts too quickly without thinking, and likes to criticize" are the most discriminating personality characteristics (all having *t*-test results in excess of 10.0). The least-discriminating personality characteristics (all having *t*-test results smaller than 7.0) include "polite, uses foul language, talks too much, can be pushed around, takes life too seriously, enthusiastic about his work, shy, energetic, lots of drive, and sticks to company rules." Although the latter traits are the least discriminating of the thirty-three measurements, all but one are statistically significant by *t*-test standards.

While many of the personality characteristics used were adapted from various personality inventories which have their own scoring systems and factor scores, it seemed potentially useful from the researcher's viewpoint to submit these items along with the items summarized earlier in Table 12 to a factor analysis,[5] which might produce certain interpretive advantages concerning the meaning of "personality." Table 13 summarizes the factor weights on the forty-one difference-score variables employed in this phase of the research. I have bracketed the factor weights of those items that appear to assist the most in interpreting the meaning of each factor.

Examination of the table reveals first of all what might be called a general personality factor (1). This factor has high loadings on such items as "moody-temperamental," "hard to talk to," "chip on shoulder," "bossy," "likes to criticize," and others in a similar vein. A supervisor scoring high on such a factor would be seen either as a generally disagreeable sort who also might tend toward autocracy or petty bossism in his approach to his employees, or as a gruff character who plays the role of "tough guy." (Overall, the first general factor accounts for 42 per cent of the variance in the matrix, as rotated. Twenty-nine of the forty-one items loaded .40 or higher on the first factor prior to rotation.)

The second factor (which accounts for 22 per cent of the variance of the matrix) appears to reflect what some writers

[5] In other words, a factor analysis was designed using as variables the difference scores on each of forty-one variables. The difference scores reflect the difference on each dimension between the first-choice foremen and the last-choice foreman. These forty-one difference scores were computed for each of the seventy-three individual workers and a 41 by 41 correlation matrix ($N = 73$) on the difference scores was computed. This matrix of difference scores then was subjected to a factor analysis. Four factors were interpretable out of the five originally rotated. It should be emphasized that the four factors are not empirically orthogonal. The factor analysis was conducted at the Cornell Computing Center using the FACTESSO program available in the Center's program library. The correlation matrix and methodological details on the factor-analytic procedure may be examined by the interested reader in Appendix I.

Table 13. Factor structure of 41 scales showing dimensions on which workers differentiate between "most"- and "least"-preferred foremen*

Factor and scale †	Factor and weight			
	(1)	(2)	(3)	(4)
(1) General personality				
Likes to criticize	81	−12	00	00
Bossy	77	−29	00	−12
Has a chip on his shoulder	75	−06	−15	[32]
Flies off the handle	73	−07	−25	15
Hard to talk to	70	−24	−10	13
Acts too quickly without thinking	65	−04	[−43]	−16
Moody-temperamental	64	−22	−12	09
Things have to be done *his* way	63	−16	−01	[−21]
Changes his mind	63	08	−26	11
His personality (pleasant–unpleasant)	−44	39	31	[−32]
Shows off his upholstering skills	35	14	−26	−04
Talks too much	33	11	−29	17
Looks for fights	25	08	08	[25]
Uses foul language	23	17	00	−19
(2) Employee-centeredness				
Good listener	−22	72	13	−03
Can take criticism	−22	61	09	06
Makes men feel important	−35	55	12	01
Friendly	−37	53	18	05
Polite	−26	51	10	[−43]
Interested in his men	−28	48	05	−01
Energetic, lots of drive	26	48	−12	[−40]
Ability to get along with the union	−28	42	30	[−36]
The way he treats his men (easy-going vs. strict)	−40	41	01	−07
(3) Initiation of structure and stress management				
Handles emergencies	−17	[43]	72	10
Avoids problems he should handle	20	02	−63	04
Ability to plan and organize the work	−18	30	61	[−26]
Is relaxed	04	15	60	19
Can be pushed around	16	15	−58	[25]
Gets upset	40	12	−52	−07
Ability to get things for his men from management	−10	[46]	48	[−23]
Puts his own problems ahead of his men's	38	−03	−43	03
His length of service	01	−04	42	−13
(4) Motivation to lead				
His skill as an upholsterer	−18	31	14	90
Extent of his job knowledge	−15	30	35	75
Sticks to company rules	28	22	−03	−38
Enthusiastic about his work	02	12	17	−24

* Based on all the upholsterers who were present for the second questionnaire administration.

† "Shy" failed to load on all four factors.

have called "employee-centeredness" or "consideration." Notice the high loadings of such characteristics as "good listener," "can take criticism," "makes men feel important," "friendly," "polite," and "interested in his men." This factor also seems to incorporate the supervisor's "ability to get things for his men from management," his "ability to get along with the union," and how "strict" or "easy-going" he is in the way he treats his men. "Ability to get things for his men from management," in this particular setting, is seen as part of the consideration dimension rather than as a separate "influence" dimension as posited by Pelz (1951).

The third factor (accounting for 23 per cent of the variance) can be interpreted as a combination of initiation of structure, the handling of stress created by the technological environment, and technical-administrative competence. High positive factor loadings appear for "handling emergencies," "ability to plan and organize the work," and "is relaxed." High negative loadings appear for "can be pushed around," "gets upset," "takes life too seriously," and "avoids problems he should handle." Notice also that supervisors scoring high on such a factor would *not* be characterized by frequent changes of mind, flying off the handle, or grouchy-grumpiness. Finally, ability to get things for his men from management, job knowledge, and length of service also appear to load on this particular factor. On balance, the factor seems to reflect initiation of structure, the ability to adapt to stress and technological-administrative competence.

The fourth factor on which the workers appear to discriminate between most- and least-preferred foremen seems somewhat unique insofar as recent research literature is concerned, although Kahn and Katz (1960) identified it several years ago. This factor (which accounts for only 12 per cent of the variance) is concerned with the foreman's ability or willingness to develop role differentiation between his supervisory role and the role of the worker. Thus, a supervisor scoring low on role differentiation appears to be quite knowledgeable about the work (factor weight = .75) and has considerable upholstering skill personally (factor weight = .90). These characteristics, of course, were paramount in the minds of top management when most of these foremen were promoted from their ranks. Supervisors who do not differentiate their role in their subordinates' eyes, however, also tend to be "*un*-enthusiastic about the work," do *not* "take life too seriously," are *not* "energetic" and are *low* on "drive," are easy to "push around," do *not* "act better than their men," do *not* "stick to company rules," are *not* "polite," have "*dis*-agreeable personalities," and "do *not* get along" well with the union. Moreover, such men are seen as "having a chip on their shoulder" and as people who "look for fights." On balance, such a person sounds like one who has not accepted the responsibilities of his formal leadership role, although he is a highly competent upholsterer.[6] He is either unable or unwilling to assume the proper leadership responsibilities. I believe, however, that this dimension is primarily a motivational one, reflecting the extent to which the appointed leader really wants to lead. The descriptive terms relating

[6] The reader probably has seen this pattern in a variety of settings. It may occur in universities where department heads or deans find it difficult or do not wish to give up their research and teaching interests. It also occurs in industrial technical professional groups where promotions are made from within on the basis of past technical performance. Interim player-managers in professional athletics also have difficulty with this problem. In this study this factor was probably highly specific to one particular foreman (and partially applicable to one other). Post-experimental interviews with the first man revealed to me that he was generally dissatisfied with his job and hostile toward the company because of a number of changes affecting him adversely in the past. Actually, he appeared merely to be going through the motions of supervising his group. At an earlier time he had worked on, and later supervised, one of the company's high-quality (special-product line) upholstering groups; his upholstering skill and knowledge of the craft were beyond question. Subsequent to the experiment, this man was switched to a different supervisory position much more to his liking. His performance and general outlook have improved accordingly.

to the dimension, and their algebraic signs, support this interpretation.

It is not surprising that workers themselves would have such a dimension in mind when evaluating the differences between most- and least-preferred foreman; the presence of an important financial incentive system, coupled with the workers' obvious interest in money and the leadership requirements of the foreman's job, should heighten its saliency. In other words, the emergence of this factor adds further support to the experimental results reported earlier. Supervisors in this department are judged by workers in terms of their perceived willingness and ability to help them achieve their group goals, which are, by and large, congruent with those of the employer.

It also is worth pointing out that "personality" (pleasant-unpleasant), the original variable with which we started, loads approximately to the same extent on all four factors in this factor analysis, although its algebraic sign varies from one factor to the next. Thus, in the workers' minds, "personality" is associated with general overall unpleasantness and gruffness, employee-centeredness or consideration, handling structure and stress, and role differentiation.

Overall, Table 13 gives us a reasonably parsimonious picture of what the major independent variable in this experiment was all about. By reassigning foremen on the basis of worker preferences, we presumably were manipulating the four supervisory dimensions reflected in the table.[7]

---

[7] Since this factor structure emerged from data collected *after* the experimental change, however, it must be conceded that all the factors might not have existed so clearly prior to the experiment. The experimental experience may have helped to create the structure. It also is important to note that factor 1 correlates −.77 and −.85, respectively, with factors 2 and 3. Factors 2 and 3 correlate .74, while 4 correlates .51 with 1, −.69 with 2, and −.57 with 3. The magnitudes of these correlations and the pattern of factor weights in Table 20 indicate a substantial halo effect in the data. An overall, general impression or response set colors all the responses to the specific items.

The workers apparently discriminate between good and poor foremen on the basis of (1) general personality considerations, (2) employee-centeredness or consideration, (3) technological-administrative competence and structure coupled with good stress management, and (4) willingness to accept managerial role responsibilities. These are the leadership characteristics that *apparently* influenced the workers' preference rankings and status consensus developments described earlier in this chapter. Perhaps the data to be reported in Chapter 5 will permit us to be somewhat more definitive about this.

In answer, then, to the question whether any of the relevant group indexes exhibited change following the introduction of the experimental foreman reassignments, we can list five major findings:

1. Group productivity levels, which had been quite stable prior to the experiment, changed considerably. The previously stable rank order of the groups was broken almost completely during the first few weeks after the foreman change. However, a stable rank order gradually emerged, although the groups' new relative productivity positions were a good deal different from their initial positions. It is clear that equilibrium was lost initially and a new equilibrium state developed over time. Data for comparable time periods during the year preceding the experiment and the year following the experiment showed no such pattern.

2. The groups differed significantly in the extent to which they changed productivity levels.

3. The groups' relative preferences for their foremen, measured one year prior to the experiment and again ten weeks after the foremen had been reassigned, by and large remained stable. On the other hand, status consensus (degree of agreement within group) on the new foremen was quite unstable. Considerable shifting of opinion and perceptions within the groups occurred. Moreover, while the groups'

relative positions on their over-all mean foreman popularity indexes did not change much, their absolute levels tended to improve in most groups.

4. Because of the changes indicated above, we must conclude that the original independent variable on which the experiment was based also changed materially over time.

5. The group attraction variable, also measured before and after the experimental manipulation, changed dramatically over time. Some groups became more attractive while others revealed the opposite pattern.

On balance it is quite clear that the Upholstering Department, comprised of the seven groups in this study plus one more, changed drastically following the introduction of wholesale foreman reassignments on short notice. It is quite likely that the changes summarized above were triggered by the experimental manipulation. However, we cannot yet identify the ways in which the several variables may have been influenced. That will be our task in the next chapter.

Our examination of the data comparing the workers' criteria for group and foreman preferences before and after the experimental change has uncovered five additional results:

1. The workers discriminated, in general, less between their most- and least-preferred groups after the experiment than they had before the experiment.

2. The most salient discriminating dimensions, both before and after the experiment, are "the amount of money you can make" and "speed of work pace." In other words, the data suggest that the group attraction data are affected by group performance levels, which are directly geared to money and speed through the company's financial incentive system.

3. The data also suggest that the workers became somewhat more conscious of intrinsic work characteristics associated with the technological requirements on the respective lines, without changing their continuing concern over

money. Presumably this had something to do with their experiences in coping with the technological stresses created when the leaders were switched around.

4. Contrary to the group attraction–cohesion data reported above, the workers became more, not less, discriminating after the experiment when describing most- and least-preferred foremen.

5. While foreman "personality" (pleasant-unpleasant) was the most discriminating dimension both before and after the experiment, the perceived technological-administrative skills of the foremen seemed to assume greater importance after the experiment than before the reassignments. This finding suggests that the new foremen were judged at least partly on their ability to help their groups re-establish equilibrium following the foreman reassignments.

We have also seen from results of a factor analysis designed to identify the major dimensions used by the workers when differentiating between most- and least-preferred foremen, that four sensible factors emerged: (1) general personality, (2) Employee-centeredness or consideration, (3) technological-administrative competence and initiation of structure, coupled with job-related stress management, and (4) role differentiation, or, willingness to accept managerial role responsibilities. These findings, like some of the others reported above, also suggest that the new foremen were judged at least partly on their ability to help their groups re-establish equilibrium following the technological disruptions created by the foreman reassignments. Thus, a foreman's popularity (mean preference rank) in his group would be affected by his behavior relative to at least the above four dimensions. Similarly, the degree of status consensus he would develop also would be affected by such matters.

This chapter has demonstrated that important changes occurred in the Upholstering Department following the foreman reassignments. It also has suggested some possible ways in which these changes may be related to worker perceptions. The causal linkages among these variables, however, are no more clear in this study, so far, than in most cross-sectional studies criticized in Chapter 1. Let us turn, therefore, to some more convincing evidence, whose persuasive power stems from the longitudinal nature of the experimental design.

CHAPTER 5

Testing Alternative Hypotheses

We have seen that numerous changes occurred in the Upholstering Department, presumably as a result of the foreman reassignments, and we have considered a broad outline of possible explanations. We can now devote our attention to a more systematic analysis of the experimental results. First, we shall test the two oversimplified alternative hypotheses, discussed in Chapter 1, that stimulated the research initially—"leader as cause" versus "performance levels as cause." Next, we shall examine the findings in relation to the more complex systems-equilibrium theory, also described briefly in Chapter 1. Finally, we shall examine the question of "Hawthorne effect" or demand characteristics as it relates to the outcome of this experiment. The major variables to be considered are: pre- and post-experimental group attraction ($\overline{X}$ preference rank in each group); pre- and post-experimental group foreman preference ($\overline{X}$ preference rank in each group); pre- and post-experimental status consensus on new foreman (standard deviation of foreman preference ranks in each group—an agreement index); and percentage change in productivity.

ANALYTICAL STRATEGY: COMPARING TWO HYPOTHESES

The reader may recall from Chapter 1 that two major hypotheses guided the development and execution of this experiment. The first of these might be labeled "the leader as cause," while the second may be called "performance levels as cause." The leader-as-cause hypothesis stipulates that a favorable foreman change (in the eyes of his subordinates) will lead directly to improved group attraction and consensus with concomitant group performance improvements. Similarly, a leadership change that is unfavorable in the eyes of group members should lead to decreased consensus, group attraction, and performance. This hypothesis, prior to the experiment, was supported by a correlational analysis revealing a consistent set of positive relationships among productivity levels, group attraction, status consensus, and foreman preferences.

The performance-levels-as-cause hypothesis assumes that the consistent relationships referred to above arise from a different time sequence among the variables. Specifically, this hypothesis states that pre-experimental group perceptions of leadership behavior will break down in the face of first-hand experiences following reassignments of the various foremen. Further, new perceptions will emerge and will be influenced primarily by group performance levels following the reassignments. In other words, this hypothesis assumes that in work teams characterized by technological interdependence and geared to objectives defined as desirable by the group members (money linked to productivity through a financial incentive system), the group members are likely to judge their leader (foreman) in terms of how well they think he helps them reach their objectives. Moreover, while he has only limited ability either to help or to hinder his subordinates, the foreman is likely to be the recipient of many perceptions that grow out of the general level of satisfaction that the group has with its circumstances. This general level of satisfaction, of course, is heavily influenced by the group's perceived degree of success, given the incentive system.

The design of the experiment permits us to test both the above hypotheses. Figure 5 reveals how this was arranged. The timetable for data collection made it possible to test the causal relationship of the independent variable, measured

April, 1963	Elapsed time 1 year + →	April, 1964	Elapsed time 10 weeks →	June 1964	+6 more weeks →
First measurement of group attraction or group cohesion, foreman preferences, status consensus on foremen, and related items	Assumption: Variable system remained stable during this time period	Introduction of foreman reassignments on Monday A.M.	Collection of productivity data from records to serve as dependent variable for hypothesis 1 and as independent variable for hypothesis 2	Second measurement of group attraction, foreman preferences, status consensus on foremen, and related items	Further collection of productivity data to ascertain whether any experimental effects picked up in June were lasting

Figure 5. Timetable for the experiment

in April, 1963, and manipulated in April, 1964, to the ten weeks of group productivity ensuing immediately after the experimental manipulation. The independent variable also can be correlated against the second measurement of group attraction taken in June, 1964. The above analyses would exhaust our tests on hypothesis 1, leadership behavior as cause. The performance-as-cause hypothesis can be tested by treating the ten weeks of elapsed productivity between April, 1964, and June, 1964, as the independent variable to predict group attraction, foreman preferences, and status consensus, as measured in June, 1964. If the observed correlations within one of these analytical schemes tend to be larger than in the other, the corresponding hypothesis would be supported. In other words, if the original independent variable predicts subsequent changes in productivity and group attraction, the leader-as-cause hypothesis will be supported. On the other hand, if the independent variable is *not* predictive and at the same time we find that the first several weeks of performance data predict subsequent changes in group attraction, foremen preferences, and status consensus, we would have support for hypothesis 2, performance as cause.

RESULTS

The empirical results related to these two hypotheses are summarized by Table 14. The reader should begin his examination of that table by comparing the correlations in the two enclosed boxes connected by a diagonal arrow. This portion of the table shows that the leader-as-cause hypothesis receives less support from the empirical data than the productivity-as-cause hypothesis. That is, the original experimental variable of the study, perceptions of the old foreman versus the new, correlates only .25 with the first ten weeks of productivity-change data following the experimental manipulation. When we turn the causal sequence around, treating the first ten weeks of productivity data as the independent variable, we find that this variable correlates only slightly

Table 14. Correlations among selected variables to test alternative hypotheses 1 and 2

Variable	Post-experimental foreman preference (X_3)	Post-experimental status consensus on foreman (X_5)	1st 10 weeks of productivity change (X_{13})	Post-experimental group attraction (X_7)
(X_1) independent variable, old foreman vs. new	.64	.63		$\begin{bmatrix} .33 \\ \updownarrow \\ .54 \end{bmatrix}$
(X_{13}) independent variable, 1st 10 weeks of productivity change	.29	.67	.25	

better (.29) with the post-experimental foreman preference ranking. On the other hand, it correlates .67 with the post-experimental status consensus on the new foremen. Given the fact that status consensus, as indicated in Chapter 4, changed quite substantially during the course of this experiment, the latter finding is quite instructional. The correlation of .67 strongly suggests that much of the within-group consensus change that took place during the process of consensus formation on the new foremen was influenced by the groups' performance achievements sometime during the first ten weeks following the experimental manipulation.[1]

On the right-hand side of Table 14 the reader may make a vertical comparison between the relative predictive powers of the initial experimental variable and early performance levels in relation to post-experimental group attraction or cohesion. The table shows that this post-experimental group measure seems to correlate more highly with the preceding productivity changes than with the original experimental variable of the study. That is, the experimental variable with which we started correlates with post-experimental group attraction only .33. On the other hand, if one uses the first ten weeks of productivity change data as a predictor, this variable correlates .54 with subsequent group attraction.

While only one of the correlations in Table 14 approaches statistical significance at the .05 level, the pattern of the data seems fairly clear-cut. On balance, it would appear that, in this case, group attraction, and, to a somewhat lesser extent, foreman preferences are influenced at least as much by the performance levels of the groups as by pre-experimental expectations about the foremen themselves. The pre-experi-

[1] The fact that post-experimental foreman preferences (X_3) correlates only .29 with the preceding performance changes may be explained by range-restriction. Table 10 in Chapter 4 shows that six of the seven foremen received relatively high *mean* rankings from their respective groups when this measurement was taken in week eleven. Variation on status consensus (standard deviations) among the groups, however, remained high and provided considerable range.

mental expectations about foremen, however, as indicated by X_1 in Table 14, do not disappear altogether from the system we are examining. As shown in Chapter 4, the groups' preferences toward their new foremen measured before the experiment correlated .71 with their preferences measured eleven weeks after the experiment began. Table 14 shows that the experimental variable, old foremen versus new, correlates .64 and .63 respectively with post-experimental foremen preferences and foreman status consensus. Overall, then, the findings suggest that the consensus-formation process around the new foremen is influenced heavily *both* by group achievements and by the groups' previous expectations about their new foremen. Group attraction, however, appears to be more strongly influenced by group achievements than by previous expectations.

The above results lend substantial support to the various findings reported in the previous chapter. That is, the self-report data that the workers gave us when describing their most- and least-preferred work groups strongly suggested that they discriminate on the basis of money-making potential. The longitudinal findings in Table 14 corroborate these data. Similarly, extensive data reported in Chapter 4 indicated that group leaders (foremen) are evaluated by work groups at least in part as a function of the extent to which they are perceived as helping the group reach its goals. Again, the data in Table 14 corroborate this finding.

Before leaving this analysis for another, we should note that the post-experimental correlations of the foreman preference and group attraction–cohesion variables were higher with *percentage changes* in productivity during the first ten weeks following the experimental manipulation than they were with productivity averages. This finding supports the assumption made in Chapter 4, which is restated above in Figure 5, that most of the attitude changes that occurred developed *after* the foremen were reassigned rather than during the one-year interval between the initial measurements of the attitudes and the introduction of the foremen assignments. The foremen assignments, made with no, or very little, advance warning, apparently made the workers conscious of their group performance levels and increased the saliency of the entire productivity-attitudinal complex. This salience facilitated comparison in the workers' minds between pre-change and post-change performance and earnings. These comparisons, in turn, are reflected by the correlations summarized in Table 14. It is likely that such comparisons were quite salient because the quarterly earnings reports on each man and group were posted routinely and conspicuously on the respective group bulletin boards within a few days of the experimental change and therefore could be compared easily with ensuing weekly paychecks.

ANOTHER ANALYTICAL STRATEGY:
SYSTEMS-EQUILIBRIUM THEORY

The systems-equilibrium theory of formal organization treats the organization as a dynamic and complex set of functionally related variables that interact with each other as the total organization strives to reach its various objectives.[2] In the process, imbalances are generated (from within the variable system or from environmental factors outside the system) which produce internal tensions and pressures. A few, several, or perhaps many of the variables within the system, depending on the seriousness of the tensions, then begin to exert added or reduced influence on each other to facilitate the reduction of tension. This view of organizations sees them as constantly seeking equilibrium because something in the system is almost always changing, thereby creating needs for adjustment. Many changes that occur, of course, are relatively mild and do not produce great tension. In fact, many organizations seem to arrive at a state, sooner or later, in

[2] See Katz and Kahn (1966) for a thorough exposition of systems-equilibrium theory as applied to formal organization.

which variations from equilibrium are small and infrequent. On the other hand, some organizations are characterized by relatively large variations and much different threshold levels than are observed in their more static counterparts.

The nation's airlines, despite their growth and dynamism, provide a nice illustration of how systems-equilibrium theory operates, at least in the short run. One can conceive of the total domestic passenger-airline industry as an organizational system. In the absence of bad weather, major strikes, large-scale fleet changeovers, and so on, the system is in a satisfactory equilibrium state, although minor tensions develop from occasional mechanical problems or scheduling errors. Such minor problems on, say, one airline may create adjustment problems for others serving the same or related routes because of the need to move unexpected passengers at unexpected times. Should a major snowstorm occur, however, simultaneously closing several large metropolitan airports, a serious disequilibrium state will develop. Almost all component variables in the system will show changes, if measured, as the system attempts to right itself. First of all, energy will be mobilized throughout the system; key reservation and ticket clerks will work harder and longer hours, as will maintenance and baggage-handling crews. (See Stagner [1951] for a discussion of energy mobilization at the individual personality level of analysis.) Dispatchers, control-tower personnel, and flight crews will all make various special efforts to return to normal schedules. The list could be expanded to include airport restaurant personnel, hotel keepers, catering services, limousine and taxi drivers, plus others. Even airlines not directly servicing the snow-stricken cities are likely to feel the effects. They also may initiate actions to help the overall industry return to equilibrium.

The industry will, of course, get back to its normal schedules. However, each such experience, including the storm and all the direct and indirect concomitants of dealing with it, will leave the internal condition of the system at least a little different than it was before. Interpersonal relations among employees, group cohesion, supervisory behaviors, attitudes toward supervisors, customer behaviors, customer attitudes toward specific airlines, employee attitudes toward customers, and so on are all likely to change in one way or another, as a function of the ways they influenced each other during the crisis.

A systems-equilibrium view of the Upholstering Department in this study (as indicated previously in Chapter 1) assumes that several dimensions of the groups, plus various technological-administrative factors, are related to each other in complex ways and exert mutual influences on each other. (This assumption is at least partly supported by the web of consistent correlations among productivity, group attraction, foreman preference, and status consensus variables described in Chapter 3.) The systems view further assumes that a major change in such an interconnected system (imposed from top management in this case) will produce disequilibrium followed by a variety of interrelated, tension-reducing reactions. Through these reactions the overall system eventually will return to a balanced state, although, as in the airlines example, the composition of that balance may be somewhat different from the original. In the process of seeking equilibrium, supervisory behavior, group attraction–cohesion, and group performance (success in achieving goals) are all likely to influence each other, provided that the initial disequilibrium state is sufficiently severe.

Given the above conceptualization, the following paragraphs outline the first two of several major assumptions and predictions that we must support to demonstrate the adequacy of the model in this experiment:

1. Prior to the experimental manipulation the system (the upholstery groups and their interconnected variables) was in equilibrium. This assumption is supported by the fact that these groups of considerable experience and tenure had been

working "as usual" for a long time. There were no unusual stresses in the environment or within the groups. Working hours and work load were regular, there were no technological or administrative changes of any import, and labor turnover (group membership changes) was virtually nil.[3] Moreover, a highly stable group hierarchy on the productivity dimension had emerged. Finally, five of the seven groups seemed to accept their foreman; only one group showed evidence of actively disliking theirs.

2. Since the foreman reassignments were introduced more than a year after the initial research and without the presence of researcher intervention, the people involved should react as they normally would to this major administrative change imposed arbitrarily and on short notice by top management. Such changes traditionally are made (in our culture, at least) only when higher authorities are dissatisfied with performance levels of subordinates. Therefore, the employees should show a "pressure" reaction. Three specific things should happen: (*a*) The groups should feel threatened in inverse relation to their customary performance levels. (*b*) Adaptation problems should occur early, given the foreman's role as expeditor in emergencies and as the group's external representative. His relative lack of technological-product information appropriate to his new assignment also should make a big initial difference. In short, the system should be knocked out of equilibrium due to a drastic change in leadership. Finally, (c) The money motive of the employees, originally measured before the experimental change, should increase its saliency because the new foremen, in five of seven groups, will be seen as inferior to the old one; he probably will not be seen by the workers as having immediate and necessary trans-

[3] One foreman reassignment involving one of our experimental foremen was initiated by the plant manager about seven months prior to the major experimental changes. However, the effects of this change had ample time to settle down before the experiment began.

ferable skills (for example, when a couch line receives a chair-line foreman). The increased saliency of the money motive should reflect the mobilization of energy to return to equilibrium. We already have seen in Chapter 4 that predictions a and b, are strongly supported by the data. The lowest-producing groups before the experiment showed the largest percentage gains following the leadership change, while every one of the seven groups showed an increase during the first week or two. Moreover, the stability of the group's productivity ranks broke down, and a new and considerably (but not totally) different hierarchy developed later.

The "money motive" or energy mobilization prediction (c) was tested after an appropriate index to measure this phenomenon was developed. The variable was measured a year before the experiment by having each worker describe, on seven-point scales, "the amount of money you can make" on his most- and least-preferred upholstering lines. For the purpose at hand, these data were converted into an index for each group. There is variation among the groups on "money motivation," and the index constructed from the pre-experimental data correlates highly (Rho = .79) with its counterpart measured in the eleventh week following the experimental change. Hence, the index is reliable. (See Appendix J for further methodological details.)

As predicted in statement c, the group "money motivation" index correlated highly with group productivity percentage changes (Rho = .71) and productivity levels (Rho = .64) during the first ten weeks of the experiment. That is, the more money motivated the group, the greater its percentage productivity increase and the higher its productivity level during the first ten weeks following the foreman switch. Interestingly enough, the "money motivation" index did *not* correlate with group productivity levels *before* the experiment (Rho = .03). The sudden introduction of the leadership crisis apparently activiated its influence, which previously was at rest during equilibrium.[4] And, this variable made its influence felt as early as the third week following the foreman changes. (See Table 15, X_9.)

Now that we have demonstrated the occurrence of disequilibrium followed by the mobilization of energy to seek a new equilibrium, it would be helpful to show that a new equilibrium state actually was reached in this experiment. This was partly demonstrated in Chapter 4 through the data presented in Table 8. That table revealed that the initially low correlations between adjacent productivity time periods immediately following the experimental manipulation began to increase and eventually leveled off in the .70's about the sixth or seventh week. Thus, a new productivity equilibrium level was reached for the component parts (work groups) of the organizational system we are examining.

Now let us examine our other group variables. In Chapter 3 we showed the following matrix of rank-order correlations among the variables, foreman preference, status consensus on foreman, and group attraction and group consensus, all measured a year before the experimental manipulations:

Pre-experimental	X_1	X_2	X_3
Foreman preference (X_1)	1.00	.93	.83
Status consensus (X_2)			.79
Group attraction (X_3)			

This is, as was pointed out earlier, a very consistent set of correlations and presumably reflects the equilibrium state that existed at that time. On the other hand, despite substantial changes in group measurements on these variables when comparing the pre-experimental measurements with their post-experimental counterparts, the post-experimental measurements showed the same kind of consistent intercon-

[4] Unfortunately, a comparative analysis of the several work groups on such variables as age, length of service, and family size revealed no explanation as to why the groups differed on money motivation to begin with.

nected pattern, although not quite as well developed. The
following matrix illustrates this point:

Post-experimental	X_1	X_2	X_3
Foreman preference (X_1)	1.00	.54	.62
Status consensus (X_2)			.83
Group attraction (X_3)			

While the degree of interconnectedness is not as high (possibly because of post-experimental range restriction on X_1) as
was the case when we measured these variables prior to the
experiment, it is evidence of the equilibrium-seeking nature
of a complex social system. What we are saying here is that
the group attitudinal variable measurements changed over
time, but the new levels (measurements) that emerged for
the groups remained fairly highly correlated. The major
difference between the two matrixes lies in the nature of the
foreman-preference and status-consensus variables. While
status consensus did change considerably, most of the within-
group change took place in those groups receiving favorable
changes in foremen in accordance with pre-experimental expectations. The new matrix also is affected by the fact that
group attraction was more susceptible to the influence of the
intervening productivity and earnings experiences of the
groups than was the foreman-preference dimension.

The fact that a new, stable productivity hierarchy developed among the groups coupled with a new, but consistent
set of correlations among the group attitudinal indexes is
important. Despite all the changes occurring among the
groups on these dimensions, the *pattern* of the variable interrelationships was not seriously disturbed. These variables
apparently bear relationships to one another, within this
small organizational subsystem, which act as forces toward
equilibrium.

The apparent result of equilibrium-seeking summarized
above would be more convincing as support for the systems
equilibrium model if we could show that the equilibrium-

seeking process began several weeks prior to the post-experimental measurements. Certain special research methods would have been required for such a demonstration. "Planted" participant observers, for example, perhaps one on every other line, could have obtained invaluable information during the crisis and subsequent adaptation stages. However, trained observers who also could have performed satisfactory upholstering work were unavailable. Ordinary research observers, of course, were ruled out by the scary results in the "non-experiment." I firmly believed that the groups had to be left to their own devices if we were to learn anything valid about the leadership-change effects. Such a decision does involve a sacrifice, however, since our data permit only inferences on the group adjustment process, not direct evidence.

One other possible strategy that theoretically might have provided such "process" information would have employed repeated measurements on group cohesion–attraction, foreman preferences, and status consensus at regular, frequent intervals following the foreman reassignments. Repeated questionnaire administrations, however, clearly would have tipped our hand. Moreover, general "panelitis" problems (see Remmers [1954]) probably would have introduced further error.

The question is, then: How can we demonstrate that the workers were assessing the new foremen in the light of performance levels *prior* to the second round of attitude measurements on Monday of the eleventh week? Can we show any kind of legitimate trend data that will reveal the disintegration, over time, of pre-experimental variables and the emergence, over time, of their post-experimental counterparts?

Figures 6 through 8 provide such trend data through what may be called a "poor man's" longitudinal analysis. Procedurally, the writer merely calculated the relationships between the pre-experimental and post-experimental group attitude measures, on the one hand, and the productivity percentage change index, on the other hand, *at two week intervals* following the foreman reassignments. For example,

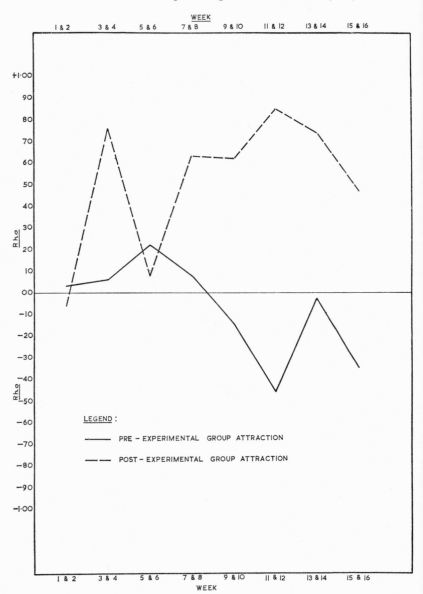

Figure 6. Correlation (Rho) of pre- and post-experimental group attraction with productivity changes, at two-week intervals

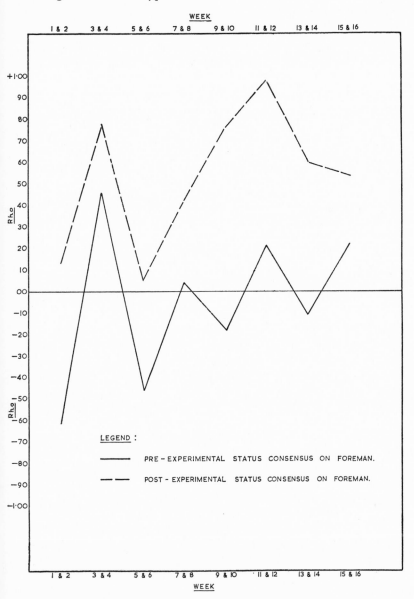

Figure 7. Correlation (Rho) of pre- and post-experimental status consensus on foreman with productivity changes, at two-week intervals

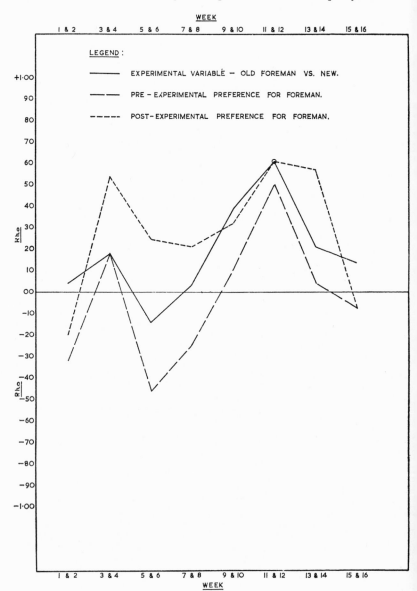

Figure 8. Correlation of pre- and post-experimental foreman preferences with productivity changes, at two-week intervals

Figure 6 shows how well the pre-experimental group attraction index correlates with productivity change in each of several two-week periods following the experiment. It also shows the comparable data for *post*-experimental group attraction measured on Monday of the eleventh week. Figures 7 and 8 were developed in the same way.

The trends in the graphs, especially Figures 6 and 7, strongly suggest that the equilibrium-seeking process began *before* the second round of measurements were taken in the eleventh week. The graphs reveal a system developing a new equilibrium state after a "crisis." The correlations of the pre-experimental variables with performance "faded away" as new ones developed. (Note in Figure 6, for example, how the correlation of pre-experimental group attraction with productivity change gradually diminished in the first several weeks following the experimental change while the opposite trend developed for post-experimental group attraction.) In the process it is likely that the several variables influenced each other, given their pre- and post-experimental correlations.

THE AFTERMATH

An obvious question to raise now is whether the new status-consensus, foreman-preference, and group-attraction variables have any implications in relation to productivity change following the measurement of these group variables on Monday of the eleventh week. That is: Will any of these variables predict subsequent productivity developments? While the post-experimental foremen preference variable $\overline{X}$) correlates with percentage productivity changes during weeks 11 through 16 only .36, post-experimental status consensus (sd) on the foreman correlates with the same productivity change index .85. Similarly, post-experimental group attraction predicts subsequent performance changes .83. It seems, therefore, on the basis of these correlations and those in Table 14, that leadership consensus and group attraction are both responsive to past accomplishments *and* predictive of future accomplishments. Moreover, the correlation between post-experimental status consensus on the leader and post-experimental group attraction is .83. Considering that these two variables were as highly correlated *before* the experiment began, given the changes that occurred in them over time, and considering their mutual relationships to performance changes, it would seem that these are "systems" variables that interact with each other reciprocally.

It should be stressed that post-experimental status consensus on leader and group attraction, while correlated more highly with the ten weeks of performance change immediately preceding their measurement than with the original experimental variable, were even more highly correlated with later performance accomplishments. It seems, therefore, that in this research setting we have found an instance where selected elements of job satisfaction are in fact related to performance—and causally, to some extent. This finding, which runs counter to the general body of literature on job satisfaction and performance relationships (see Brayfield and Crockett [1955] or Vroom [1964]), will be explicated in Chapter 8.

DISCUSSION OF THE SYSTEMS-EQUILIBRIUM DATA

The system-equilibrium conceptualization and its supporting data reported above seem analogous to what happens when a football coach (the "researcher") asks his players whether they can "live with" the new quarterback (following an injury to the old one) after the new quarterback's second or third game of the season. Their team performance comparisons (under the new and the previous quarterbacks) and comparisons (of traits and behaviors) with other quarterbacks they have known will lead the players to close ranks around him to some extent or another. Their advance expectations about him, as was the case in this experiment, also are likely to affect how he is perceived in these comparisons and consequently will affect the degree of consensus on him. The entire process will be affected by the extent to which the team is motivated to win ("money motivation" or "acceptance of company goals"). This variable is likely to be affected by the initial emergency (the injury) so that extra team energy will be mobilized in the first place in direct proportion to motivation level.

The final data of this experiment (weeks 11–16) suggest that the *next* development will be enhanced or ragged performance as a result of the degree of consensus on the new leader. The loop, at this point, is now closed; perceived leadership behavior, group attraction, and group achievement of goals are inextricably bound together in a circular relationship. A change in any part of this system is likely to produce changes elsewhere.

The observer of political process in relation to the behavior of elected leaders also may see this experiment in analogous terms. The second measurement in the experiment is analogous to a vote for a second term in office. The degree of consensus depends on the leader's past performance in relation to the electorate's needs and his perceived personality characteristics. The development of consensus seems to enhance the leader's future influence on achievement. In the political process, of course, the leader receives feedback on "consensus" from the election results. While I did not provide such feedback to the foremen in the experiment, it is likely that the workers let them know informally how the "vote" turned out. It also is likely that the workers discussed their rankings among themselves after the questionnaire was administered, thus facilitating the consensus-formation process and enhancing the relationships found in weeks 11 through 16.

STATUS CONSENSUS AND EQUILIBRIUM

The fact that the status consensus index proved to be a critical variable in the experiment will surprise no one who is familiar with the work of Bales and his colleagues at Harvard, the experimental work on "autokinetic effect" by Sherif (1935), and the conformity research by Asch and Crutchfield (summarized by Krech *et al.* [1962]). The evidence is quite clear that individuals' perception of stimuli are affected by others' judgments; group pressures play a significant role in the process, as do stimulus properties, individual differences of various kinds among group members, structural characteristics of the group, and so on.

The results of this industrial field experiment, coupled with the "conformity" literature and other research bearing on status consensus, suggest that leadership status consensus, as measured herein, may be a direct index of group equilibrium. Thus, if group members cannot reach substantial internal agreement on their attitudes toward and perceptions of their formal leader, the group would be classified, by definition, as out of equilibrium, especially if the group's task requires that the formal leader perform significant functions. The failure to achieve consensus might be a function of the leader himself, characteristics of other members, group structural problems, or some combination of these factors. Without a suitable combination, however, consensus will not be reached. Concomitantly we are likely to find low morale or cohesion, which, for interdependent task groups, probably will affect adversely the coordination of members' efforts and the strength of individuals' motivation toward formal goals.

Thus, when we arbitrarily remove leaders from groups characterized by substantial positive leadership consensus (as happened in most of the groups in this experiment) and replace them with leaders about whom there is far less advance agreement, disequilibrium is a likely result. A new consensus, and therefore the return to equilibrium, will occur only if a variety of factors, mentioned above, happen to combine properly. If they do not, disequilibrium will remain. The fact that the post-experimental status-consensus index in this study correlated .85 with subsequent productivity percentage changes supports this argument. Group effectiveness on the designated task improved in direct proportion to the degree of consensus on the leader that had developed and was expressed by the eleventh week.

SOME COMMENTS ON DEMAND CHARACTERISTICS
AND HAWTHORNE EFFECT

The reader may recall from Table 9 in Chapter 4 that in addition to the sharp increases in productivity that occurred in the first week or two following the experimental change, another large increase developed during weeks 11 and 12, immediately after a research team had remeasured the various employee attitude dimensions. At first glance this may sound like traditional "Hawthorne effect." Table 15 may shed further light on the matter. The table shows the correlations between all of our pre-experimental and post-experimental group variables, on the one hand, with post-experimental percentage changes in productivity on the other—at two-week intervals. Notice the large magnitudes of the relationships during weeks 11 and 12. This was the only time during the sixteen-week experiment when the original independent variable showed a marked relationship to productivity. The pattern of the data suggests that our appearance on the scene as researchers helped produce understanding of the reassignments for the first time, which then was translated, subsequent to that Monday afternoon, into productivity changes. The time sequence here is clear. It is possible that this strong relationship would have developed in the eleventh week without our entering the plant with the questionnaire, but this seems doubtful. It is more likely that the "lights went on" for these upholstery workers when we showed up with the same questions about foremen and work groups that they had answered previously and easily could recognize on the second occasion. It also seems plausible that the measurement process coupled with the related discussions that the workers must have had among themselves after the research team left may

Table 15. Rank-order correlations of several relevant variables with post-experimental changes in productivity,* at two-week intervals

Variable	Time period and rank order correlation							
	Weeks 1–2	Weeks 3–4	Weeks 5–6	Weeks 7–8	Weeks 9–10	Weeks 11–12	Weeks 13–14	Weeks 15–16
(X_1) experimental variable, old foreman vs. new	.04	.18	−.14	.03	.39	.61 / .74‡	.21	.14
(X_2) pre-experimental preference toward new foreman	−.32	.18	−.46	−.25	.11	.50 / .63‡	.04	−.07
(X_3) post-experimental preference toward new foreman	−.20	.54	.25	.21	.32	.61 / .54‡	.57	−.25
(X_4) pre-experimental status consensus, new foreman	−.61	.46	−.46	.04	−.18	.21 / .13‡	−.11	.21
(X_5) post-experimental status consensus, new foreman	.13	.78	.06	.42	.76	.99 / .92‡	.60	.54
(X_6) pre-experimental group attraction	.03	.06	.22	.08	−.15	−.46 / −.80‡	−.03	−.35
(X_7) post-experimental group attraction	−.06	.76	.08	.63	.62	.85 / .70‡	.74	.47
(X_8) pre-experimental base productivity level	−.67	.04	−.53	−.33	−.47	−.44 / −.62‡	−.26	−.72
(X_9) pre-experimental money motive	.29	.71	.55	.86	.79	.57 / .17‡	.93	.11

* Computed as follows: pre-experimental twelve-week base productivity level − two-week productivity level ÷ pre-experimental twelve-week base productivity level × 100. Each of these was assigned a rank from 1 to 7 every two weeks. See Table 9.
‡ For week 11 only.

well have contributed to the consensus-formation process. In other words, the second questionnaire administration may have been perceived as a formal, organizational symbol that signified the "end" of the experiment and stimulated the consensus-formation process. This may account for the strikingly large correlations between the consensus and group attraction indexes, on the one hand, and percentage changes in group performance during weeks 11 through 16 (especially weeks 11 and 12), on the other.

The disciples of Martin Orne will draw great sustenance from these data. It certainly seems that the decision to remain away from the experimental plant and to maintain secrecy about the experiment was a sound one in the light of this particular set of results. Had the workers known from the outset what our objectives were, it is possible that the pattern observed for weeks 11 and 12 might have occurred earlier, thus giving us an entirely different picture of the experimental impact. On the other hand, one might argue that the change methods used here were too dramatic and thereby obfuscated the real experimental variable; this serious methodological issue, among others, will be discussed in Chapter 8.

In any event, despite the dramatic data for weeks 11 and 12, the *trends* appear to have started *before* we re-entered the plant. Figures 6 and 7 show that the correlations between the pre-experimental attitudinal-perceptual variables and performance changes started to break down shortly after the foreman reassignments were made and gradually declined to nonsignificant or negative levels. The newly emerging attitudinal-perceptual variables, as measured in week 11, began to show positive correlations with performance after about the first six weeks had transpired following the foreman reassignments. The reader should note that the timing of this correlational development corresponds with the reliability trend data reported in Chapter 4 (see Table 8). *That is, the relationships between group attraction and status consensus, on the one hand, and performance change on the other hand, apparently began to crystalize at the same time (weeks 7–8) that the groups' productivity levels began to stabilize after their initial disruption.* Therefore, the changes that occurred cannot reasonably be written off entirely as mere "Hawthorne effect" or demand characteristics stemming from the research operations used.

SUMMARY

The design of this experiment enabled us to test two oversimplified but competing hypotheses—"leader as cause" versus "group performance as cause—which conceivably can explain a large number of research study findings in recent years. The data in this experiment are at least as friendly to the performance-as-cause hypothesis as to the leader-as-cause hypothesis. Performance levels following the experimental manipulation predict later measures of group attraction and status consensus on foremen better than does the original independent variable of the experiment, pre-experimental foreman preferences. Moreover, the original independent variable apparently did not predict subsequent performance levels or percentage performance changes. However, pre-experimental expectations about the new foreman do appear to influence the development of later status-consensus changes, and status consensus appears to be a crucial variable in the total system.

A complex systems-equilibrium model was proposed as a more sophisticated explanation of the experiment. The data support this model surprisingly well, considering the relative lack of rigor in this field experiment as contrasted with laboratory conditions. We found evidence to support the following-systems-equilibrium propositions: (1) a previously stable system was knocked out of equilibrium by a major leadership change; (2) energy was mobilized to bring the system back into equilibrium; (3) a new equilibrium state was reached; and (4) the equilibrium-seeking process began prior to the second round of attitude measurements, thereby precluding an explanation of the results entirely as an artifact of the research process.

The data also suggest that once the new equilibrium was reached and formalized through the second round of questionnaire responses, subsequent productivity effects developed. Thus, the new status consensus on the new foreman correlated .85 with later productivity increases; that is, the more each group agreed that "this is our leader" the more performance improvement it showed in the next several weeks. The consensus-formation phenomenon can be compared with analogous leadership-replacement phenomena in athletic teams and with the political process surrounding elected officials. The data herein and related arguments seem to support the view that group attraction, subordinates' perceptions of their leader's behavior, and performance levels exert mutual influences on each other. It would be difficult, indeed impossible, to identify one of these variables as "causal" in the formal organization.

Let us now return to the Northeast Plant to learn more about this remarkably resilient department.

CHAPTER 6

The Search for a Spurious Variable

The operations to be described in this chapter were generated from two major and related considerations. First, it seemed reasonable to expect that some of the experimental results reported previously could be enhanced upon being presented in a feedback meeting to the foremen who participated in the experiment. Insights from the foremen's personal experiences during the experiment quite possibly could provide further research leads. Second, there always was the nagging suspicion that some spurious variable might have accounted for much of the productivity change that took place, thereby influencing the workers' perceptions of their foremen and groups.[1] In the absence of any major managerial, organizational, or technological change, the leading contender as a spurious variable had to be some aspect of the production-scheduling operation. In other words, it seemed possible that some aspect of the production-scheduling process might have changed during the experiment in such a way as to create unfair advantages for certain upholstery groups. Such advantages theoretically might have made it easier for some groups than others to increase their productivity. It was hoped that the feedback process would provide insights

[1] Such a process would resemble what must have happened in the early part of the Great Depression. President Herbert Hoover was blamed for it by many people, although the major causes probably lay elsewhere. Later, of course, Roosevelt received credit, only some of which was deserved, from many citizens for getting us out of the depression.

into this matter. This chapter, then, is concerned with the feedback of some of the experimental results to the foremen, consideration of the foremen's reactions to these data, and a description of subsequently generated research work to check up on the question of production-scheduling influences.

RETURNING TO THE LIONS' DEN

Feedback Meeting. Approximately one year following the conclusion of the sixteen-week experiment I fulfilled my one obligation to the plant manager. In return for J. R.'s cooperation, I had promised to conduct a training meeting with the factory's foremen—those who had been in the experiment plus many others. The meeting was arranged at a local country steak house, where approximately thirty men were wined and dined at company expense prior to a two-hour meeting. The audience included two representatives from the corporate headquarters who had been invited by J. R. specifically for this meeting. The entire management structure of the Northeast Plant also attended.

During that meeting selected tables (in Chapters 3 and 4) were presented on a blackboard. The pre-experimental relationships between group attitudes on the one hand and productivity on the other were illustrated first. The "chicken and egg" phenomenon was explained next as a justification for the experiment, followed by a presentation of the factors on which the workers discriminated between effective and less effective foremen. It was emphasized, of course, that since these were ranking data the foreman who was ranked last prior to the experiment was not necessarily a poor foreman. The basis for the experiment was also explained. I then presented the results, emphasizing Table 9 (in Chapter 4), which shows the percentage changes in productivity that occurred after the supervisory reassignments. (The identities of the various groups and foremen, of course, were kept confidential during the entire presentation.) Considerable emphasis also was placed during this presentation on the differences between the workers and the foremen in the ways in which they discriminated between effective and less effective supervisors. There was lively discussion among the managers present upon the conclusion of this presentation.

During the discussion phase, some of the men raised questions about production-scheduling differences among the groups. I explained the assumption of long-term equivalency that had been made before conducting the research and the reasons behind that assumption. The chief production dispatcher and various other managers present all spoke up in support of the assumption that scheduling differences do get "randomized out" over a period of time. While this seemed to satisfy the other supervisors present, the discussion stimulated further exploration of the matter.

Following the discussion of the experiment and its results, a small group-dynamics laboratory demonstration was conducted using volunteer groups from the audience. This demonstration involved the construction of towers from children's blocks under certain controlled circumstances. Four-man groups were used and a "foreman" was appointed for each. An incentive system was employed (beer being the reward) and a ten-minute time limit was imposed. After watching three groups perform under these circumstances, the audience participated in developing a list of variables that had potential influence over the effectiveness of these groups. They easily saw the relevance of leadership, raw material characteristics, other task characteristics (such as time pressure), group structural characteristics (including size, personality composition, and individual abilities), motivational-incentive variables, and the overall environment in which the groups operated. The most obvious generalization that develops from such a demonstration, and which these men easily could see, is that group effectiveness is a function of a large number of variables, many of which are beyond the control of the formal group leader. This demonstration was deliberately arranged in this particular meeting so that none of the upholstering foremen would feel too put upon by the factory experiment that had been performed. That is to say, by stressing publicly in front of their local and corporate-level managers that the foreman is only one source of variance in group effectiveness, I hoped to take the sting out of the experiment for certain of the supervisors involved. I also hoped to reduce, if not eliminate, the possibility that the local plant management would be overly impressed by the importance of foreman rotation.

OBSERVATIONS OF UPHOLSTERY FOREMEN IN ACTION

During the meeting, it was agreed that I might spend several full work days in the Upholstering Department, observing directly the activities of the individual foremen. The upholstering foremen who were present, although perhaps under the influence of too many beers, agreed to my presence and expressed a willingness to be interviewed during the process. Consequently, I spent at least two hours observing each man in action with his group. During those two hours several questions were asked of each foreman in an informal, on-the-job interview. The questions were designed to get at the following: (1) How had they introduced themselves to the new group upon being reassigned and what was the worker reaction to the change? (2) How did they look at their relationship to their group and to what extent did they think they, as individual foremen, were important to group success? (3) How accurate did they consider the assumption of scheduling equivalence among the lines to be? These three questions do not exhaust the agenda, but they do reflect the more important interests that were pursued at the time.

The first foreman that I observed and talked with informed me that several of the upholstering workers with whom he was acquainted believed that the foremen reassignments were made by the top management as a means of "disciplining the foremen." This seems to be in line with the general interpretation in Chapters 4 and 5 that the groups appeared to respond to that change as a pressure device. This foreman also believed that changes in furniture styles and in the difficulty of the work, rather than the foremen themselves, brought about the productivity changes in the groups. He also pointed out (along with the local union president in a separate interview) that a shortage of space in the shipping area sometimes holds up the exit of completed material from the upholstering lines, thereby forcing the upholstering lines to slow down or even stop work. This is an important point to which we will return in Chapter 7, when we analyze production-scheduling operations, which clearly are affected by the space problem.

This foreman also indicated several factors that he thinks are characteristic of a "good" foreman. Among other things he indicated that a good foreman helps his men make money, but not at the expense of quality. He emphasized, however, that a good foreman must be conscious of his worker's earnings. This is merely one more corroboration of the importance of incentive earnings to these employees. It also illustrates that this foreman was aware of the fact that his leadership influence depended at least in part upon his ability to help his subordinates achieve their goals. The data in Chapters 4 and 5, as we already have seen, demonstrate the validity of his judgment.

The second supervisor I observed had a different view of his job, and several incidents that occurred during the few hours that I watched him perform with his group deserve elaboration. The first incident involved a component piece in certain pieces of furniture known as a "back-pull stretcher." This is a piece of cloth that certain workers on the line have to grab firmly and pull in order to get an appropriate level of tautness in the back of the furniture. While I was watching this group, a long set of furniture pieces began moving down the line. Part way through the order, the back-makers discovered that the back-pull-stretcher dimension in these pieces had suddenly changed (part way through the order) to six inches from the originally specified nine inches. This reduction in size made it difficult for the upholsterers to grip the back-pull stretcher. Upon discovering this they literally yelled for their foreman. They held a heated discussion with him in which they gesticulated and made considerable noise. The reluctant foreman eventually sought out the quality control supervisor in plain view of his group members in a manner much like that a baseball manager uses toward an umpire on the ball field in view of his team. Upon getting no action from the quality control supervisor, the foreman told his men that he was "powerless" and suggested that if they were still upset about the matter they make use of the formal grievance procedure. In case the reader has not already recognized this fact, it might be pointed out that this was one of the least cohesive groups during the experiment and its foreman was not at all well accepted by the group, according to the data collected a year prior to this particular incident.

On the same occasion the researcher observed that several of the men on this line were quite hostile in a variety of ways. The hostility clearly was being directed at the foreman, although I had the feeling that some of it was being done for my benefit. They deliberately jammed up completed furniture near the end of the upholstering line, which required action from the foreman. He was pressured to take action by the loud hollering of various group members because the log jam was preventing them from speedy operation. Eventually he reluctantly moved several heavy pieces of furniture himself in order to solve the problem.

On another occasion, a worker found that he had a jammed pneumatic staple gun. He threw it approximately fifteen feet through the air to the foreman after giving him little warning that the missile was coming. The gun must weigh at least eight pounds. The foreman tried to repair the gun but could not. As a hostile conference about this matter between the foreman and the worker ended, the worker returned to his work place. In the process, however, he managed to bump into the foreman quite hard and, in my opinion, deliberately. I considered this a provocative action which deserved disciplinary action. In fact, all three of the episodes (the back-pull stretcher incident, the jamming of furniture on the line, and the bumping incident) required firmer and more willing action from the foreman. His behavior in these instances is illustrative of "low role differentiation," as described in Chapter 5. The bumping episode, I believe, is representative of the atmosphere that existed in this group. It should be emphasized, however, that not all the workers on this line had such hostile feelings about this man.

When I interviewed this foreman, I learned from him that "several foremen around here are not interested in their jobs." He added that he personally would quit "if something better came along." It may be worth pointing out that when he was asked, "Who is your best worker?" he responded, "They are all good." He tended to focus his dissatisfaction on the technological aspects of this particular line, which he saw as being different from his previous assignment. His dissatisfaction stemmed primarily from what he considered to be much heavier requirements for chasing and being an errand boy coupled with the sheer physical requirements placed upon him by the weight of the furniture. He revealed no complaints about the workers in his crew.

Another foreman told me that first-off, on the day of the foreman reassignments, he had held a group meeting with his new group in the foreman's office. He had used this meeting essentially to set up expectations on "who is the boss." He reported that he spent considerable time in that meeting stressing the importance of workers moving from one job position to another on the line (from back-maker to seat-maker, for example) as the occasion requires. This man reported that he asks one or another of his workers from time to time to go and obtain material needed by the line. Normally the foreman does this himself although there is no reason why this task cannot be delegated to a subordinate if his group enjoys sufficient cohesion. He emphasized that he was always careful whom he picked for such assignments, however brief, because some individuals resent this type of interruption more than others. This strategic thinking suggests an ability to discriminate perceptually among his subordinates in addition to a willingness to share leadership responsibilities. I believe, however, that he delegated in this way partly because of personal health problems. At the time of my interview with him, he no longer was supervising an upholstery line and had been moved into a department as supervisor where there were fewer physical requirements placed upon him.

One foreman indicated to me that the workers on his newly assigned line in the experiment had heard in advance by the grapevine that he was "hard to get along with." Another foreman told me that one of his men whom he had supervised several years previously in another group commented to him on the renewal of their relationship, "You have changed!" These episodes suggest that at least in some cases the foremen did receive feedback from the bottom up as to how well they were going over or were expected to go over with their new groups. This supports some of the arguments made in Chapter 5, where the question of consensus formation was discussed.

This last foreman emphasized in his interview with me that he is a strict disciplinarian and feels that this is a necessary aspect of his role. His emphasis on disciplinary activity may have been his way of telling me that he knew he wasn't overly popular with his men, but that he could explain it in terms of a deliberate choice of supervisory actions rather than as some aspect of his own personality.

Another man who was not expected to be well liked by his new group described himself in terms suggesting that he was highly conscientious from a managerial viewpoint. He reported to me that he "supervises" men on neighboring lines or even other departments if he sees them doing something wrong. He maintained that being "right" was more important to him than being popular. This individual was particularly preoccupied with the technological assumption problem. He insisted that increasing style complexity had been affecting production results. He also stated that for the past eight months, excluding the one during which this interview was conducted, his line has been getting all the "shit" and no long runs. (By "long runs" I refer to the number of consecutive furniture pieces coming down the production line that are identical to each other.)

While explaining to me his philosophy of being fair to the men while at the same time being fair to the company, one foreman told me that every foreman must "negotiate" whether a man will receive pay for repairing his own faulty work. This bit of information made me particularly conscious of certain activities that I had noticed on the preceding day. That is, at the end of the work day just before the whistle blows, there normally is a fair degree of conversation between each foreman and at least one or two of his work-group subordinates while they examine a small form known as the Daily Production Report. This report is made out by the foreman and reflects upon his group and himself. The deliberations here also appear to have a bearing on the earnings of the employees, in the light of what the above-mentioned foreman told me about "negotiations." It seems that these foremen do in fact have some influence over a major incentive relevant to the motives of their subordinates. In other words, they are in a position to reward and punish through their administration of company policy on payment for the repair of faulty work. They also are in a similar position with respect to their recording of "down time," reflecting those periods of the day when there are material shortages or other problems preventing the worker from working on his normal incentive-paid activities. While the research worker may notice that conversations do take place between foremen and workers on incentive operations at the close of the work day, he is not likely to gain much insight into the dynamics of these negotiations as an outside observer. When one tries to get close enough to these conversations to hear them, the conversations seem to dry up, for obvious reasons. It therefore is possible that the popularity levels of foremen in this instance can be explained at least in part by the extent to which they are liberal in administering these policies. The plant management knows about the problem and controls it rather tightly by studiously preparing weekly statistics on "down time" and repair time. The groups are compared at frequent intervals and the plant manager personally pressures any foreman who appears to be getting out of line. The control process therefore prevents large differences from developing between groups. However, this does not prevent the foreman from showing a certain amount of favoritism toward individuals *within* his group if he is so inclined.

The last two foremen that I observed and interviewed both reported that when they took over their new groups after the experimental change they found considerable bickering among the group members and complaints about the previous foremen. In one case the new foreman arranged a meeting on the first day following his reassignment in order to discuss these matters and begin to improve interpersonal relations in his group. He took special pains to explain the necessity of moving from one job position to another on the line in order to keep a smooth flow of production. Their mutual recognition of the relationship between group cohesion and timely movement from one job position to another quite possibly explains a lot about the popularity and effectiveness of these foremen in this department. They were the two most highly rated foremen both before and after the experiment.

DISPATCHING

The reader probably has noticed that at least some of the foremen stressed technological–production-scheduling matters in speaking with me about their operations. I therefore spent some time with the chief dispatcher in the plant, who is responsible for allocating work to the various upholstering lines. He indicated that there are "infinite" numbers of style variations when one takes into account the variations in furniture-covering material (colors, weaves, fibers), shapes, sizes, and types of furniture. Style variations also are related to the component materials used, such as cotton, cardboard, and different types of foam rubber. Finally, styles vary on the extent to which the covers are fitted tightly or loosely on the furniture. The chief dispatcher maintained on this occasion, as he had on previous occasions, that he balances out style variations between the lines over a period of time. He seemed to be aware of giving groups difficult products to work on. If he has been providing "shit" for an unusually long period of time, he automatically tries to balance this out subsequently by giving a line what is known as a "good lay." (This is furniture-manufacturing lingo referring to how easily a group can make incentive earnings on a product run.)

Despite the chief dispatcher's firm insistence that no group is disadvantaged for an extended period of time, I felt that production scheduling deserved greater attention in connection with this research project. Therefore, the analysis of certain records, an example of which appears in Figure 9, was initiated. Figure 9 is a fairly typical Daily Production Record, showing the variety of production occurring on a particular upholstering line on one day. The reader may observe the number of style numbers worked on by the group on that date and the number of units (quantity column) manufactured for each style number. Quantitative research on product mix required a hand tabulation of this kind of data because the data are not summarized in any weekly or monthly report. Thus, the material that follows in the next several pages is based upon painstaking, painful, and time-consuming analyses of these daily reports that could not have been conducted without the patience and hard work of Nick Yarmoshuk.

DAILY PRODUCTION REPORT

Line No. ___7___   Date __6-12-65__

2 Pc. Suites _____   Sectionals _____

Hi Chairs _____   _____

PAY SUMMARY

Style	No. of Pcs.	Total Rate	Amount
8330-83	3	I 750	6
8340-53	1	I 451	2
4	8	''	8
1080-4	3	I 758	3
82	3	''	6
4280-4	2	''	2
52	1	''	2
4280-65	4	''	8
91	2	''	4
8380-4	9	I 736	9
83	2	''	4
66	3	''	6
7	3	''	4½

FORM GP 25   Total (Per Oper.) __64½__

Figure 9. Typical daily production report

Data were examined for all eight work groups on a daily basis for one hundred and forty working days during the experimental year. This includes the sixty work days preceding the foreman reassignments (the pre-experimental base period) and the eighty days following the change. To check on the comparability of the data during the experimental year with that from other years, we found it desirable to conduct parallel analyses for the same one hundred forty days in the preceding year and the same one hundred forty days in the following year.[2] Overall, then, well over three thousand daily report forms like the one in Figure 9 had to be examined.

PRODUCT MIX AND GROUP PRODUCTIVITY:
A STATISTICAL ANALYSIS OF THREE VARIABLES

Examination of the contents of the Daily Production Reports suggested the extraction of three potentially meaningful quantitative indexes. These are labeled "number of product types," "style variations," and "run length." "Product type" refers to whether a particular piece coming down a production line is a couch, sectional couch, sleeper bed, chair, or suite (combination chair and couch). The index derived for product type was simply the raw number of different product types worked on by a line on a weekly basis. This required that we observe each week on the Daily Production Reports all of the product-type numbers appearing on these forms for each group and simply count the number of *different* ones that appeared during the week. Thus, during a given week one line may have worked exclusively on chairs. Consequently its product type score would have been 1. Another line might have produced

[2] The experiment began in early April, 1964. The pre-experimental base period was January through March. The same periods of time in 1963 and 1964 were examined to determine whether there are regular cyclical shifts that might explain the experimental data better than the analysis presented in Chapter 5.

chairs, couches, and a few sectionals. Its score would have been 3. The index here reflects nothing more than the number of different kinds of furniture worked on by a line during a specified time period. Theoretically this index should relate negatively to productivity.

"Style variations" refer to such design dimensions as early American and contemporary, size, minor shape or raw-material variations, and so on. The quantitative index for style variations was simply a raw count on the number of different styles worked on by a line during a given time period. This variable was expected to relate negatively to productivity.

Finally, an index called "run length" was developed. This reflects essentially the extent to which a group during a given time period is permitted to work on a single product and style without interruption. This index was derived by looking at the Daily Production Report and finding the largest number on the report representing the number of units produced of a particular product and style. Thus, in Figure 9 the longest run was for product and style number 8380-4, where, as the reader may see on that date, 9 units were produced. In other words, nine was the longest production run for this group on that particular date. To get a weekly or bi-monthly index the daily longest-run figures were averaged. Thus the run length variable as an index of product mix is nothing more than the average length of longest production run for a particular period of time.

This index seemed to be of high potential value in explaining productivity variance among the work groups. It seemed likely that a work group would derive great benefit from practice effect if given the advantage of long production runs; frequent short runs which involve many chopped-up orders would necessitate many changes of pace by the workers.

Once the above product-mix dimensions were identified and operationalized, it became possible to study their behavior in relation to each other and in relation to group productivity levels. Each group received a score on all three product-mix indexes for various time periods. The scores were then converted to ranks. Thus, the groups were ranked from 1 through 7 on average run length, for example. Once the rankings were available, intercorrelation analyses were conducted. These analyses are described below, prior to an assessment of their potential contribution as spurious variables that might account for the experimental results discussed in Chapters 4 and 5.

Table 16 summarizes an analysis bearing on the intercorrelations of the three product-mix variables and produc-

Table 16. Intercorrelations* of group product-mix and
productivity indexes during twelve-week
pre-experimental base period

Variable	X_1	X_2	X_3	X_0
(X_1) number of products		.79	−.29	−.13
(X_2) number of styles			.00	−.09
(X_3) mean run length				.79 †
(X_0) productivity (% of base)				

* Rank-order correlations based on seven pairs of group measurements in all cases.

† When eight groups are used, this Rho increases to .86.

tivity. It is clear from the table that two of the group product-mix indexes, number of products and number of styles, did not correlate significantly with group productivity levels prior to the conduct of the experiment, even though they correlated highly with each other. On the other hand, group average product run length (X_3) correlated very highly (.79) with group productivity levels.[3] In other words, the longer the product runs a group customarily received, the more productive it was. The high correlation (.79) between

[3] The analysis reported here is based upon only the seven groups used in the experiment. If one includes the eighth group that works in this department, the correlation of .79 increases to .86.

run length and group productivity levels before the experiment, especially since run length was not correlated significantly with number of styles or products, is difficult to interpret. In the absence of further information, one doesn't know whether the receipt of long runs (for reasons as yet unspecified) leads to high group productivity or whether high productivity leads to receipt of long-run work assignments. The large correlation, however, certainly suggests that production-scheduling factors somehow were related to task difficulty and productivity differences among the groups before the foremen were reassigned. The large correlation also suggests that to the extent that group attraction, foreman preference, and status consensus on foreman are influenced by performance levels, a spurious variable (run length) may well be responsible.

THE CASE AGAINST PRODUCT MIX
AS A SPURIOUS EXPERIMENTAL VARIABLE

Table 17 summarizes an intercorrelational analysis for the product-mix indexes conducted for the sixteen-week time period *following* the foremen's reassignments. (This table may be compared directly with Table 16, representing the *pre*-experimental analysis.) The data in Table 17 reveal a pattern that is only partly similar to what occurred prior to the experiment. Neither number of products nor number of styles worked on was related to productivity. However,

Table 17. Intercorrelations* of group product-mix
and productivity indexes during post-
experimental time period

Variable	X_1	X_2	X_3	X_0
(X_1) number of products		.89	−.45	−.14
(X_2) number of styles			−.43	.07
(X_3) mean run length				.32
(X_0) productivity (weeks 1–16)				

* Rank order r based on seven groups.

the run-length variable, contrary to the case before the experiment, was virtually uncorrelated with group productivity levels after the foreman reassignments. (The correlation between run length and productivity during post-experimental weeks 1 through 10 was .21; for weeks 11 through 16 it was .39.) The sharp reduction (from .79 to .32) of the relationship between run length and productivity during the sixteen-week post-experimental time period suggests that run length as a product-mix index did *not* exert a spurious influence on the experimental data described in Chapters 4 and 5.[4]

Additional data lend further support to this interpretation. These data reflect the stability of the product-mix indexes when the group measurements taken in the pre-experimental base period are compared with the group measurements taken in the sixteen weeks following the foremen reassignments. Thus, number of products, as a group index measured prior to the experiment (twelve-week base period), correlates (Rho) .91 with its repeated measurement during the sixteen-week experimental period. Similarly, number of styles also is quite stable (Rho = .95). In other words, the groups' relative positions on average number of products and styles did not change after the foreman reassignments. While run length is not as stable as the other two (Rho = .68), it is rather high and suggests that the groups did not change much relative to each other on the number of interruptions typically encountered in the production process. (When eight groups are used, rather than seven,

[4] Note also in Table 17 that number of products and number of styles worked on, while not related to productivity in the post-experimental period, show a suggestive although nonsignificant relationship to run length (about −.45). Run length showed no such relationship to style and product mix in the preceding twelve weeks. This suggests that run length was affected by somewhat different factors after the foreman reassignments than before. As the reader will see in Chapter 7, the odds are that this is explained best by referring to the lines' various product specialties and market factors.

this Rho increases to .79.) It should be emphasized that although these group product-mix indexes were very stable over the time period spanning the twelve pre-experimental and sixteen post-experimental weeks, the group productivity levels were far less stable (Rho = .46). This suggests, then, that foreman reassignment effects occurred *in spite of* stable product-mix differences among the groups, *not because* of product-mix changes.

DISCUSSION

This chapter has reported information bearing on the experiment obtained through a fairly elaborate feedback process. Meetings, interviews, and direct observations of the foremen provided qualitative data that corroborate much of the quantitative evidence reported in previous chapters. A major point that emerged is that several of the foremen do in fact see their role as requiring them to assist their subordinates' goal-directed efforts—to produce and make money.

This chapter also has described a detailed analysis of production-scheduling records to determine whether a spurious technological–market-conditions factor might explain the post-experimental productivity changes better than the motivational explanation developed in Chapter 5. Considering the data in summary fashion, it would appear that production-control factors did *not* play a substantial role in the experimental results. That is to say, no major production-scheduling changes occurred that could have caused the productivity changes reported in Chapters 4 and 5. Indeed, the stability of run length and other product-mix indexes on the various groups underscores the seriousness of the motivational explanation. Since run length during the pre-experimental base period was highly correlated with run length during the sixteen-week post-experimental period, the productivity effects were achieved in spite of strong technological constraints. It is clear that an unusual amount of energy must have been expended. It also is clear that stable production-scheduling variables may well account for a major finding reported in Chapter 4—the post-experimental productivity levels of the groups correlated approximately .50 with their pre-experimental starting points. Thus, the new equilibrium state that they reached was not totally different from their previous equilibrium state, presumably because of scheduling considerations that did not change much over time. In other words, production-scheduling variables comprise a system that impinges on the group-dynamics system previously discussed in earlier chapters.

It would be possible for us to end this report here. The experiment has been described, the hypotheses have been tested, the results seem to be reasonable, and the most likely spurious variable has been ruled out. However, the production-scheduling data raise some intriguing questions from a systems-equilibrium theory viewpoint. Specifically, why was there such a strong relationship between run length and productivity levels before the experiment? Why did this strong relationship weaken sharply following the foreman reassignment? What factors control the very stable (over time) hierarchy among the lines on product-mix dimensions; that is, why do certain lines consistently have longer or shorter runs, more or fewer styles, and more or fewer products than other lines? In short, how do production-scheduling variables operate within the organizational subsystem we are examining? In what ways do they contribute to the equilibrium-seeking process?

These seem to be important questions whose answers might enlarge our knowledge of this system and perhaps others as well. Consequently, Nick Yarmoshuk was dispatched to the Northeast Plant for one week of observational and interviewing work from which we hoped to extract some answers. The next chapter is devoted to a freely edited account of his activities and observations during four work days. This will be followed by some overall conclusions on relevant systems variables

Production Scheduling as
a Systems Variable

Nick Yarmoshuk spent four consecutive work days in the Northeast Plant. He arrived at the plant before the chief dispatcher each day and remained until the chief dispatcher left. Yarmoshuk virtually lived with the man during working hours for most of the week.

The material that follows represents my freely edited version of Yarmoshuk's 120 pages of field notes. Wherever possible, repetitious material and descriptions of routine events that do not bear directly on the problem at hand have been removed. Numerous passages have been italicized to emphasize certain events for the reader. The italicized sections relate, in most cases, to the several questions raised at the end of Chapter 6. Except in the case of bracketed passages, the language is Yarmoshuk's as edited by me. Quotation marks enclose the language of Northeast employees whenever such material appears. Initials and fictitious names have been substituted for actual names and line designations, where necessary, to insure anonymity for the corporation and to prevent embarassment to individuals.

The material on all four days is included to minimize the possibility of nonrepresentative observations. Moreover, the format employed should permit the reader to draw his own conclusions from the data in case he disagrees with the author's.

THE FIRST DAY

I arrived at the plant shortly before seven on Monday morning. My intentions were to go to "Rick Collins'" office immediately, introduce myself to him, and start my observations of what he did, when he did it, whom he met, and under what conditions of time, place, and circumstance.

R. C.'s office is situated at the foot of the frame assembly line. This is the line on which all of the frames for the furniture produced at Northeast are assembled from pre-formed pieces of wood. His office is a cubicle measuring approximately fifteen feet square. R. C. shares this space with the foreman in charge of the frame assembly line. The foot of the frame assembly line feeds directly into the frame storage area, which is at the head of the several upholstery lines in which we are interested.

R. C. arrived in his office at approximately 7:25. When he entered the office, he gave no indication that he was or was not surprised to see me there. In fact, he tended totally to ignore my presence. I began the conversation by remarking, "I assume you are R. C."

"Yes, I'm R. C. and who are you?"

"My name is Nick Yarmoshuk and I am from Cornell University." He looked at me as if to say, "Yeah, so what?" I replied by saying, "I assume that J. R. [the plant manager] has explained to you my presence here this morning."

"No, J. R. has not explained anything like that to me. He was away on Friday. He was taken ill."

Given that statement, I immediately responded that we had been in touch with J. R. late the previous week and had requested his permission for my entry into the plant to observe R. C.'s work as a *scheduler of operations. He corrected me by saying that he was the chief dispatcher and that the real schedulers were in the main office.* [Note that R. C.'s scheduling powers are circumscribed.] He then said that J. R. had mentioned some time ago that Ned Rosen and the people at Cornell were interested in the relationship between the way lines operate and the scheduling function. I emphasized that I was also interested in other functions that the dispatcher carried out in addition to those which concerned the upholstering lines. I said that my main interest was in his job. If in the course of learning about his job, I found that one aspect of it appeared to be more important than some other to the total plant functioning, then we could focus on that aspect. His only comment to that was a seemingly doubtful "Oh," and then silence. At this point, I indicated briefly the objective of my trip. He seemed satisfied with my explanation and agreed that there was some similarity between his dispatching operation and dispatching operations in similar semibulk, semiunit operations. He remarked further: "Other students from Cornell have been in the plant previously. It seemed that the plant management was very satisfied to have the tourists on board." Consequently, he would agree to having me follow him throughout the day.

R. C. explained that his first task every morning is to go into the Sewing Department to pick up the production tickets of the units that had been completed there on the previous day. He said that he would use the tickets as the basis for his production-planning operation; that is, *he would assign work to the various lines on the basis of completed cuttings and in order number sequence.* He left his office to go to the Sewing and Cutting Departments. He spent approximately ten minutes on the plant floor, returned to his own office, and began to sort out the tickets. Shortly after his return to the office, he was called to the telephone there and was asked to come to J. R.'s [Plant Manager] office. R. C. turned to me and said, "I certainly expect that J. R. will be looking for me since he probably wants to tell me that if you are not here now, you will be here shortly." In J. R.'s office, the plant manager apologized to R. C. that he had not let him know of my plans, but said that it was all right for me to follow him around, if R. C. was agreeable; J. R. said that he held no secrets from us at Cornell and that this was not an evaluation practice but one in which I (Nick) was trying to learn all the plant's operations.

R. C., in his office after the talk with J. R., mentioned the existence of three specific lines of furniture made at Northeast. He also explained that in the event that there is a shortage of work or if he has given too much work to one line, he takes work away from one line and gives it to some other one. In his words, "The main part of the furniture-dispatching operation is to know what covers have been produced by the Sewing Department and to know whether the associated frames are also available. When they are, there is no difficulty in bringing all the remaining pieces together to have a smoothly running operation." R. C. pointed out voluntarily that the fact that he shares the office space with the frame foreman is conducive to easy scheduling. He said that the frame foreman keeps his records of completed work on a pegboard attached just over his (the frame foreman's) desk. To get immediate information on what frames are available or to learn of the state of completeness of the frames for a specific order, he has but to look on the board. By keeping in close verbal touch with the Sewing Department, he said that he has his two major functions well in hand. There are other operations which he said also were important. One of these is the cotton-batten group, which cuts the larger pieces of cotton from which the arms and backs are made. The remaining operations, such as providing the metal springs, are influenced more by outside job-lot subcontractors than by any operation inside the plant.

On returning to his office after his brisk walk to the Sewing Department, R. C. said that he saw from the number of work orders that appeared on the work order desk for line 5 that the line was short of work; he said that he would have to attend to that immediately. He picked up a handful of orders, seemingly at random, but actually *the next in nu-*

merical sequence, left the office, and deposited them on line 5's order desk. [Each line has its own work order desk at the beginning of the line.]

After depositing the work orders, he returned to his own office and continued sorting the orders that he had picked up on the first trip to the Sewing Department. He volunteered that there existed a number of problems for him regarding some orders that he had in his hand. He said that he had two "big schedules" which he did not know how to assign. (The expression "big schedules" is analogous to our term, "length of run.") I questioned him on the meaning of this term "big schedule." He explained it in these terms: The central scheduling office takes all similar units ordered by various customers and holds them [for efficiency reasons] until a large number of identical style types are assembled; the only difference between individual units that are assembled would be the color involved on the covering. Otherwise, all units of the big schedule are identical. Since the orders he had on hand were suites consisting of two pieces and identical in most respects, they should be produced at the same time. Therefore, he would assign them to two adjacent lines; lines 5 and 6 in this case. This means that he would have to make sure that the work of these two lines was balanced before he gave them the big schedule. *He said he would assign this work to these two lines because they were very reliable ones and would probably produce the work very quickly and that the materials would probably come off at the end of the line together.* Besides, he said, these lines seemed to be short of work at the moment.

At approximately 8:30 R. C. left his office and deposited some orders for a line explaining to me in the process that this line and one next to it are the sectional lines. He tries to assign sectionals to both those lines. I inquired why it was that one line was the bed line, another line was the high quality line, and two others sectional lines. R. C.'s response was that somehow long ago it was started that way and it seems to have continued with *people expecting to get large proportions of one kind of work or another.* [Notice that he implies workers have possessive attitudes regarding furniture types.] He said that despite the fact that lines had these identifications, he tries to balance out the work for all of them. He then took two orders that he identified to me as "specials" and deposited them on the order desk for line 5. In doing this he explained that line 5 appeared to be a fast line and hence could be depended upon to produce the orders quickly. He explained that he relied upon information from all the other foremen, especially those who are producing component parts, to tell him the state of their orders. If they are delayed, he said that he can find out most readily by these people telling him first.

Approximately half an hour after R. C. mentioned that he was going to give the big schedules to lines 5 and 6, I asked him, "Why are you giving them to lines 5 and 6? Why don't you give them to lines 1 and 2?" I realized immediately that this may have been a hasty question, but it was interesting that up to that point the big schedules had not yet been assigned. R. C. seemed to stand his ground and said that the only reason for doing what he did was on the basis of expediency. *He said that he will assign those things to lines that he could depend upon.* I let the matter drop. R. C. returned to his paperwork and said that he was preparing time sheets for his subordinates. His subordinates are a team of seventeen expediters and five or six other workers who work in supporting departments such as Cotton Cutting.

R. C. showed me the daily production record sheets and explained their use. At 9 A.M., R. C. received a telephone message asking him to appear in D. R.'s (the assistant plant manager's) office.

From D. R.'s office we went to see C. H. (the manufacturing superintendent). C. H.'s office and an adjoining room is the supervisors' gathering place; present there besides R. C. and myself were the foremen from the Sewing Department, the woodwork superintendent, the plant manager, an upholstery foreman, a corporate headquarters engineer, and the quality control supervisor. While we were talking and having coffee with this group, the quality control supervisor told R. C. that the foreman of line 6 was not very happy about the fact that his line had been asked to do some work on a new product. Apparently line 6 had had a certain difficult product assigned to it previously; when asked to work on this product again, *the men expressed their displeasure to the foreman.* [This, in turn, was passed along through the quality control supervisor to R. C.]

Back in his own office after the coffee break (it was now 9:30), R. C. voluntarily pointed out that he had no special reason to give this unpopular work to line 6. He continued that he wanted to be as fair among the lines as possible. He said that on any one day (or any one week) the amount of work that he assigns to one line might be somewhat different than the work that he assigns to another line. But *what he did assign to a line he believed to be a function of the capacity of that line to produce.* He said that over a two- or three-month period, and certainly over six months, the distribution of products and big schedules should be fairly consistent for all the lines. *He said that he certainly could not afford to show any kind of favoritism among the lines. He said that if he did this, it would be deadly to his position in the plant and that it would cause more problems than he would know what to do with.* [Our statistical records, of course, indicate long-term stable differences among the lines on "big schedules."]

At approximately 9:45, R. C. left his office to tour various departments in the plant. He stopped briefly at an upholstery line; he stopped at the Sewing Department to talk to a foreman about some orders that he was going to put on to the upholstery lines; in his comments to the foreman he emphasized the need for all parts to be available since a lack of components will cause a backlog of frames at the head of the line. R. C. then proceeded around the plant, returning to his own office at 10:15. In walking through the plant, he surveyed the production lines to see how "things were going." It should not be misinterpreted here that we walked up and down the production lines. He walked along the feet and the heads of the lines. At no time did he pass along the length of them. [He thereby "looks things over" without interacting with the individual group members. This minimizes workers' chances to pressure him regarding scheduling.]

R. C. returned to his office at 10:18 after the brief inspection at the head of the frame line; he told me that he was going to assign the big schedule that was bothering him earlier this morning to lines 1 and 2 [instead of 5 and 6]. He said that this last tour had told him that "they [lines 1 and 2] are running faster than he had originally anticipated they would." Consequently he was going to let them have the big schedule. *He said that he wanted to assign this big schedule to adjacent lines because this work would be handled by one expediter.* [Note how the staffing arrangement— one expediter for every two lines—interacts with schedule size and probably product specialization to influence scheduling decisions. Note also how his scheduling decisions are responsive to group speed.]

R. C. sorted the cards on his desk, selected some work for a line, and at 10:32 left his office to deposit this work at the work desk for line 7. In response to my question, "Why did you give that work to line 7 at this time," R. C. replied that he did this because in his tour he noted that line 7 was running short of work and he picked out five hours' work for them from the first group of orders that appeared on his desk.

R. C. explained that he sorted his orders as he got them from the cutting tables according to the numerical sequence. The way the orders are coded, he said, allowed them to be placed in numerical sequence. By doing this he said, he is making maximum use of the original scheduling (explained earlier) that has been accomplished for him in the main office. Once that work is done, his sole function is to see that the work reaches the assembly line (the upholstery lines) in "proper sequence so that the upholsterer's sole concern should be with building the furniture." In response to my question, "How much of your time on the average is devoted to seeing that the lines have enough work as opposed to coordinating materials flow?" R. C. replied that he spent about half of his time being concerned about the volume of work that the upholstery lines had and the other half of his time on making sure that all the other components are flowing smoothly in the plant.

While depositing work on line 7 he looked at another line and received some information that there was a shortage of frames. He returned to his own office very quickly and determined with the frame foreman what was holding up the production of these frames.

R. C. made a comment to me that lines 5, 6 and 7 seemed to be running short of work. Consequently, he pulled out some work for each of these lines. He assigned the largest schedule [meaning the longest run], to line 5, a somewhat shorter schedule to line 6 and the smallest one to line 7. I noted specifically that although 5, 6 and 7 come in sequence, he did not select in the same sequence the work for lines 5, 6 and 7. If he had, he would have given the shortest run to line 5 and the longest run to line 7. I did not question him on this, but he maintained that he had assigned the work as it came along. [Of course, this is not consistent with his contention that he does not discriminate among the lines. It is consistent, however, with his belief (supported by our statistics) that line 5 works faster than lines 6 and 7. In assigning work on the basis of line speed, presumably he expected all three lines to complete these three schedules simultaneously. In this way, he probably assumes that he has balanced operations.]

When R. C. took this work to the appropriate work tables,

the dispatcher from line 5 saw the large bundle that was being placed on the table and said, "Oh, the gravy train?" When I asked R. C. what it meant to be on the gravy train, he said that it would make his expediter's job a lot easier. Since the expediter was paid on a cash basis, it meant that his work would be easier now that much of it came from the same source and was the same kind of unit. [At least two interpretations of this response are possible. From the dispatcher's point of view, in thinking of his own work he might have believed that he would not have to work hard since he knew that all the frames were located in one place. Since dispatchers are *not* paid on an incentive basis, however, "gravy" does not appear to be a germane term. On the other hand, his language might mean that he thought line 5 was going to be able to get some extra pay from this batch because they could really make out on the longer run. The latter probably is what the man had in mind when referring to the "gravy train."]

R. C. returned to his office and worked there for a half hour, looking through the work orders and filling out various forms. He then took some orders with him, orders which he said were for beds and *matching* chairs, and said that he would assign the beds to one line and the chairs to another. He said that he was quite confident that the chairs and the beds would be produced so that they emerged at the shipping area of the plant simultaneously. [Note this environmental constraint on the scheduling process. Matching pieces must be completed simultaneously to avoid confusion in shipping.] On returning to his office, he first stopped at C. H.'s office and looked at the daily absence report. He noted that line 7 had two men absent and said to me that he will have to assign less work to these people because they are short staffed and cannot produce as much [another constraint].

After he reached his office, he continued working on some papers. The foreman for one of the upholstery lines entered and complained loudly about some work that the floor sweepers had done. Apparently, the floor sweepers had swept up a pile of debris and left it in a position where it would disturb the work of this foreman's men. This was the third time that this foreman has been either in direct communication or had had opportunity to discuss things with R. C. on this morning. The first time occurred in C. H.'s office. The second time occurred on the floor when this foreman happened to be there when R. C. passed and they exchanged brief pleasantries about the weather. The third time was this direct confrontation of R. C. by the line foreman with regard to the work of R. C.'s subordinates. (R. C. is responsible for the Maintenance Department in addition to supervising the cotton-cutting operation and being the chief dispatcher.)

R. C. volunteered that he saw this foreman somewhat more frequently than he did any other foreman. (In fact, he said that he rarely saw any of the other foremen.) *He said that the only reason for this was because this foreman is the biggest complainer of all the foremen in the plant. R. C. cautioned that this should not be interpreted as a derogatory statement. He added that if anything ever occurred that might in some way influence this foreman's line's ability to work effectively, this foreman would quickly make the difficulty known.* [Note that the foreman being discussed here is the most popular line foreman in the Upholstering Department according to the worker rankings. Also, before the experiment began he supervised the highest-producing line in the department. The line he took over when he was reassigned wanted him more than any other foreman. They closed ranks around him, increased their group cohesion, and showed a nice productivity increase after getting him.]

R. C. planned to go to lunch at noon with the Cutting and Sewing Department supervisor. I asked if they would mind my accompanying them. R. C.'s response "No" was coupled with a statement that included the following facts: he often brought a sandwich with him which he consumed in his car while he and his companion drove into town to a bar; lunch usually consisted of three or four glasses of beer; food was available at the bar; his companion usually purchased some food—other than beer—at the bar.

The afternoon period seemed, by and large, to be very relaxed for R. C. His general method of operation was to walk by the head of each line, leaf through the number of orders that were lying on the desk, decide on a very loose basis of approximately ten units per hour how much work the line had, and return to his office. There, by some internal ranking that (to me) seemed to be absolutely random, he selected pieces of work for each of the lines. The only work that he selected in the afternoon was for lines 6, 7, and 8. The rest of the time was spent at his desk going through his orders, filling out various forms, and answering questions regarding his plans regarding order distribution for the rest of the afternoon and for the morning. These questions were put to him by the sewing foreman and the frame foreman. In addition, he spent considerable time going through the records of the frame department.

THE SECOND DAY

Although this day commenced the same way as Monday, by R. C. going into the cutting and sewing area to get the production tickets representing material that had been cut in the Cutting Department, it may be characterized by the fact that the plant faced an emergency throughout the morning and into the middle of the afternoon. The emergency was caused by a threatened shortage of a key piece of material, a spring which is used in almost all the furniture produced in any one day. The emergency was resolved when the supplier finally met his commitment on delivery date, but late in the day. More interesting than the resolution of the problem is the effect that it had on the chief dispatcher and upon the foremen. In addition to a description of these circumstances, other information will be provided including a summary of the total day's operation.

When I entered the plant, I found that R. C. had not arrived and was not expected for another half hour. I took advantage of the half hour to speak in very general terms with one of the frame dispatchers. The frame dispatcher is responsible for two upholstery lines. It is his job to deliver the frames to the end of the line as they are required. *This man has limited influence on the selection process of the orders as far as I can see.* His only potential effect on productivity would occur if he were to carry out his job too slowly. The dispatcher with whom I spoke was a man about fifty-five years old, and he had been with the company a considerable length of time. He said that he rarely had to deal with the line foreman, in fact, he sees him "only once a month if that much." He said that if he is doing his job properly, neither the line workers nor the foreman have any recourse to him or reason to call attention to his work to R. C., his primary boss. He said that if anything does go wrong with the line's production, the foreman will immediately seek R. C. This dispatcher said that in addition to making sure that the frames are set up ahead of the time that the line workers actually require them, he tries to assist the line workers in "small" ways, such as supplying them with important parts as they may become necessary. For example, he said that he may obtain staples for them whenever the workers run out of them. He will pick up a piece of cotton and cover if the regular dispatcher for the task happens to be otherwise occupied. He said that this was not really his job and no one really expected him to do it. But, in the interest of cooperating with fellows, he did this. The dispatcher pointed out that he tries to run the orders in the same sequence in which they are presented to him. But in the event that there might be unexpected problems such as a shortage of trucks (the dollies on which the pieces of furniture rest as they are pushed down the production line), he obtains R. C.'s and the line foreman's permission to alter the sequence of the orders.

Planning by R. C. in the morning was highly influenced by two events. First of all, there appeared to be a lack of trucks for moving furniture along the lines. Second, there was the shortage of springs. *The first problem originated around the fact that within recent months there seemed to be an increase in the number of chairs which were being sold by the sales force.* Although there was a sufficient number of trucks in which to rest the chairs as they were being worked upon, there was an insufficient number of trucks to be used for planning purposes; that is, for resting the frames at the head of the line prior to the time at which the frames are required by the upholsterers. Before additional chairs can be put on a line, the available trucks must be returned from the chairs that are presently on the line. As a result of the truck shortage, the new chair orders were held back by R. C. This caused him to assign other kinds of furniture than he usually assigns to certain groups. [This problem illustrates how a market trend can influence the behavior of people within the organization. Due to the shortage of trucks appropriate for chairs, normal product-specialty distinctions between groups had to be ignored. This had a direct bearing on productivity, because of skill differences associated with product specialization. Productivity, in turn, affects the workers' pocketbooks, which leads, in turn, to perceptions about their foreman and their group.]

The second problem, caused by the lack of springs, was something beyond the control of the dispatcher. R. C. made frequent attempts to learn from the purchasing agent when the required items might arrive; *at the same time he was being asked a number of questions by the expediter in the main office who had made delivery date promises to some of the customers.* [Note pressure from front office.]

The main group at coffee this morning consisted of the supervisor of the cutting operation, the acting superintendent, the plant manager, the quality inspector, several fore-men, and R. C. Prior to R. C.'s leaving the coffee break, he, the plant manager, and the acting superintendent talked at some length about the problem caused by the lack of trucks. In their discussion they finally agreed that a more versatile vehicle should be found for this purpose, one which could be adapted for both davenport and chair use.

After coffee an amusing, informal quality-control situation arose. One of the [very popular] upholstery line foremen is in the habit of testing the strength of the furniture that his line manufactures. He performs this test by jumping on a piece after it has been completed. This morning in carrying out this act, the foreman broke several supporting members at the base of one piece of furniture. This was attributed to the poor quality of wood that was being used by the Frame Department. The foreman, although his action had been condoned by the plant manager, nevertheless appeared to be disconsolate about the fact that he had broken those pieces and had alienated the frame foreman. His comment to me was: "I am in deep shit now with the Frame Department, but I can't help it. I believe I am right in what I did. If the furniture we make can't stand up to my test in the plant it's better we find out here than when the customers' kids do it at home or on the dealer's floor. That's the only way to run a furniture business; fix your poor workmanship in the plant before the furniture leaves, not after it leaves."

During the afternoon a meeting was called by the Assistant Plant Manager. The meeting dealt with a special order that was to be completed by February 5. It was supposed to be delivered to an office in Philadelphia on February 7. D. R. emphasized that not only must they meet the delivery date, but that this was work of the highest priority and required highest quality. Consequently, he expected all members present (the quality control man, R. C., the cutting room supervisor, and the frame supervisor) to meet their respective commitments as well as possible. [Note that the assistant plant manager exercises a direct influence over production scheduling when the occasion demands.] The result of this talk was that the cutting room supervisor, the frame supervisor, and R. C. all literally dashed out of the meeting to see if patterns were available for the various pieces, to check on specifications, and to see if any extra orders had to be made before the work could be assembled. (As the week wore on, we learned that this special panic had been canceled by the salesman. The pieces would still be produced, but they would not be shipped; they would be maintained for stock in the plant.)

Following this meeting, R. C. proceeded to make alternate plans in case the needed springs failed to arrive in time. It appeared that the various lines had sufficient work to carry them to the end of the afternoon, but R. C. had doubts about how many lines could be kept functioning on the following day. In response to my question, "What will happen if the springs do not arrive?" R. C. replied that if the springs had not arrived by morning, then the men would be given the work to do that was available. If such work were no longer available, the men would have to be sent home and the lines shut down. In making his plans, R. C. first determined what orders were available that did not require the missing springs. He then determined from the frame foreman the state of completion of various frames. He then went to the Cutting Department, determined the state of cutting for the frames that would match the available springs, and then he suggested that some effort be made to expedite the production of these other pieces so that in the event that the mass of springs did not arrive, they could put the substitute plan into effect.

To everyone's relief, the springs arrived at approximately 2 P.M. The emergency plan did not have to be put into effect. Rather, R. C. proceeded to assign work in the normal manner.

Later in the day, R. C. volunteered that the very big schedules bother him, in that he does not necessarily want to assign an entire one to a line. Normally, he tries to split a big schedule among two adjacent lines. He explained that if a line happens to be on a long schedule, he would not assign a single special to it; this would disrupt a line's production. But, in the event that he had two long schedules and some singles, he would insert the singles *between* the two big schedules and in this way get the particular line to do the specials *without complaint.*

In listening to R. C. talk and describe his plans for the day, *I was struck by the fact that he never refers to a line by using its foreman's name.* When he assigns something, he says that he assigns it to "line number 1" or "line number 2." This phenomenon led me to ask him to tell me what foreman was in charge of which line. *R. C. had considerable difficulty in remembering the names of the foremen associated with given lines. This makes me believe that this man does not think about lines in terms of foremen but simply in terms of a group of men.* [In other words, this suggests that the run length is not influenced by special efforts of the chief dispatcher to help out certain foremen. His emphasis on *line* rather than foreman characteristics also suggests that he does not switch his scheduling around deliberately to meet perceived characteristics of foremen.]

R. C. again summarized his views on scheduling work by saying that it is a matter of keeping the amount of work balanced. Of equal importance is to make certain that suites and other units of the same style appear simultaneously at the end of the production lines; when they do not appear simultaneously at the end of the production lines, warehousing problems and unnecessary movement of finished furniture occurs. This leads to damaged goods. R. C. said that his prime concerns were to avoid showing favoritism and to make certain that work is balanced on the lines. [This appears to be a nice summary statement of the major technological constraints that control this man's ability to respond to worker or foreman pressures.]

THE THIRD DAY

When he arrived in his office this morning, R. C. looked through the papers on top of his desk to see what orders he had on hand. He immediately said that he was going to pick up his orders from the Cutting Department; he would check to see whether or not his people (the dispatchers) were all in this morning and he would see how things were going on the upholstery lines.

R. C. checked four times with the frame foreman on the status of specific orders and finally commented that there would be many chairs coming up during the day. He also stated that there might be a problem caused by a shortage of chair trucks and that the ABC Company order that he had on his schedule would be required soon. He said that in the first schedule for the day there were approximately five hours of chairs to be produced and that there would be more chairs to do later on in the day. He then referred to his preference for small schedules over big schedules, saying that big schedules give him problems and that he prefers to have several lays of orders with smaller schedules than one large lay with a large schedule. *He said that smaller schedules make for more flexibility in his own operation and prevent the build-up of frames and other materials around the head of the upholstery lines.* [It is clear that R. C.'s preference on schedule size conflicts directly with that of front office personnel who like the overall efficiency involved in processing big schedules throughout the plant. Thus, his technological need for flexibility is incompatible both with front office and worker pressures.]

At 7:45 he left his office for the production floor. While on the upholstery floor, R. C. met two of his subordinates who are dispatchers. He also met the cutting room foreman;

he talked to the foreman about progress of cutting for the ABC *davenports*. He wanted to get these into production so that the shortage of chair dollies would be bypassed.

He then returned to the office, where he remained for some time, except for a few brief excursions to the factory floor, sorting cards that he had brought from the sewing room first thing that morning. In sorting these cards, he put them into numerical order. This is the same order in which the schedules are prepared in the main office.

R. C. left his office for the floor at 8:45 A.M. While on the floor he received a telephone call from the front office expediter. R. C. gave the expediter information on the kinds of styles and schedules which were being run that day and he reassured him that deliveries promised for that day would be filled. [Note pressure from the front office.]

R. C. was in the assistant plant manager's office from 8:49 to 9:05. On returning, he volunteered that they had talked about the special orders that must be shipped on Friday. They had also talked about a large order for Philadelphia.

In his own office, R. C. looked at the finished framework records which hang beside the frame foreman's desk, saw what he was concerned about, and prepared a special cut for a special one-item schedule. R. C. volunteered that he would give this special order to line 6 because he dispatches the orders in the sequence in which they are placed on his desk, and his estimate of the work that was on the floor now is that line 6 would probably be able to finish it first. *R. C. said that he did not interrupt other lines which might be working on big schedules by inserting smaller specials within long-runs; he assigns these specials to those lines which will probably turn them out first.* [This is consistent with what he said the previous day. The reader should note the circular relationship between the lines' characteristics and the scheduling process. The laws of chance indicate that lines typically getting long runs are less likely to get "specials" than lines typically getting short runs.]

Later in the morning R. C. left for the floor and gave a big schedule with many lays to line 7. While he was on the floor, he saw a cutting foreman, bumped into one of his dispatchers, looked at the work on lines 1, 2, and 3, and informed me, *"The men on all the upholstery lines are very heavily money-oriented. These men will do almost anything for money; they will even take on evening jobs for some of the specialized manufacturers around town."* [This is one more piece of evidence to support the quantitative data in Chapters 3, 4, and 5.]

The lunchtime conversation was initiated by F. J., the Cutting Department foreman. It dealt with new products which had to be produced in the next few days. These new products were essentially *velvet-covered* furniture. *F. J. told R. C. that the use of velvet presents some specific problems regarding storage of cut materials.* He asked R. C. if it would be possible to schedule the orders at a time that was convenient for the cutting and sewing operation. In essence, F. J. said that velvet is a very delicate material: "You know that velvet cannot be folded or creased in any way. It comes to us in rolls. After you cut it, the only way to store the velvet is to drape it over bars or on carts. Once you start draping and letting the material lie around for a day or so, you can get into some real problems. The quality of the finished product will surely suffer. We can't afford that in this business. You know that there are fads; if we produce these new products well now, we may get more of these same orders —if we do a poor job, then we lose that portion of this new market." [Note this production foreman's concern over future sales.]

R. C. replied that he couldn't make a promise on this issue at the moment because his action would depend on what the rest of the schedules required. But he said if this work presents a severe problem they will have to work it out together. [We shall revisit this problem on the following day, when F. J. takes unauthorized action.]

R. C. and I returned to his office at 1. P.M. While in his office, R. C. sorted through orders that he had put aside the day before and estimated work available on the basis of so many units for each piece. *He told me that he would give some short schedules to line 6 and some bigger schedules to line 5. He said that this is done very consciously. The day before line 5 had had chairs which were difficult to produce. He would attempt to balance the work now. He said that any line would start to holler if it received too many chairs or too many short orders. But, he continued, he tries to balance out the work.* Regarding work group complaints, R. C. believes that workers have a short-term view of the products that they work on; however, he said that he has a longer perspective of the work that he assigns. He realizes that it is easy for lines to submit a grievance against him and that from time to time complaints about the way he assigns work do go in to the superintendent's office. He explained that if he is called into the front office, he always looks at the background of past work and sees that he has an alibi for doing what he had done. His approach is to point to necessary technological factors considered at the time that the work was being assigned. He is helped in this by a crude record of work assignments that he maintains. *He told me many times that his main criterion for operating is the date promised on the factory master schedule showing the due dates of all orders.*

Later R. C. volunteered some further thoughts: *"You know, lines compete for the privilege of doing work which is normally theirs.* Let me give you an example of what happened in the early part of 1964. Two of the line foremen used to fight over the distribution of work. Each thought the other was receiving work that was rightly his group's. The problem came to me through the plant superintendent. I report to the plant superintendent daily when he is here. He is sick now, so I act more on my own. In this case, I learned from him that he had discovered the fighting between the lines. He told me that it may help relations between lines if they got that which they thought was theirs as long as it did not upset production. *The image that lines are sectionals (specialized) was reinforced for me.*" [Thus, despite the fact that some groups typically get shorter runs than others, they may not mind so long as they always work on the same basic type of furniture.] R. C. continued his free associations: "I have frequent discussions with the superintendent about scheduling, but the assigning is done on the basis of schedules that come from the head office; they are distributed in the sequence in which they come. I distribute the orders so that congestion is minimized at both ends of the upholstery line. Whatever instructions I do get from the superintendent really pertain to maintaining the demands of the front office and to maintaining the demands of maximum efficiency of the work distribution."

R. C. left the plant floor, deposited work on line 3's work order desk, returned to his own office, and continued his talking: "Line 8 has not had chairs assigned to it for quite a long time, I'd better give them some; but I really can't, because I don't have enough trucks."

During the afternoon break, the following episode occurred in the foremen's room. Notice that this conversation refers to a similar issue presented to R. C. by the quality control inspector in behalf of line 6 on Monday. Remember we are dealing with line 9 now.

Line foreman: "Did they jump you on that shit yesterday?"

R. C.: "No. No one jumped me."

Line foreman: "Those men were going to file a grievance the way you were running the zero-defect patterns yesterday. Apparently, they had one the previous day and that slowed them down; they received another one yesterday as well. This really got them mad."

R. C.: "Well, I can't remember whether or not I realized I gave them a second hard pattern. I suppose it did happen. You must remember that we almost shut down some upholstery lines yesterday for lack of springs. It was really touch and go." [Notice the neat and potent alibi.]

A silence ensued between the two men.

Nick: (Addressing myself to the line foreman) "What do you mean by, 'Did they jump you yesterday'?"

Line foreman: "The men asked me yesterday if the distribution of work they were receiving was legitimate. They also asked the steward about this, and it seems that they were really mad about the kind of work that R. C. was assigning to them. They also asked the steward whether this was fair; the steward was ready to file a grievance. I asked him to hold it until I got some information, but I really expected the men to go after R. C. this afternoon when he was walking close to the lines."

R. C.: "I'm not alibiing now but there are some other problems that have occurred in the sewing operations as well. The main reason that I gave them this work yesterday was because of the shortage of springs. I just had to give them something to do and if I hadn't given them that, I wouldn't have had anything else to provide."

[Note, once again, that the groups do find ways to remind R. C. to assign work on an equitable basis.]

THE FOURTH DAY

R. C. arrived at about 7:15 and took a telephone call in his office from the front office expediter about an order that the assistant plant manager was directly interested in. R. C. patiently told the expediter that the order would be available as requested.

After looking through the orders, R. C. left his office for 45 minutes. During this time, he went to line 3 and noted that it would soon be out of work. He also noted that lines 5 and 6 had enough work to keep them busy for a while. He eventually walked into the superintendent's office. There he determined the amount of cutting that had been completed the previous day and commented that there was a considerable backlog of work in the plant.

R. C. received a telephone page from F. J. (Cutting and Sewing Room supervisor) who asked R. C. to wait for him in the Superintendent's office; R. C. agreed. F. J. arrived five minutes after his call, got his coffee and sat beside R. C. They immediately launched into F. J.'s primary concern.

F. J. told R. C. that the velvet discussed by them yesterday was now being cut, with over one hundred units involved. This meant that there was more than one day's production for one upholstery line. *F. J. said that this cutting was being carried out now because there was a momentary shortage of work in his department. He said the shortage occurred before he realized that it was going to happen.* Since folding or draping causes creases in velvet, sewing would have to start almost immediately. R. C. appeared to be calm throughout F. J.'s explanation and responded that he would accede to his request. He said that in doing so, he would really disrupt the kind of operation he would like to run because this one order did not come in sequence. F. J. continued to explain why the cutting had occurred at that time and emphasized the fragility of his velvet. R. C., in turn, pointed out that the velvet issue is not the only problem in the plant. He explained that the spring shortage in the first part of the week caused a greater backlog of work than normally would have occurred. *R. C. concluded that he would do his best to get along with F. J.'s request, but that he would have to tell D. R. (assistant plant manager) about the situation. Starting to work on the velvet order now would mean that some of D. R.'s promised orders would not be filled on time.* [This is another example of the complications affecting the production-scheduling process.]

In the process of depositing work on line 3, R. C. walked to lines 7 and 8, observed that line 8 would need work shortly, and returned to his own office. On returning to his office, he did not sort additional work orders but picked up the chair orders left over from yesterday and deposited them on lines 1 and 2. After depositing the chair orders he volunteered the following statement: "It's important for a smooth operation that this group of chairs be produced by adjacent lines. This minimizes work for my dispatchers at the head of the lines and also for the material dispatchers; they don't have to wander to various floor areas. Material and frames are brought to essentially one location. At the foot of the line, the finished product is automatically grouped in one area; this makes the warehouse man's job easier. Since the lines work at approximately the same rate, I can be certain that the two halves of any order will be finished at the same time; this further helps the warehouse people. It also helps me in planning additional work for the lines."

On completing the single orders, R. C. was summoned to the telephone again by the front office expediter. He was seeking information on a bed order promised to a customer for late that week. R. C. informed him that the bed was on a line and would be available within the hour.

Following the telephone call, R. C. delivered some small suite schedules to lines 1, 2, and 4. En route he said to me, *"This will compensate these lines for some of the chairs that they have had recently."*

After depositing the work on these lines, R. C. delivered some swatches of material to a single dispatcher. While R. C. was on the floor, a frame dispatcher inquired when a frame for a special order then on the work order desk would be available. R. C. told him that the frame was now coming off the frame line and that it could be dispatched as soon as it came off. *Notice that a rule was being broken at this point. Normally, frames are allowed to dry for some three or four hours before they are sent to the upholstery lines. The drying operation allows the glue that is used in the joints to set. Sending the frames to the upholstery line before the glue has set may result in some difficulties for the upholsterers. The difficulty will arise not from the fact that the joint may separate but from the fact that the wet glue may come off on the material and make the upholsterer's job more difficult.* [Thus, certain kinds of specials really "get in the way" of fast line work. Lines that get too many of these are penalized.]

R. C. then wrote up some work for a particular line. He volunteered to me: "These orders that I am working on now are sofas. They are next in line. Like the previous ones, they are fairly simple so this line should be able to make out on them. *I'd like to be able to beef up this line's production by giving them some easier work; but they are a slow line and I wonder if my efforts do any good for them."*
[Note how R. C. occasionally tries to help out a "weak sister" line.]

R. C. responded to a page. The shipping man who was looking for a single sofa was told which line the sofa was on. R. C. returned to his backlog of orders. He again talked to me voluntarily: "Here are some specials which are identical to a big schedule now on the floor. To get this processed quickly, I'll give it to the line [5] which has the [another] special now; this should help me and it will preclude another line's getting a single order—lines don't like singles. The next order that I have is the same style that line 9 complained about [through its foreman] yesterday. It also is the same style that I have given to line 6 twice recently. They complained about it the second time [through the quality control man]. *If I give it to 6 [a third time in such a short period] you can bet that I will really hear about it this time. You know, Nick, my philosophy is to keep them all happy."* At a later time I asked R. C. just what he meant by his expression, "I might as well keep them all happy." R. C. answered as follows: "What I mean by keeping them happy is to keep their complaining down. *They holler when the schedules are too short. They holler when they have too many specials. They holler when there are too many large schedules in a row. They complain if they have two chair orders in a row. They* like to get some gravy, easy styles. When squawking occurs, it occurs on the basis of these things."

[It is clear from R. C.'s report that the workers pressure R. C., *but they do not confine their pressure to run length alone.* Given the totality of their demands, it seems unlikely that any particular line gets a consistently good deal from R. C. on the one variable that really counts—run length.]

Later, as he sorted his orders, R. C. volunteered to me: "I will try to meet F. J.'s request for getting those velvets out today. In order to do this, I must check the frame record to see if the frames have been made. If the frames have not been made, I will tell the frame foreman to proceed with them. He will understand our problem."

A meeting on this matter was convened in the assistant plant manager's office at 9:45. R. C., D. R., and F. J., and the front office expediter were present.

This meeting was called by D. R. because R. C. had told him earlier of the rescheduling required by F. J.'s problem with the velvet. D. R. immediately challenged F. J. on the reason for the early cutting of the velvet. He told F. J. it is not his job to do scheduling; scheduling he said was solely R. C.'s responsibility. F. J. responded to D. R. by describing the serious handling problems associated with velvet. He further stated that there had been other material shortages which had upset his own planning operation; this had left him with only two alternatives, *cut the velvet* or *temporarily lay off some people.* D. R. responded that he understood all this but emphasized the promises he had made to his various customers. D. R. agreed, however, that R. C. would go ahead with the velvet scheduling now. He instructed F. J. that this problem was not to be initiated by him to R. C. in the future. D. R. said that there are many pressures upon him to meet promises which will be impossible to put through because of this problem.

(My own view of the pressures which exist on D. R. show

that they are of three kinds. Pressure from the customers is very strong. Salesmen seem to be calling him continuously. While we were in his office, he received three calls from salesmen pressuring him for orders. Shortages in raw materials inventory occur because suppliers do not meet their promised delivery dates. A third pressure results from the first two; the raw material shortages result in a backlog of orders which makes the scheduling difficult both before and after the raw material shortage is resolved. [D. R. is also the plant personnel manager and therefore receives many additional pressures.]

(Pressures on F. J. come from his own work. When there is a lack of material to be cut, he must resort to whatever he has at hand in order to keep his employees occupied. If he has to cut the most delicate fabric, there is no alternative but to use it on the furniture quickly; otherwise the fabric may be damaged in storage.)

During this entire period R. C. was relatively quiet. From 9:45 to 10:22 he spoke once: "I can schedule things to meet F. J.'s demands but it will be impossible for me to meet the other schedules. There are a hundred units in F. J.'s cutting. This will result in one day's delay in many of the orders. One hundred units operating at the rate of about eight or ten units per hour requires somewhere between ten or fifteen hours of work. This amount of work cannot be distributed to many lines; you have to keep one line or at most, two, on this special work."

(Notice that the reason for not being able to distribute this work to more than one or two lines is that there are only two dispatchers for fabrics. For one man to distribute the same fabric to many lines would involve more material handling than is safe; it may result in confusing parts or orders. Apparently the most efficient and least dangerous procedure from the point of view of material damage is to assign as much of one schedule to one line as possible. The reason for assigning work of one style to one line or two adjacent lines rests upon the need to get things done quickly, to meet the demands of the schedule, the need to have the work done accurately, and the need to balance out the work load at the output and the input ends of the line.)

R. C. left D. R.'s office at 10:23, returned to his own office, picked up some orders, and left for the floor. There he met a line foreman, who accosted him with "What are you giving us, a pile of shit?"

R. C. replied, "Oh well, it's assigned as it comes and everyone has to have their fair share."

R. C. momentarily left the area where this foreman was standing and looked at the orders on the work desk. I engaged the foreman in a brief conversation:

"What do you mean by the phrase, 'giving you a pile of shit'?"

"Oh, you know, some stuff is shit and other stuff smells nice. Some things are harder to work on than others. They don't go as smoothly. With some things you have to mess around more and it seems to influence the way the fellows work on the orders."

"Oh. What kinds of things happen when you have to work on some of this dirty stuff?"

He replied, "I have to give the workers other pieces of material or tools. The tools might be gauges for various lengths and I have to get these extra things for them."

After a pause, I asked, "Oh, can you influence how much they make in this way?"

"No, not too much. I have to anticipate it and if they don't get what they need they start bitching at me."

"Can you influence R. C. to give you less crap and more of something better?" I asked.

"No, nobody in this plant can influence what R. C. does. He has his own job to do. He has his pressures from the main office and he really gives the work to us as it comes. At least, that's what he tells us."

"How do the men react to some of the work they get?"

"Well, they complain all right and raise hell with me, but they continue to do the work as quickly as they can."

"What do you do when they complain?"

"There is nothing I can do about it. All that I can do is give them a pile of shit back just like I get from R. C. They quiet down after a while. As far as I'm concerned, there is not too much that I can do to influence how these fellows work except by bringing them the odd pieces of materials and tools they need. They have their own mind. They all know how much money they want to make. Most of them try to make as much as possible, but they all work at their own pace."

At 10:30 I noticed R. C. talking to F. J. The subject was velvet. R. C. volunteered to me: "I checked lines 1, 4, 5, and 6 to see how much work they need. I don't want to put the velvet on line 2 because of that line's relative inexperience in the process, and line 5 is lowest on the amount of work left on their table. The damned little davenports are nasty to work on from a quality point of view; and then I have more sectionals coming. I really can't decide what to do."

At this juncture I asked R. C. to rank the lines for me in terms of which would be most likely to receive the new (velvet) work. He responded, "Well, you have to eliminate lines A, B, X, and Y. Line B because they have their own work to do, line A because it does only our high-quality production work, and lines X and Y because they are the slowest. You have to eliminate lines G and F because they are the sectional lines. This leaves me lines L, J, M, and O. Line L is probably the fastest line now, so that if I wanted things done in a hurry I would probably assign it to them. Line O is almost as fast but for some reason I believe L is a little faster. There is not much to choose between the lines (L and O) on quality. *I am more concerned about the rate of production than I am about quality.* Quality is a foreman's responsibility. All I do on a very special piece where quality is extra important is tell the foreman what the problem is and leave it in his hands. [Line L finally got the velvet order. He stuck to his criterion of speed presumably because he wanted to get this job out of his hair and get back on schedule. Note that it was a very long run, too; 100 units. Thus, speed begets long runs which in turn beget speed.]

DISCUSSION

Observations based on four days of production-scheduling activities in the Northeast Plant reveal that twelve factors influence the assignment of work to the upholstering lines: (1) the master schedules made up in the front office reflecting market factors and matters of overall factory efficiency; (2) frequent pressures from front office officials reflecting special promises made to customers; (3) space limitations at each end of upholstery lines which affect amount of raw material (frames) and finished product that can be accommodated without inefficient congestion; (4) the need for all elements in a customer order to be kept together to avoid shipping errors and excessive handling; (5) availability of raw materials; (6) timeliness and coordination of efforts by supporting departments; (7) availability of vehicles on which various products must be transported while moving down assembly lines; (8) attributes of raw materials—for example, fragility of cover material; (9) customary product specialties associated with each line and the work groups' related possessive attitudes; (10) speed levels of the various lines as perceived by the chief dispatcher; (11) absenteeism on lines; and (12) the pressures brought to bear by the work groups on the chief dispatcher via line foremen and others. These pressures stem from workers' reactions to product-mix factors. Moreover, since they complain about having "too many long runs" *and* too few, it is clear that there is no simple formula that can be applied to keep them happy. It would seem that they want the money that long runs lead to, but that they compromise on money to some extent in the interest of variety.

In addition to the above production-scheduling findings, Yarmoshuk's notes also reveal a very important factor that probably affected the work groups' motivation levels when the foremen were reassigned. Specifically, the amount of work and number of "fat" assignments in the plant at any given time are fixed—the groups play a zero-sum game. The more long runs assigned to one line, the fewer are available to others. Thus, when confronted with the threatening foreman reassignments as a new complication in their work it is no wonder that "survival" motivation appeared among the upholsterers and became salient on the lines.

With the above facts in view, we now may return to the several questions at the end of Chapter 6 that generated the field observations in the first place. The most obvious conclusion to be drawn is that the production-scheduling process in the Upholstering Department system plays a major role in its equilibrium-seeking activities. Market conditions, specific customer demands, suppliers from outside the plant and functionally related departments inside the plant continually provide inputs that force adjustments within the system; that is, the system is almost always bouncing in and out of equilibrium. A number of internal factors within the system interact with these inputs to aggravate or relieve their effects. Included are such factors as floor space, availability of "trucks," work-group notions of equitable treatment, traditional product specialization on the various lines, and differential tendencies of the various line foremen to stick up for their men.

It seems reasonable to conclude that the high pre-experimental correlation between run length and group productivity can be explained primarily in terms of two phenomena. First, the faster lines get the longer runs to work on, while the slower lines tend to get a disproportionate share of singles and special orders. This occurs because the chief dispatcher must keep things moving smoothly and minimize handling and shipping problems. Second, certain kinds of furniture products year in and year out are more popular in the market place than others. Hence, the traditional line specializations lead to some groups' regularly receiving somewhat shorter runs than others. Both of the above factors, it would seem, explain the stable differences over time on run length among the lines.

The remaining unanswered question is: Why did the correlation between run length and productivity drop so sharply (from .79 to .32) during the sixteen weeks following the foreman reassignments? Since the chief dispatcher normally reacts to line speed, one would have expected him to reinforce the improving lines with longer runs. This apparently did not happen readily, presumably because of his long-standing perceptions of the various lines. Hence, lines that became more productive did so in spite of shorter runs, by and large, not because of them. Therefore, the correlation between run length and productivity broke down. This condition, however, is unlikely to prevail over a very lengthy time period because sooner or later the chief dispatcher is likely to notice the rapidity with which order slips disappear from each line's order desk. Market conditions and traditional product specialization among the lines, however, would restrict his ability to adapt to changes in line speed.

On balance, it seems that the production-scheduling–dispatching process is another open subsystem which is analogous to, and closely interwoven with, the subsystem encompassing leader-group relations. There are many variables that have a reciprocal influence on each other. A change in one can have far-reaching effects on all or many of the others, although homeostatic tendencies will tend to bring the system into balance again. Moreover, while it is theoretically possible that group productivity, cohesion, and relevant perceived leadership behaviors can be influenced substantially through direct manipulation of work assignment variables (especially run length), the equilibrium-seeking forces of group pressure are likely to prevent such manipulation in the long run. Nevertheless, it is clear that technological factors in the scheduling process, market demands, available floor space, and similar matters influence run length. This, in turn, influences (and is influenced by) group productivity, which in turn influences group attraction, cohesion, and perceptions of foremen.

CHAPTER 8

Summary and Conclusions

The previous chapters have described a small-scale, programmatic study of leadership and work-group behavior in the upholstering department of a furniture-manufacturing factory. The overall purpose of the research was to examine, experimentally, certain relationships among leadership behavior, group cohesion, and group performance variables frequently reported in cross-sectional studies. More precisely, the research problem herein stems from the difficulty of interpreting the "causal" direction of these relationships, which, in turn, creates both theoretical and practical problems. The vast field research literature in this area has not made clear whether leadership (supervisory) behavior, especially when measured via subordinate perceptions, causes variance in such indexes as group cohesion and productivity or whether perceived supervisory behavior is responsive to the latter variables. The major purpose of this research program was to build an experiment incorporating longitudinal features so that the two competing hypotheses—"leader as cause" versus "performance levels as cause," could be tested.

The experimental design also enabled a test on certain central propositions flowing from systems-equilibrium theory, a potentially more rewarding approach to leader-group relationships. Thus, it was hypothesized that a major leadership change would push the groups out of equilibrium, that energy would be mobilized to bring the system back into equilibrium, and that a new equilibrium state would be reached. The systems model, rather than relying on either of the two oversimplified causal hypotheses ("leader as cause" vs. "performance as cause") assumes that the variables in question exert reciprocal influences on each other.

The overall research program consisted of five phases. The first phase incorporated the collection of base line data, the development of operational measures (largely through a questionnaire), the conditioning of the plant for research operations, and a special preliminary (placebo) experiment to determine how the workers in question would react to being human guinea-pigs. The preliminary experiment was a critical step because a decision was necessary on whether to conduct the later leadership experiment as a publicly acknowledged, jointly sponsored company-university research project *or* strictly as a management-sponsored internal change with no visible research or university involvement. Suffice it to say at this point of our summary that both the quantitative and qualitative results of the preliminary experiment suggested that the workers indeed were likely to distort their behavior strictly as a function of being research subjects. Consequently, it was decided to forgo the advantage, in the later leadership experiment, of placing observers in the plant. In fact, the later experiment was conducted "in camera."

Phase 1 lasted six weeks. A little over a year later, Phase 2 was entered. During the intervening year, various data analyses were conducted to assess the reliability and utility (for experimental purposes) of several potentially important measures. The leadership experiment also was planned during this period. Phase 2 included the introduction of the foreman reassignments and the collection of productivity data to assess certain results of the leadership changes.

The third phase involved the collection of a second round of measurements on certain attitudinal variables. This permitted a further assessment of the leadership-change impact.

The repeated measurements were taken ten weeks following the supervisor reassignments. Approximately one year later, Phase 4 was entered. This included feedback of the experimental results to the participants, coupled with the collection of qualitative data on foreman behavior as a supplement to the quantitative experimental results. The fifth and final phase occurred six months later, when an intensive study was made of the production-scheduling function. This phase was designed to follow through on the possibility of a spurious variable in the experiment and to learn how production-scheduling variables enter the systems-equilibrium model.

The following is a list of the major variables incorporated in the leadership experiment and the operations used to measure them:

a. Pre- and post-experimental group attraction ($\overline{X}$ preference rank assigned to own group by members, before and after the foreman reassignments).

b. Pre- and post-experimental foreman preference ($\overline{X}$ preference rank assigned to new foreman, before and after his arrival in group, within each group).

c. Pre- and post-experimental status consensus on foreman (standard deviation within each group on preference ranks individual members assigned the foreman, before and after his arrival in group).

d. Discrepancy between preference for original foreman and preference for new foreman (as measured before the experiment by examining the $\overline{X}$ ranks assigned within each group to their current foreman and all others in the department. The experimental reassignments were made on the basis of maximizing these discrepancies; that is, some groups lost their favorite foreman and received the one they liked least as a replacement; others lost what appeared to be unpopular foremen and received much better liked ones as replacements).

e. Group money motivation (an index of potential energy

mobilization measured by extent to which each group discriminated between its most- and least-preferred groups in
terms of money-making prospects. This measurement was
taken prior to the experiment).

f. Pre- and post-experimental group productivity levels ($\overline{X}$
percentage of incentive base rate achieved by each group
during selected time periods).

g. Post-experimental percentage change in group productivity (as measured by comparing post-experimental productivity levels with a pre-experimental twelve-week base line
period).

The operations and variable system were quite straightforward. All measures were tied to groups as the appropriate
unit of analysis in a leadership study. While only seven
groups (with from eight to ten members each) were involved,
the measures used appear to be reliable and the small number
of groups enabled a high degree of experimental control for
a field study.

It should be emphasized that the experimental variable
mentioned in paragraph *d* was justified both in terms of the
empirical literature in this problem area and on the basis of
our pre-experimental data analysis. That is, when the pre-
experimental base line data were collected, a consistent set
of positive relationships (correlations) was found among
group attraction, foreman preferences, status consensus on
foreman, and group productivity levels. Moreover, worker
preferences for foremen were correlated with the same kinds
of perceived leadership-behavior dimensions reported in the
literature, and group attraction was closely related to perceived money making potential via the incentive system used
in this plant. Therefore, it seemed that foreman reassignments based upon work-group preferences would provide a
test on the causal direction and systems-equilibrium hypotheses described earlier; a change in such a highly interconnected set of variables should have triggered reactions
throughout.

EXPERIMENTAL FINDINGS

Data presented in Chapter 4 indicate that the department under study changed considerably following the introduction by the plant manager of seven simultaneous foreman reassignments on short notice. Relative group productivity levels, which had been quite stable prior to the experiment, changed sharply. Later, a new stable rank order gradually emerged among the groups' productivity levels, although it bore some resemblance to the original. It is clear that equilibrium was lost initially, while a new equilibrium state developed over time.

Status consensus on the new foreman which was low in all the groups before they received their new foremen, also changed a good deal over time. Some groups closed ranks tightly around their new leaders, some did not close ranks at all, and one showed even less consensus after the leadership change than before. On the other hand, the groups' *relative* positions on their *mean* foreman preference indexes did not change very much. However, the absolute levels of these mean ranks increased in most cases. In other words, within-group change occurred, and most groups, on the average, decided they liked their new foreman better after having direct experience with him than they had thought they would much earlier. In any event, it is clear that the experimental variable guiding the original leader reassignments changed over time.

Finally, the group attraction variable changed even more. Some groups became more attractive to their members after the foreman reassignments, while others revealed the opposite tendency.

Chapter 5 presented an analysis to test alternative hypothetical explanations of the above findings. The data were found to be at least as friendly to the "performance as cause" hypothesis as to the "perceived leader behavior as cause" hypothesis. In fact, performance of the groups *following* the foreman reassignments turned out to be a stronger correlate of post-experimental group cohesion, for example, than the initial experimental variable. Thus, the greater the increase in productivity (and therefore pay) of each group during the first several weeks following the foreman reassignments, the more favorable the later group-attraction and foreman-preference attitudes became. However, pre-experimental expectations about the new foreman did appear to influence the development of later status-consensus changes. Therefore, the original experimental variable did have influence in the overall system.

A complex systems-equilibrium model was proposed as a more appropriate and fuller explanation of the experiment than was available through the two oversimplified hypotheses discussed above. The data support this model surprisingly well, considering the relative lack of rigor in this field experiment as contrasted with laboratory conditions. Evidence was found to support systems-equilibrium theory as follows: (1) a previously stable system was knocked out of equilibrium by a major leadership change; (2) energy was mobilized to bring the system back into equilibrium; (3) a new equilibrium state was reached; and (4) the equilibrium-seeking process apparently began prior to the second round of attitude measurements, thereby precluding an explanation of the results entirely as an artifact of the research process.

The data also suggest that once the new equilibrium was reached and formalized through the second round of questionnaire responses, subsequent productivity effects developed. Thus, the new status consensus (measured eleven weeks after the experimental manipulation) on the new foreman correlated .85 with later productivity increases; that is, the more the group agreed that "this is our leader," the more performance improvement they showed in the next several weeks (weeks 11 through 16). This finding seems to correspond with research results reported by Pryer, Flint, and Bass (1962), who conclude from some small group experimentation: "Our results suggest that groups are most likely to become more effective if they reach early agreement on who shall lead. Once this interaction problem is solved without further contest, the groups can move to a higher state of task effectiveness." Thus, the consensus-formation phenomenon seems analogous to leadership-replacement phenomena in athletic teams and to the political process surrounding elected officials.

Some of the data—questionnaire responses from the group members before and after the experimental change—have a direct bearing on the nature and importance of relevant perceived-leadership-behavior dimensions. Thus, while foreman "personality" (pleasant-unpleasant) was the most discriminating of several dimensions *both* before and after the experiment (as determined by comparing the workers' descriptions of most- and least-preferred foremen), the perceived technological-administrative skills of the foremen seemed to assume greater importance after the experiment than before the reassignments.

Finally, the results of a factor analysis designed to identify the major dimensions used by the workers when differentiating between most- and least-preferred foremen indicated four sensible factors: (1) general personality; (2) employee-centeredness or consideration; (3) technological-administrative competence or initiation of structure, coupled with job-related stress management; and (4) role differentiation or willingness to accept managerial role responsibilities. These findings, like some of the others reported above, also suggest that the new foremen were judged at least partly on their ability to help their groups reestablish equilibrium following the (technological) disruptions created by the foreman reassignments. Thus, a foreman's popularity (mean preference rank) in his group would be affected by his behavior relative to at least the above four dimensions. Similarly, the degree of status consensus he would develop also would be affected by such dimensions. It should be remembered that group-member perceptions of their foremen on these dimensions apparently were influenced *both* by their post-change, direct experiences with their foremen *and* by their pre-experimental expectations of them.

PRODUCTION SCHEDULING: A SPURIOUS VARIABLE?

Given the apparent influence of percentage changes in group performance levels (directly geared to the size of each worker's paycheck) on group attraction and status consensus on foreman, one must ask what created the productivity changes in the first place. The data suggest that initially the groups responded as if the leadership change were a management pressure device; *all* the groups increased, but the lowest-producing groups showed the largest percentage increases. It also was shown that after the first two weeks, the money-motivation variable (paragraph *e*, above) became salient. Thus, the groups apparently made efforts to cope with the leadership-replacement "emergency" (which presumably created technological problems because the foreman's role is highly integrated in each group) in direct proportion to their interest in making money. This was not a perfect relationship, however, and the possibility of some unknown spurious variable was always present. Subsequent inquiry during Phase 4 suggested that some aspects of the production-scheduling process (which can affect task difficulty) might have been at least partly responsible for the experimental productivity changes, rather than motivational-leadership variables. Therefore, an extensive analysis of production-scheduling factors was undertaken.

This analysis produced extensive quantitative data strongly suggesting that spurious production-scheduling factors did *not* have a substantial impact on the experimental results. Indeed, the stability of certain product-mix indexes (described in Chapter 6) underscores the motivational explanation for the experimental results described earlier; productivity improvements were achieved in spite of strong technological constraints. It was found, however, that average length of product run over a given period of time is an important factor to consider because the longer the run, other things being equal, the more speed a group can develop. Like other systems variables, though, this one was found to be involved in two-way causal relationships. Groups work faster when they get long runs, but, fast, highly motivated groups tend to get longer run assignments to begin with (see Chapter 7).

The detailed analysis of the production-scheduling process led to the conclusion that this process plays a major role in the equilibrium-seeking activities of the Upholstering Department. Market conditions, specific customer demands, suppliers from outside the plant and functionally related departments inside the plant continually provide inputs that force adjustments within the system; the system is almost always bouncing in and out of equilibrium, or at least it fluctuates frequently between its equilibrium limits. A number of internal factors within the system interact with these inputs to aggravate or relieve their effects. Included are such factors as floor space, availability of "trucks," work-group notions of equitable treatment, traditional product specialization on the various lines, and differential tendencies of the various line foremen to stick up for their men. On balance, it seems that the production-scheduling–dispatching process is another open subsystem which is analogous to, and closely interwoven with, the subsystem encompassing leader-group relations.

DEMAND CHARACTERISTICS

The "placebo" or "non-experiment" referred to above and described in Chapter 2 clearly showed that the factory-worker subjects in the study did not react passively to the research process. The mere presence of two observers in the department for two weeks coupled with occasional interviews and eventually a questionnaire administration led to individual differences in productivity among the workers. Younger, urban, low F-scale-score workers and active unionists tended to restrict output during the two-week placebo period whereas older, rural, high F-scale, inactive union workers showed increases. These statistically significant results did not appear to be of practical magnitude on their face. They became more important, however, when considered in combination with the qualitative interview and observational data reported by the two researchers who were on the scene. One of the most frequent categories of worker comments made to the field researchers, for example, reflected clear attempts to define the graduate students' effective institutional identification or loyalty *and to establish their real purpose in being present.* It also was observed that many workers were concerned with *how well they were playing their role of research subject.* Thus, many workers asked, sometimes more than once, "Are you getting what you want?"

These early findings acquire still further importance in the light of later developments during the leadership experiment. Thus, when the foreman reassignments were introduced simultaneously and on short notice by the top management, the groups showed a "pressure from management" reaction, described above. That is, before they found out about the link between the foreman reassignments and the previous university research project (over one year earlier), they interpreted the changes as management-initiated and responded accordingly—all groups increased, although the largest percentage increases occurred in the lowest (pre-experimental) producing groups. On the other hand, when the workers learned ten weeks later of the university research project relationship, they apparently manipulated (for only two weeks) their group performance levels in direct relation to the original experimental variable. In other words, when they realized what the actual basis of the foreman reassignments had been (worker preferences, not management pressure), they supported (either consciously or otherwise) the experimental hypothesis, but only for two weeks. Presumably they didn't keep it up because new attitudes had formed during the period of time when they were assuming the "wrong" reason for the leadership change. We shall return to the experimental design problems posed by this phenomenon in a later section of this chapter.

DISCUSSION

The substantive findings of this experiment, when viewed within the context of systems-equilibrium theory, seem realistic and understandable. They suggest that leadership-behavior variables have an impact on other group variables, but that changes throughout the entire variable system can be activated by externally imposed change. Under such conditions, group attraction, follower perceptions of leadership behavior, and performance variables all seem to vary together and exert reciprocal influences on each other until a new equilibrium is established.

The more theoretically oriented reader may ask what specific psychological mechanisms are involved here. I believe that we must draw on at least two kinds of mechanisms for an adequate explanation of the findings; perception and reinforcement. Thus, the various environmental cues associated with the leadership change were integrated through the *organizing principles of perception theory* and resulted in systematic interpretations, by the workers and their foremen, of the reasons for the change. These perceptions had motivational implications for the work groups. While acting on the basis of these motivational implications, the groups were more or less effective in pursuing their goals (in this case, increase in, or at least protection of, productivity level).

The groups' effectiveness (performance levels) in coping with disequilibrium apparently influenced their cohesion (attraction) through psychological *reinforcement*. Thus, those that were successful were rewarded by the incentive system (and also, perhaps, by satisfaction with an accomplishment) and developed stronger internal ties. Groups not receiving such reinforcement became or remained relatively noncohesive.[1]

We might also surmise that to the extent that the new leader was perceived to be helpful to the group in pursuing its goals, he came to be accepted by the group; that is, a high degree of status consensus developed. This, like cohesion, presumably occurred as a function of reinforcement. However, given the workers' emphasis on personality characteristics when evaluating foremen, the *stimulus* characteristics of the leader's personality may tend to overshadow any objective ability he shows at helping his group reach its goals.

The leader's ability, as perceived by his subordinates, to help his group reach its goals also is likely to be affected by *stimulus generalization* phenomena. Thus, if the group turns out to be effective in dealing with an externally imposed change, its cohesive and satisfied members are likely to "include" their leader in the group as a full-fledged member, giving him part of the credit for their accomplishments whether he deserves it or not. If the group fails to accomplish its objective, of course, the leader may well take the rap, even though his own positive contributions and attributes were substantial.

The status-consensus phenomenon emerges noticeably from this study and deserves emphasis before we move on to other matters. The data suggest that this variable (degree of internal agreement about the leader) is critical in understanding leadership effectiveness. This underscores the need to consider simultaneously not only the leader's objective characteristics, but also how they are perceived by his subordinates. The development and integration of such perceptions, as we know from the social perception literature cited

---

[1] Wolman (1960) has shown in the laboratory that task failure affects group cohesion negatively. This phenomenon is observed regularly, of course, in athletic teams and other kinds of groups.

in Chapter 5, are affected by group variables. Therefore, if we wish to gain more insight into the conditions under which groups do or do not reach consensus on their supervisory leaders, further research will be needed. Group and leadership characteristics will have to be considered simultaneously. It might be worthwhile, for example, to determine whether certain kinds of leadership stimulus characteristics are more amenable to group consensus than others. More specifically, which of the four leadership-behavior dimensions (personality, initiation of structure, employee centeredness, role differentiation) identified herein (or others) is the most salient in this connection? Indeed, industrial psychologists might consider resurrecting personality measurement, using status consensus within groups as a criterion measure, rather than traditional performance ratings by superiors, when making predictions from personality scores.[2] Various group membership characteristics and other group variables would be employed as moderator variables.

The reader may have noted that none of the seven groups herein exhibited consensus (agreement) that its leader was a poor one. Thus, status consensus ranged only from high agreement in one group that the leader was "good" to substantial disagreement on the leader in the low-consensus group. The absence of the lowest possible extreme—consensus that the leader is "bad"—merely may reflect normal range restriction is a viable work organization; any leader (foreman) uniformly perceived as ineffective by his subordinates probably would have been replaced by the manage-

---

[2] Essentially this is another way of saying that we need to devote further effort to the study of "successful" leadership (as defined by Bass [1960]) as a prelude to improving leadership effectiveness. That is, the consensus-formation process apparent in this study is intimately bound together with social influence. If we can identify the leadership characteristics that produce (in combination with group-moderator variables) status consensus among group members, we should find a key to leadership influence over groups and, consequently, group effectiveness.

ment before this study was undertaken. On the other hand, perhaps few such circumstances ever develop. Complete unanimity within a group that its leader is incompetent or undesirable may be unlikely given the heavy personality component in the system, which leads to ambiguous perceptions or at least to differences in personal preferences. In any event, this matter also deserves further study. It should be said here, however, that this apparent range restriction problem did not seem to influence unduly the outcome of the experiment. Both status consensus and group mean foreman preferences were highly correlated with other variables prior to the experiment. Undue range restriction would have prevented the development of such correlations.

The absence of leaders perceived uniformly as ineffective opens the larger question of the generalizability of this experiment's results. In the absence of such conditions in the experiment, we cannot say what might happen where they would occur, if in fact they ever do occur. Moreover, it must be emphasized that each group herein is characterized by a high degree of role interdependence among its members because of the technological requirements in the Northeast Upholstering Department. The groups are legitimate *teams,* not mere collectivities. The results of leadership reassignments in relatively noninterdependent groups (such as steno pools) might be different. Moreover, the groups herein strive for a highly visible performance criterion which is clearly related to their efforts. Continuous feedback and reinforcement on performance, therefore, are present. Many work groups, however, either have no such visible performance criterion or receive much more intermittent or zero reinforcement. Thus, possible range restriction on leadership behavior, task interdependence, the availability of a visible criterion, and the criterion's reinforcement value and reinforcement schedule are all potentially limiting conditions. We might add the partially competitive relationship among the upholstery groups to this list; given the relatively fixed amount of work available in this plant during a given time period, one group can improve its performance only at the partial expense of one or more other groups (see Chapter 7). If we are to understand fully the relationships among leadership, group-attraction, and performance variables, we probably shall have to take all the above variables into account as moderators. The present experiment's results certainly may not be generalized safely, and additional studies are needed. It is likely, however, that this study provided a conservative test of supervisory influence because of the high degree of task structure in the work and the high levels of team experience and skill.

METHODOLOGICAL ISSUES

The findings of this study re-emphasize the very real dilemma in social research that initially stimulated the experiment. The data in Chapter 5 suggest that the subjects, when responding to questionnaire items about their groups and supervisors, apparently were influenced by comparisons they made between their performance levels (income) before and after the experimental change. Moreover, in Chapter 3 we found in a cross-sectional correlational analysis that group attraction and foremen preferences were correlated with productivity; however, the productivity measure was based on the several-week period immediately *preceding* the questionnaire administration. The same attitudinal measures did *not* correlate with productivity *following* the questionnaire administration. All this suggests that, at least in groups characterized by visible performance criteria, correlations between attitude responses and performance must be interpreted with great restraint. The chicken-egg problem is real. Cross-sectional studies will rarely do more than provide suggestions in this connection, although some researchers have managed to get around this problem through creative data analyses. See, for example, Melbin (1961) and Kendall and Lazersfeld (1950).

While cross-sectional studies have their weaknesses, so do field experiments. The experiment herein, for example, relied heavily on a systems-equilibrium model both because of its conceptual appeal and the difficulty of measuring important variables on a repeated basis. While the data are instructional and support the model, we are still a long way from knowing what variables are relatively more likely than others to be necessary and sufficient to start or inhibit chain reactions in a system. One reason that it will be difficult to analyze systems through field experiments more fruitfully stems from the perceptual mechanisms inherent in all social systems. For example, if we introduce an experimental-variable manipulation as interventionist researchers known to the subjects, we may very well become victimized by "demand characteristics." On the other hand, if we introduce change "naturally," as was done in this study, we find that the subjects will interpret the change in unintended ways. Both possibilities arise as a function of the apparent universal tendency among humans to impose perceptual structure on environmental events. In either case, the intended independent variable may be obfuscated. Assuming a choice of strategies has to be made, the writer prefers the "natural" introduction without known researcher involvement where possible. (In the best of all possible worlds, we would introduce the same experiment in different ways to comparable groups so that the method of intervention would be controlled in the experimental design.) Considering the experiment described in this book, however, there can be little question that the way in which the independent variable was introduced had a great deal to do with the ultimate results. If the changes had been introduced more gradually (say two foreman reassignments at a time) instead of simultaneously, it is likely that less pressure would have been perceived by the groups. On the other hand, serious timetable problems would have occurred and comparable production records would have been a problem. Had more advance warning been provided (which is not the plant manager's *modus operandi*), the employees and foremen would have had more time to speculate about, and perhaps guess, the true purpose of the change. The future experimenter will have to choose which of these problems he wants to live with.

Still additional experimental design problems emerged from this study. Since the data strongly suggest that the group members' new attitudes and perceptions were closely related to their percentage gains in productivity, it seems likely that when responding to the second questionnaire they compared their post-foreman-reassignment performance levels with their previous levels to ascertain how well they had done under the new foreman's leadership. To the extent that they made such comparisons, some of the groups may have been misled because of "ceiling effect." That is, some groups started out as high producers and presumably had less room for improvement than those starting out at low pre-experimental performance levels. High initial producers, then, may not have been as satisfied with their improvements as low initial producers. Thus, post-experimental group attraction and status consensus on foremen may have been affected by a faulty experimental design. Ideally, the groups should have been paired or matched on initial productivity levels to eliminate this problem. The availability of only seven groups, however, precluded such a design. In fact, it is unlikely that any experimenter will find sufficient groups for such a design in field settings, although it is quite feasible in the laboratory. The absence of this design feature in the present study, however, does not alter the basic implications of the finding that performance levels influence attitudes and member perceptions of group leaders.

Design problems also arise from the proximity in space of subject groups and their opportunity to communicate with each other. Close proximity, small size of floor space, the presence of car pools, long tenure of workers throughout the department, and the nature of the surrounding, nonurban community all contributed to substantial communication and interaction in the Northeast Plant. This, in fact, helps explain the consistency of the variable relationships found throughout the Upholstering Department prior to the foreman experiment (see Chapter 3). For some experimental purposes, however, it might be better to deal with groups that are isolated from each other. This probably would require the investigator to locate "comparable" groups in separate organizational components—decentralized sister plants, regional offices, and so on. Experience here, however, showed that so-called technologically "comparable" groups in a sister plant were not comparable at all. The same may be true in many other far-flung organizations. Thus, it will not be easy to build insulated groups into a field experiment in formal organizations.

At least one other methodological issue deserves mention. Given the finding herein that at least four leadership-behavior dimensions (admittedly correlated with each other) apparently bore some relationship to the development of status consensus, how can we manipulate these dimensions in future research to facilitate hypothesis testing on their individual and combined effects? Such research probably is possible only in the experimental laboratory.

CONCLUSIONS

The following conclusions seem defensible on the basis of the experimental results reported previously:

1. Within the technological constraints imposed on the groups in this study (for example, task interdependence), simultaneous reassignments of several group leaders on short notice has pronounced effects on a system of variables including productivity and group attraction. The extent of the supervisor's direct impact through subordinate-perceived behavioral dimensions such as initiation of structure and employee centeredness, or through his general personality characteristics, still is not clear. The data suggest, however,

that such perceived leadership variables influence the development of within-group agreement on the leader (status consensus), which, in turn, has a positive impact on productivity and is related positively to group attraction. It seems fair to say, then, that even in the highly structured furniture-upholstering technology studied here, the group leader's image is not without influence. The influence occurs, however, through a complex social process of consensus formation which relates to group attraction and performance.

2. The findings suggest overall that the search for "causal" relationships between organizational variables may not be promising. A systems-equilibrium model, coupled with a search both for equilibrium-disturbing variables and equilibrium-restoration variables should be more fruitful. The results here, especially the production-scheduling-dispatching observations reported in Chapter 7, show that many organizational-technological variables will have to be included in the system.

3. Within-group status consensus (agreement among members) appears to be a critical variable in the study of leadership and group behavior. The more closely that group members agree that they value their leader, the more viable the group is likely to be. The status-consensus formation *process* deserves further research so that we may learn how to control it.

4. Group cohesion or attraction, as shown earlier by Seashore (1954), clearly emerges as a critical variable having implications for productivity and general administrative practice. In this study, group cohesion was directly related to performance levels and appeared to be both a *result* of performance changes through reinforcement mechanisms, and a cause. In any event, this experiment provides one setting where selected elements of job satisfaction, namely group attraction and status consensus on the leader, bear a strong relationship to performance. While the reviews by Brayfield and Crockett (1955) and Vroom (1964) conclude

that there is no necessary relationship between job satisfaction and performance, the task and administrative circumstances inherent in this situation allowed such a relationship to develop. It is entirely possible that group attraction (and possibly additional elements of job satisfaction) would relate to performance in other settings, *where interdependent group members share common norms about the value of rewards available to them through high performance*. It should be re-emphasized, moreover, that in this study, while group attraction did appear to be responsive to performance accomplishments prior to the measurement of group attraction (Rho = .54), this satisfaction variable *also* predicted subsequent performance changes (Rho = .83). Status consensus, similarly, predicted subsequent performance changes (Rho = .85). It would seem, therefore, that we cannot yet write off satisfaction with the leader or group attraction as being unimportant, either theoretically or practically speaking, as a cause or consequence of performance.

5. The above analysis, of course, would be modified by the extent to which groups value or are motivated by the formal organization's performance goals. Seashore (1954) also has pointed this out. Our experimental findings support his cross-sectional data in showing that the more money-motivated the group (and therefore the more productivity-oriented in this case), the more performance improvement it shows in the face of pressure from management.

6. "Demand characteristics" represent distinct problems for the field experimenter. The way in which an independent variable is introduced to an organization can have profound effects on the outcome of an experiment.

Many additional problems confront us. I hope that they will not overwhelm us in our quest for fuller understanding of group process in formal organizations.

Worker Booklet, Pre-experimental

New York State School of Industrial and Labor Relations

A Contract College of the State University

Cornell University   Ithaca, New York 14850

April 15, 1963

To Northeast Upholsterers and Foremen:

We are about to ask you a number of questions on a questionnaire. There are no "right" or "wrong" answers to these questions—they are all a matter of personal opinion for research purposes only.

Many of the questions are quite personal or private. For this reason we want to tell you again that nobody at Northeast (managers, foremen, fellow workers, or union officials) will ever see your answers. The only people who will see them will be Professor Ned Rosen at Cornell and me. Any reports to the company or union will be based on combined answers and percentages. No individual's name will be identified in any way.

Your name is on the outside of your envelope so that we can come back to see you in case we need to. This also will make it possible for us to link together certain information that we otherwise would not be able to do. Thus, we need your name for *research* purposes only.

Thank you again for all your assistance.

Cordially yours,
Walter Nord

Leadership Opinion Questionnaire
[By E. Fleishman]

[This forty-item instrument by Fleishman, which is not reproduced here, was administered to the workers immediately after they read the above covering letter. The workers were asked to indicate how the ideal foreman *should* act in relation to the forty questions.]

Survey of Furniture Worker Preferences in the Work Situation

1a. Pretend you can form a new upholstering line. Choose the 10 men you would most want to work with you. You may choose only from among the 80 or so men who work on the several upholstering lines presently, including your own line. Please ignore the job titles which they now have; thus it would be possible for you to select all the present back-springers, for example, to be on the line. Print the first and last names of the men you would select in the order of your choice.

Name	*Name*
1st choice _____	6th choice _____
2nd choice _____	7th choice _____
3rd choice _____	8th choice _____
4th choice _____	9th choice _____
5th choice _____	10th choice _____

1b. Now, again pretend that you can form a new upholstering line. This time, however, you may choose only from those 8 or 10 men *now working on your present line.* Which 3 men would you most like to keep with you? Print their names below in the order of your choice.

1st choice _____
2nd choice _____
3rd choice _____

1c. How would you describe the *first* man you picked above (item 1b)? (Circle the appropriate number on each of the following scales.)

(*a*) The amount of cooperation
he gives supervisors   A lot 7 6 5 4 3 2 1 A little

(*b*) His speed at work   Very fast 7 6 5 4 3 2 1 Average to
                                                              slow

(*c*) Your personal feelings   Like him 7 6 5 4 3 2 1 Don't like
                     personally   him per-
                                                        sonally

(*d*) The quality of his work-   Very good 7 6 5 4 3 2 1 Average to
      manship   poor

(*e*) Extent to which he gets   Very well 7 6 5 4 3 2 1 Not liked
      along with other workers   liked by other   by other
                            workers   workers

(*f*) Amount of help he gives
      other workers when they
      get behind   A lot 7 6 5 4 3 2 1 Very little

(*g*) Ability to "take charge"
      when foreman is absent   A lot 7 6 5 4 3 2 1 Very little

(*h*) _____ Other?   7 6 5 4 3 2 1
      (write in)

1d. How would you describe the *second* man you picked above (item 1b)? (Circle the appropriate number on each of the following scales.)

(*a*) The amount of cooperation
      he gives supervisors   A lot 7 6 5 4 3 2 1 A little

(*b*) His speed at work   Very fast 7 6 5 4 3 2 1 Average to
                                                 slow

(*c*) Your personal feelings   Like him 7 6 5 4 3 2 1 Don't like
                      personally   him per-
                                                       sonally

(*d*) The quality of his work-   Very good 7 6 5 4 3 2 1 Average to
      manship   poor

(*e*) Extent to which he gets   Very well 7 6 5 4 3 2 1 Not liked
      along with other workers   liked by other   by other
                            workers   workers

(*f*) Amount of help he gives
      other workers when they
      get behind   A lot 7 6 5 4 3 2 1 Very little

(*g*) Ability to "take charge"
    when foreman is absent   A lot 7 6 5 4 3 2 1 Very little

(*h*) _____ Other?   7 6 5 4 3 2 1
    (write in)

1e. How would you describe the *third* man you picked above (item 1b)? (Circle the appropriate number on each of the following scales.)

(*a*) The amount of cooperation
    he gives supervisors   A lot 7 6 5 4 3 2 1 A little

(*b*) His speed at work   Very fast 7 6 5 4 3 2 1 Average to
                                      slow

(*c*) Your personal feelings   Like him 7 6 5 4 3 2 1 Don't like
                        personally   him per-
                                              sonally

(*d*) The quality of his work- Very good 7 6 5 4 3 2 1 Average to
    manship   poor

(*e*) Extent to which he gets   Very well 7 6 5 4 3 2 1 Not liked
    along with other workers liked by other   by other
                            workers   workers

(*f*) Amount of help he gives
    other workers when they
    get behind   A lot 7 6 5 4 3 2 1 Very little

(*g*) Ability to "take charge"
    when foreman is absent   A lot 7 6 5 4 3 2 1 Very little

(*h*) _____ Other?   7 6 5 4 3 2 1
    (write in)

1f. Please print the names of the *first three* persons presently on your line that you think your regular *foreman* would choose to put on this new upholstery line if he were to be its foreman. Please list his first three choices in the order you think he would choose them. You may include your own name if you think your foreman would choose you.

Name (first and last)

1. _____

2. _____

3. _____

2a. Of the eight upholstering lines listed below, indicate the one which you would most like to work on, if you had your choice, by placing a *1* next to this line. Then place a *2* next to the line which would be your second choice. Continue in this manner until you have ranked all eight lines.

Rank order of preferred lines I'd like to work on:

_____ line   3—J. Smith's line
_____ line   4—G. Gary's line
_____ line   5—W. Jones' line
_____ line   6—B. Gray's line
_____ line   7—I. Brown's line
_____ line   8—J. Steel's line
_____ line   9—T. Cronin's line
_____ line 10—E. Mayo's line

[These are not the actual names of the foremen.]

2b. Describe the *first*-place line you picked above (item 2a) by drawing a circle around the appropriate number on each of the following rating scales. Be sure to do *all* of them.

(*a*) Amount of money you can make on this line	A lot 7 6 5 4 3 2 1	Average or below
(*b*) Friendliness of the workers on this line	Very friendly 7 6 5 4 3 2 1	Very unfriendly
(*c*) Amount of skill required	A lot 7 6 5 4 3 2 1	A little
(*d*) Amount of physical effort required	A lot 7 6 5 4 3 2 1	A little
(*e*) The amount of variety in the work	A lot 7 6 5 4 3 2 1	A little
(*f*) Amount of freedom to work at own pace	A lot 7 6 5 4 3 2 1	A little

(*g*) Amount of opportunity to use your head   A lot 7 6 5 4 3 2 1 A little

(*h*) Amount of opportunity to talk to other workers   A lot 7 6 5 4 3 2 1 A little

(*i*) Amount of cooperation among the workers on this line   A lot 7 6 5 4 3 2 1 A little

(*j*) Speed of work pace   Very fast 7 6 5 4 3 2 1 Average to slow

(*k*) Fairness of rates on most furniture run on line   Very fair 7 6 5 4 3 2 1 Very unfair

2c. Now describe the *second*-place line you picked above (item 2a) on the following scales by drawing a circle around the appropriate number on each.

(*a*) Amount of money you can make on this line   A lot 7 6 5 4 3 2 1 Average or below

(*b*) Friendliness of the workers on this line   Very friendly 7 6 5 4 3 2 1 Very unfriendly

(*c*) Amount of skill required   A lot 7 6 5 4 3 2 1 A little

(*d*) Amount of physical effort required   A lot 7 6 5 4 3 2 1 A little

(*e*) The amount of variety in the work   A lot 7 6 5 4 3 2 1 A little

(*f*) Amount of freedom to work at own pace   A lot 7 6 5 4 3 2 1 A little

(*g*) Amount of opportunity to use your head   A lot 7 6 5 4 3 2 1 A little

(*h*) Amount of opportunity to talk to other workers   A lot 7 6 5 4 3 2 1 A little

(*i*) Amount of cooperation among the workers on this line   A lot 7 6 5 4 3 2 1 A little

(*j*) Speed of work pace   Very fast 7 6 5 4 3 2 1 Average to slow

(*k*) Fairness of rates on most fur-
niture run on line   Very fair 7 6 5 4 3 2 1 Very unfair

2d. Now describe the *last*-place line you picked, above (item 2a) on the
following scales by drawing a circle around the appropriate number on
each.

(*a*) Amount of money you can   A lot 7 6 5 4 3 2 1 Average or
make on this line   below

(*b*) Friendliness of the workers on   Very 7 6 5 4 3 2 1 Very
this line   friendly   unfriendly

(*c*) Amount of skill required   A lot 7 6 5 4 3 2 1 A little

(*d*) Amount of physical effort re-
quired   A lot 7 6 5 4 3 2 1 A little

(*e*) The amount of variety in the
work   A lot 7 6 5 4 3 2 1 A little

(*f*) Amount of freedom to work
at own pace   A lot 7 6 5 4 3 2 1 A little

(*g*) Amount of opportunity to use
your head   A lot 7 6 5 4 3 2 1 A little

(*h*) Amount of opportunity to
talk to other workers   A lot 7 6 5 4 3 2 1 A little

(*i*) Amount of cooperation among
the workers on this line   A lot 7 6 5 4 3 2 1 A little

(*j*) Speed of work pace   Very fast 7 6 5 4 3 2 1 Average to
                                                           slow

(*k*) Fairness of rates on most fur-
niture run on line   Very fair 7 6 5 4 3 2 1 Very unfair

3a. Listed below are the names of the upholstering-line supervisors in
your plant. Some of them probably are better than others. Place a *1*
before the person who you believe is the *best* supervisor, a *2* before the
second best, and so forth until you have ranked all the men from 1
through 8.

Rank

_____ J. Smith

_____ G. Gary

_____ W. Jones

_____ B. Gray

_____ I. Brown

_____ J. Steel

_____ T. Cronin

_____ E. Mayo

If there is anyone else who is now working on *your* line whom you would like to have as foreman (do *not* list yourself), please print his name below:

Name: _____

3b. Now describe your *first* choice of foreman above (item 3a) by drawing a circle around the appropriate number on each of the following scales.

(*a*) The way he treats his men   Easy-going 7 6 5 4 3 2 1 Strict

(*b*) His knowledge of his job and   Lots 7 6 5 4 3 2 1 **Average or**
the work   little

(*c*) His ability to plan and organize the work   Lots 7 6 5 4 3 2 1 Little

(*d*) His ability to get things for
his men from management   Lots 7 6 5 4 3 2 1 Little

(*e*) His length of service   Long 7 6 5 4 3 2 1 Short

(*f*) His ability to get along with
the union   Lots 7 6 5 4 3 2 1 Little

(*g*) His skill as an upholsterer   High 7 6 5 4 3 2 1 Low

(*h*) His personality   Pleasant 7 6 5 4 3 2 1 Unpleasant

3c. Now describe your *last* choice of foreman above (item 3a) by drawing a circle around the appropriate number on each of the following scales.

(*a*) The way he treats his men   Easy-going 7 6 5 4 3 2 1 Strict

(*b*) His knowledge of his job and   Lots 7 6 5 4 3 2 1 Average or
the work   little

(c) His ability to plan and organize the work   Lots 7 6 5 4 3 2 1 Little

(d) His ability to get things for his
men from management   Lots 7 6 5 4 3 2 1 Little

(e) His length of service   Long 7 6 5 4 3 2 1 Short

(f) His ability to get along with
the union   Lots 7 6 5 4 3 2 1 Little

(g) His skill as an upholsterer   High 7 6 5 4 3 2 1 Low

(h) His personality   Pleasant 7 6 5 4 3 2 1 Unpleasant

4a. Pretend again that you are going to form a new line. Please **print** the name (first and last) of the upholsterer (*not* the foreman) who **is** now working on your present upholstering line whom you would *least* like to have on your new line.

Name: _____

4b. How would you describe the above-named man (item 4a)? (Circle appropriate numbers on each of the following scales.)

(a) The amount of cooperation
he gives supervisors   A lot 7 6 5 4 3 2 1 A little

(b) His speed at work   Very fast 7 6 5 4 3 2 1 Average to slow

(c) Your personal feelings   Like him 7 6 5 4 3 2 1 Don't like him personally / him personally

(d) The quality of his work-
manship   Very good 7 6 5 4 3 2 1 Average to poor

(e) Extent to which he gets
along with other workers   Very well liked by other workers 7 6 5 4 3 2 1 Not liked by other workers

(f) Amount of help he gives
other workers when they
get behind   A lot 7 6 5 4 3 2 1 Very little

(g) Ability to "take charge"
   when foreman is absent   A lot 7 6 5 4 3 2 1 Very little

(h) _____ Other?   7 6 5 4 3 2 1
   (write in)

5a. If you had your choice of any *job* on your line, which one would you choose? Show your choices by placing a *1* next to your first choice, a *2* next to your second choice, and so forth until you have *ranked* all the jobs in the order in which you would choose them.

Rank   *Jobs*
_____ back-springer
_____ seat-maker
_____ arm-maker
_____ back-maker
_____ trimmer
_____ seat-springer

5b. If you wanted to make as much money as possible (base rate plus incentive), without working too hard, which of the following jobs on *your* present line would you try to get? Place a *1* next to that job, a *2* next to the second best-paying job, and continue until you have ranked all the jobs on their income possibilities from 1 through 6. *Ties are allowed.*

Rank   *Jobs*
_____ back-springer
_____ seat-maker
_____ arm-maker
_____ back-maker
_____ trimmer
_____ seat-springer

6a. Think about your performance at the Northeast Company—(a) amount of work you usually do, (b) quality of your work, (c) your general attitude, (d) attendance record. In comparison with your fellow employees *on your line* at the Northeast Company, how would you rate yourself? (**Check one.**)

_____ Much above average
_____ Above average
_____ Slightly above average
_____ Slightly below average
_____ Below average
_____ Much below average

6b. How do you think your foreman would rate you? (Check one.)

_____ Much above average
_____ Above average
_____ Slightly above average
_____ Slightly below average
_____ Below average
_____ Much below average

Opinion Questionnaire
(Short Form of California *F*-Scale)

Please indicate your extent of agreement or disagreement to these items in the following manner: Write the corresponding number in the left hand margin according to the following scale:

No. 1 if you *strongly* disagree with the item,
No. 2 if you disagree with the item,
No. 3 if you neither agree nor disagree with the item,
No. 4 if you agree with the item,
No. 5 if you *strongly* agree with the item.

There are no right or wrong answers for these statements; all we want is your opinion.
[Thirteen items followed the instructions.]

Opinion Questionnaire II

Instructions

On the pages to follow you will find a number of statements which ask you about your beliefs and attitudes about a number of things.

After each statement there are six possible answers; your job i
to circle the answer which shows how you feel about the statement.

Example:

Competition does more harm than good.

Strongly   (Disagree)   Slightly   Slightly   Agree   Strongly
disagree   disagree   agree   agree

Example:

There are many things in life which are a lot more important than
succeeding in one's occupation.

Strongly   Disagree   Slightly   (Slightly   Agree   Strongly
disagree   disagree   agree)   agree

Some of the questions are hard to answer but try to answer every
item. Remember to answer the way *you* feel, not the way you think
other people feel. There are no right answers. Just circle the answer
that shows how you personally feel about the statement.

All answers will be kept strictly *confidential* and will not be seen
by anyone else in your company.

[Thirty questions followed these instructions, all dealing with
competition and cooperation.]

Census of Personal Histories of Furniture Workers in the U.S.

1. Please circle the last year which you have completed in school.
              1 2 3 4 5 6 7 8 9 10 11 12 13 14 15 16
Please list any other training or schooling which you may have had

2. Were your grades in school (check one):

_____ much above average?
_____ a little above average?
_____ high average?
_____ low average?
_____ a little below average?
_____ much below average?

   3. Where were you born? city _____ state _____ country _____

4. How would you describe the type of community in which you were raised? (Check one.)

_____ a farm
_____ a small town
_____ a large town
_____ a city about the size of Portsville
_____ a city much larger than Portsville

5. Please answer the following questions by checking the proper column for each person.

	In the United States	Outside the U.S.
My mother was born		
My father was born		
My mother's mother was born		
My mother's father was born		
My father's mother was born		
My father's father was born		

6. Do you own your own home? _____ yes _____ no

7. Do you own a car? _____ yes _____ no
If the answer is yes, please fill out the following chart.

	Year	*Make*	*Model*
1st car			
2nd car			

8. To the nearest whole hour, about how many hours of sleep do you get before an average work day? _____

9. Are you _____ married _____ single _____ divorced _____ widower?

10. Circle the number of childeren you have living with you at home who depend on you for financial support.

0 1 2 3 4 5 6 7 more than 7

11. Circle the number of children you have living away from home who depend on you for financial support.

0 1 2 3 4

12. Do you change clothes (other than an outer coat) after arriving at work or before leaving work for home?

___ always
___ usually
___ sometimes
___ seldom
___ never

13. Are you *now* buying anything on the installment plan (including mortgages)?

___ yes   ___ no

If yes, indicate about how much your monthly payments are.

___ $0–9	___ $50–59	___ $110–119	___ $160–169
___ $10–19	___ $60–69	___ $120–129	___ $170–179
___ $20–29	___ $70–79	___ $130–139	___ $180–189
___ $30–39	___ $80–89	___ $140–149	___ $190–200
___ $40–49	___ $90–99	___ $150–159	___ over $200
	___ $100–109		

14. In order to buy things costing over $50, I find it necessary to borrow money. (Check one.)

___ always   ___ seldom
___ usually   ___ never
___ sometimes

15. During an average year I (or my wife and I combined) save:

___ 21–25% of my (our) income.
___ 16–20% of my (our) income.
___ 11–15% of my (our) income.
___ 6–10% of my (our) income.
___ 0–5% of my (our) income.

16. Are you a member of a national political party? ___ yes ___ no

   If *yes*, is it ___ Democratic, ___ Republican, or other ___ (please specify)_____.

17. Do you normally vote for one political party in state and national elections? ___ yes ___ no

   If *yes*, is it ___ Democratic, ___ Republican, or ___ other, (please specify) _____.

18. I attend union meetings:

____ always
____ usually
____ about half of the time
____ seldom
____ never

19. How many social activities sponsored by the union do you attend?

____ all of them
____ most of them
____ about half of them
____ a few
____ none

20. How many years have you worked for this company? _____

21. About how many *days* were you temporarily laid off last year because of lack of work at the factory? _____

Work Characteristics Ratings

By this time you have had sufficient direct and indirect employment experience to give you a good idea of what is important and what isn't important in a job. The following are all characteristics of work— please indicate *how important* each characteristic is to *you personally* by drawing a circle around the appropriate number. 7 = Very Important and 1 = Very Unimportant.

	Very important	Very unimportant
Working with people a lot instead of alone	7 6 5 4 3 2 1	
Working with things instead of ideas	7 6 5 4 3 2 1	
A boss who knows his job	7 6 5 4 3 2 1	
Steady work	7 6 5 4 3 2 1	
Much travel in my work	7 6 5 4 3 2 1	

	Very important	Very unimportant
High pay	7 6 5 4 3 2 1	
Lots of freedom to be my own boss	7 6 5 4 3 2 1	
Being of service to society	7 6 5 4 3 2 1	
Lots of opportunity for promotion to higher level jobs	7 6 5 4 3 2 1	
Short work week	7 6 5 4 3 2 1	
A boss who can get what his men need from higher management	7 6 5 4 3 2 1	
Lots of responsibility	7 6 5 4 3 2 1	
Lots of recognition for a job well done	7 6 5 4 3 2 1	
A location close to my home town	7 6 5 4 3 2 1	
Work that fully uses my training, experience and abilities	7 6 5 4 3 2 1	
Work that is located in a climate that I like	7 6 5 4 3 2 1	
Fellow workers who have ability and are hard workers	7 6 5 4 3 2 1	
An understanding, sympathetic boss	7 6 5 4 3 2 1	
Work that I can forget when I go home at night	7 6 5 4 3 2 1	
A clean, quiet well-lighted place to work	7 6 5 4 3 2 1	
Lots of supervisory responsibility over others	7 6 5 4 3 2 1	
Many different kinds of duties	7 6 5 4 3 2 1	
Work that permits me to do my own planning on the job	7 6 5 4 3 2 1	
Fellow workers who get along well together	7 6 5 4 3 2 1	
Interesting work	7 6 5 4 3 2 1	
Work that doesn't demand too much of my attention	7 6 5 4 3 2 1	
A boss who knows what he wants	7 6 5 4 3 2 1	

Worker Booklet, Post-experimental

New York State School of Industrial and Labor Relations

A Contract College of the State University

Cornell University   Ithaca, New York 14850

June 25, 1964

To Northeast Upholsterers and Foremen:

We are about to ask you a few questions on a questionnaire. There are no "right" or "wrong" answers to these questions— they are all a matter of personal opinion for research purposes only.

Many of the questions are quite personal or private. For this reason we want to tell you again that nobody at Northeast (managers, foremen, fellow workers or union officials) will ever see your answers. The only people who will see them will be some of my students at Cornell and me. Any reports to the company or union will be based on combined answers and percentages. No individual's name will be identified in any way.

Your name is on the outside of your envelope so that we can come back to see you in case we need to. This also will make it possible for us to link together certain information that we otherwise would not be able to do. Thus, we need your name for *research* purposes only.

Thank you again for your assistance.

Cordially yours,
Ned A. Rosen
Assistant Professor

1a. Of the eight upholstering lines listed below, indicate the one whic. you would *most* like to work on if you had your choice, by placing a next to this line. Then place a 2 next to the line which would be you second choice. Continue in this manner until you have ranked all eigh lines.

Rank order of preferred lines I'd like to work on:

____ line   1—J. Steel's line
____ line   3—I. Brown's line
____ line   5—E. Mayo's line
____ line   6—T. Cronin's line
____ line   7—G. Gary's line
____ line   8—W. Jones' line
____ line   9—B. Gray's line
____ line 10—J. Smith's line

1b. Describe the *first*-place line you picked above (item 1a) by drawin a circle around the appropriate number on each of the following ratin scales. Be sure to do *all* of them.

(*a*) Amount of money you can make on this line

A lot 7 6 5 4 3 2 1 Average o below

(*b*) Friendliness of the workers on this line

Very 7 6 5 4 3 2 1 Very friendly   unfriendly

(*c*) Amount of skill required

A lot 7 6 5 4 3 2 1 A little

(*d*) Amount of physical effort required

A lot 7 6 5 4 3 2 1 A little

(*e*) The amount of variety in the work

A lot 7 6 5 4 3 2 1 A little

(*f*) Amount of freedom to work at own pace

A lot 7 6 5 4 3 2 1 A little

(*g*) Amount of opportunity to use your head

A lot 7 6 5 4 3 2 1 A little

(*h*) Amount of opportunity to talk to other workers

A lot 7 6 5 4 3 2 1 A little

(*i*) Amount of cooperation among the workers on this line ...... A lot 7 6 5 4 3 2 1 A little

(*j*) Speed of work pace ...... Very fast 7 6 5 4 3 2 1 Average to slow

(*k*) Fairness of rates on most furniture run on line ...... Very fair 7 6 5 4 3 2 1 Very unfair

1c. Now describe the *last*-place line you picked above (item 1a) on the following scales by drawing a circle around the appropriate number on each.

(*a*) Amount of money you can make on this line ...... A lot 7 6 5 4 3 2 1 Average or below

(*b*) Friendliness of the workers on this line ...... Very friendly 7 6 5 4 3 2 1 Very unfriendly

(*c*) Amount of skill required ...... A lot 7 6 5 4 3 2 1 A little

(*d*) Amount of physical effort required ...... A lot 7 6 5 4 3 2 1 A little

(*e*) The amount of variety in the work ...... A lot 7 6 5 4 3 2 1 A little

(*f*) Amount of freedom to work at own pace ...... A lot 7 6 5 4 3 2 1 A little

(*g*) Amount of opportunity to use your head ...... A lot 7 6 5 4 3 2 1 A little

(*h*) Amount of opportunity to talk to other workers ...... A lot 7 6 5 4 3 2 1 A little

(*i*) Amount of cooperation among the workers on this line ...... A lot 7 6 5 4 3 2 1 A little

(*j*) Speed of work pace ...... Very fast 7 6 5 4 3 2 1 Average to slow

(*k*) Fairness of rates on most furniture run on line ...... Very fair 7 6 5 4 3 2 1 Very unfair

2a. Listed below are the names of the upholstering-line supervisors in your plant. Some of them probably are better than others. Place a *1* before the person who you believe is the *best* supervisor, a *2* before the second best, and so forth until you have ranked all the men from 1 through 8.

Rank

_____ J. Smith
_____ G. Gary
_____ W. Jones
_____ B. Gray
_____ I. Brown
_____ J. Steel
_____ T. Cronin
_____ E. Mayo

2b. Now describe your *first* choice of foreman above (item 2a) by drawing a circle around the appropriate number on each of the following scales.

(*a*) The way he treats his men   Easy-going 7 6 5 4 3 2 1 Strict

(*b*) His knowledge of his job and the work   Lots 7 6 5 4 3 2 1 Average or little

(*c*) His ability to plan and organize the work   Lots 7 6 5 4 3 2 1 Little

(*d*) His ability to get things for his men from management   Lots 7 6 5 4 3 2 1 Little

(*e*) His length of service   Long 7 6 5 4 3 2 1 Short

(*f*) His ability to get along with the union   Lots 7 6 5 4 3 2 1 Little

(*g*) His skill as an upholsterer   High 7 6 5 4 3 2 1 Low

(*h*) His personality   Pleasant 7 6 5 4 3 2 1 Unpleasant

2c. Now describe your *last* choice of foreman above (item 2a) by drawing a circle around the appropriate number on each of the following scales.

(a) The way he treats his men   Easy-going 7 6 5 4 3 2 1 Strict

(b) His knowledge of his job and   Lots 7 6 5 4 3 2 1 Average or
the work   little

(c) His ability to plan and organize the work   Lots 7 6 5 4 3 2 1 Little

(d) His ability to get things for his
men from management   Lots 7 6 5 4 3 2 1 Little

(e) His length of service   Long 7 6 5 4 3 2 1 Short

(f) His ability to get along with
the union   Lots 7 6 5 4 3 2 1 Little

(g) His skill as an upholsterer   High 7 6 5 4 3 2 1 Low

(h) His personality   Pleasant 7 6 5 4 3 2 1 Unpleasant

3a. Now describe the *personality* of your *first*-choice foreman (item 2a) by drawing a circle around the appropriate number on each of the following scales.

(a) Enthusiastic about his work   Always 7 6 5 4 3 2 1 Never

(b) Changes his mind   A lot 7 6 5 4 3 2 1 Seldom

(c) Moody-temperamental   Very 7 6 5 4 3 2 1 Not at all

(d) Hard to talk to   Very 7 6 5 4 3 2 1 Not at all

(e) Likes to remind his men of their
mistakes   Always 7 6 5 4 3 2 1 Never

(f) Flies off the handle   Often 7 6 5 4 3 2 1 Never

(g) Friendly   Always 7 6 5 4 3 2 1 Seldom

(h) Takes life too seriously   Always 7 6 5 4 3 2 1 Never

(i) Grouchy-grumpy   Always 7 6 5 4 3 2 1 Never

(j) Acts too quickly without thinking   Always 7 6 5 4 3 2 1 Never

(k) Energetic, lots of drive   Always 7 6 5 4 3 2 1 Never

(*l*) Talks too much   Always 7 6 5 4 3 2 1 Never

(*m*) Makes his men feel important   Always 7 6 5 4 3 2 1 Never

(*n*) Can be "pushed around"   Always 7 6 5 4 3 2 1 Never

(*o*) Good listener   Always 7 6 5 4 3 2 1 Never

(*p*) Has a "chip on his shoulder"   Usually 7 6 5 4 3 2 1 Never

(*q*) Handles emergencies   Very well 7 6 5 4 3 2 1 Poorly

(*r*) Shy   Very 7 6 5 4 3 2 1 Not at all

(*s*) Sticks to company rules   Always 7 6 5 4 3 2 1 Never

(*t*) Can take criticism   Usually 7 6 5 4 3 2 1 Never

(*u*) Puts his own problems ahead
       of his men's   Always 7 6 5 4 3 2 1 Never

(*v*) "Bossy"   Always 7 6 5 4 3 2 1 Never

(*w*) Uses foul language   Frequently 7 6 5 4 3 2 1 Never

(*x*) Gets upset   Frequently 7 6 5 4 3 2 1 Never

(*y*) Avoids problems that he should
       tackle   Frequently 7 6 5 4 3 2 1 Never

(*z*) "Looks for fights or trouble"   Always 7 6 5 4 3 2 1 Never

(*aa*) Is relaxed   Always 7 6 5 4 3 2 1 Never

(*bb*) Things have to be done *his* way   Always 7 6 5 4 3 2 1 Never

(*cc*) Polite   Always 7 6 5 4 3 2 1 Never

(*dd*) Acts like he is "better" than his
        men   Always 7 6 5 4 3 2 1 Never

(*ee*) Interested in his men   Always 7 6 5 4 3 2 1 Never

(*ff*) Likes to criticize   Always 7 6 5 4 3 2 1 Never

(*gg*) Shows off his upholstering skill   Frequently 7 6 5 4 3 2 1 Never

3b. Now describe the personality of your *last*-choice foreman (item 2a) by drawing a circle around the appropriate number on each of the following scales.

(*a*) Enthusiastic about his work   Always 7 6 5 4 3 2 1 Never

(*b*) Changes his mind   A lot 7 6 5 4 3 2 1 Seldom

(*c*) Moody-temperamental   Very 7 6 5 4 3 2 1 Not at all

(*d*) Hard to talk to   Very 7 6 5 4 3 2 1 Not at all

(*e*) Likes to remind his men of their mistakes   Always 7 6 5 4 3 2 1 Never

(*f*) Flies off the handle   Often 7 6 5 4 3 2 1 Never

(*g*) Friendly   Always 7 6 5 4 3 2 1 Seldom

(*h*) Takes life too seriously   Always 7 6 5 4 3 2 1 Never

(*i*) Grouchy-grumpy   Always 7 6 5 4 3 2 1 Never

(*j*) Acts too quickly without thinking   Always 7 6 5 4 3 2 1 Never

(*k*) Energetic, lots of drive   Always 7 6 5 4 3 2 1 Never

(*l*) Talks too much   Always 7 6 5 4 3 2 1 Never

(*m*) Makes his men feel important   Always 7 6 5 4 3 2 1 Never

(*n*) Can be "pushed around"   Always 7 6 5 4 3 2 1 Never

(*o*) Good listener   Always 7 6 5 4 3 2 1 Never

(*p*) Has a "chip on his shoulder"   Usually 7 6 5 4 3 2 1 Never

(*q*) Handles emergencies   Very well 7 6 5 4 3 2 1 Poorly

(*r*) Shy   Very 7 6 5 4 3 2 1 Not at all

(*s*) Sticks to company rules   Always 7 6 5 4 3 2 1 Never

(*t*) Can take criticism   Usually 7 6 5 4 3 2 1 Never

(*u*) Puts his own problems ahead of his men's   Always 7 6 5 4 3 2 1 Never

(*v*) "Bossy"   Always 7 6 5 4 3 2 1 Never

(*w*) Uses foul language   Frequently 7 6 5 4 3 2 1 Never

(*x*) Gets upset   Frequently 7 6 5 4 3 2 1 Never

(*y*) Avoids problems that he should
       tackle   Frequently 7 6 5 4 3 2 1 Never

(*z*) "Looks for fights or trouble"   Always 7 6 5 4 3 2 1 Never

(*aa*) Is relaxed   Always 7 6 5 4 3 2 1 Never

(*bb*) Things have to be done *his* way   Always 7 6 5 4 3 2 1 Never

(*cc*) Polite   Always 7 6 5 4 3 2 1 Never

(*dd*) Acts like he is "better" than
       his men   Always 7 6 5 4 3 2 1 Never

(*ee*) Interested in his men   Always 7 6 5 4 3 2 1 Never

(*ff*) Likes to criticize   Always 7 6 5 4 3 2 1 Never

(*gg*) Shows off his upholstering skill   Frequently 7 6 5 4 3 2 1 Never

4a. Think about your performance at the Northeast Company—
(*a*) amount of work you usually do, (*b*) quality of work, (*c*) your
general attitude, (*d*) attendance record. In comparison with your
fellow employees on your *line* at the Northeast Company, how would
you rate yourself? (Check one.)

_____ Much above average
_____ Above average
_____ Slightly above average
_____ Slightly below average
_____ Below average
_____ Much below average

4b. How do you think your foreman would rate you? (Check one.)

_____ Much above average
_____ Above average
_____ Slightly above average
_____ Slightly below average
_____ Below average
_____ Much below average

Foreman Booklet, Pre-experimental

New York State School of Industrial and Labor Relations

A Contract College of the State University

Cornell University   Ithaca, New York 14850

April 15, 1963

To Northeast Upholsterers and Foremen:

We are about to ask you a number of questions on a questionnaire. There are no "right" or "wrong" answers to the questions —they are all a matter of personal opinion for research purposes only.

Many of the questions are quite personal or private. For this reason we want to tell you again that nobody at Northeast (managers, foremen, fellow workers or union officials) will ever see your answers. The only people who will see them will be Professor Ned Rosen at Cornell and me. Any reports to the company or union will be based on combined answers and percentages. No individual's name will be identified in any way.

Your name is on the outside of your envelope so that we can come back to see you in case we need to. This also will make it possible for us to link together certain information that we otherwise would not be able to do. Thus, we need your name for *research* purposes only.

Thank you again for all your assistance.

Cordially yours,
Walter Nord

Leadership Opinion Questionnaire

[Fleishman's forty-item instrument was administered to the foremen immediately after they read Walter Nord's covering letter.]

Survey of Supervisor Preferences in the Work Situation

1a. Pretend you can form a new upholstering line with yourself as foreman. Choose the 10 men you would most want to work under you, in the order you would select them. You many choose only from among the 80 or so men who work on the several upholstering lines presently, including your own line. Please ignore the job titles which they now have; thus it would be possible for you to select all the present back-springers, for example, to be on the line. Print the first and last names of the men you would select in the order of your choice.

Name		*Name*	
1st choice	_____	6th choice	_____
2nd choice	_____	7th choice	_____
3rd choice	_____	8th choice	_____
4th choice	_____	9th choice	_____
5th choice	_____	10th choice	_____

1b. Now, again pretend that you can form a new upholstering line. This time, however, you may choose only from those 8 or 10 men *now working on your present line.* Which 3 men would you most like to keep with you? Print their names below in the order of your choice.

Name

1st choice _____

2nd choice _____

3rd choice _____

1c. How would you describe the *first* man you picked above (item 1b)? (Circle the appropriate number on each of the following scales.)

(*a*) The amount of cooperation
he gives supervisors   A lot 7 6 5 4 3 2 1 A little

(*b*) His speed at work   Very fast 7 6 5 4 3 2 1 Average to
                                                          slow

(*c*) Your personal feelings   Like him 7 6 5 4 3 2 1 Don't like
                                               personally   him person-
                                                                            ally

(*d*) The quality of his work-   Very good 7 6 5 4 3 2 1 Average to
       manship   poor

(*e*) Extent to which he gets   Very well 7 6 5 4 3 2 1 Not liked
       along with other workers   liked by other   by other
                                               workers   workers

(*f*) Amount of help he gives
       other workers when they
       get behind   A lot 7 6 5 4 3 2 1 Very little

(*g*) Ability to "take charge"
       when foreman is absent   A lot 7 6 5 4 3 2 1 Very little

(*h*) _____ Other?   7 6 5 4 3 2 1
       (write in)

1d. How would you describe the *second* man you picked above (item 1b)? (Circle the appropriate number on each of the following scales.)

(*a*) The amount of cooperation
       he gives supervisors   A lot 7 6 5 4 3 2 1 A little

(*b*) His speed at work   Very fast 7 6 5 4 3 2 1 Average to
                                                                            slow

(*c*) Your personal feelings   Like him 7 6 5 4 3 2 1 Don't like
                                               personally   him person-
                                                                            ally

(*d*) The quality of his work-   Very good 7 6 5 4 3 2 1 Average to
       manship   poor

(*e*) Extent to which he gets   Very well 7 6 5 4 3 2 1 Not liked
       along with other workers   liked by other   by other
                                               workers   workers

(*f*) Amount of help he gives
       other workers when they
       get behind   A lot 7 6 5 4 3 2 1 Very little

(*g*) Ability to "take charge"
when foreman is absent   A lot 7 6 5 4 3 2 1 Very little

(*h*) _____ Other?   7 6 5 4 3 2 1
(write in)

1e. How would you describe the *third* man you picked above (item 1b)? (Circle the appropriate number on each of the following scales.)

(*a*) The amount of cooperation
he gives supervisors   A lot 7 6 5 4 3 2 1 A little

(*b*) His speed at work   Very fast 7 6 5 4 3 2 1 Average to
slow

(*c*) Your personal feelings   Like him 7 6 5 4 3 2 1 Don't like
personally   him person-
ally

(*d*) The quality of his work- Very good 7 6 5 4 3 2 1 Average to
manship   poor

(*e*) Extent to which he gets   Very well 7 6 5 4 3 2 1 Not liked
along with other workers   liked by other   by other
workers   workers

(*f*) Amount of help he gives
other workers when they
get behind   A lot 7 6 5 4 3 2 1 Very little

(*g*) Ability to "take charge"
when foreman is absent   A lot 7 6 5 4 3 2 1 Very little

(*h*) _____ Other?   7 6 5 4 3 2 1
(write in)

2a. Suppose you had your choice of supervising any one of the present upholstering lines as they are now set up. Place a *1* next to the line you would like to have most, a *2* next to your second choice, and so on until you have ranked all eight lines.

Rank order of lines I'd like to supervise:

_____ line 3—J. Smith's line
_____ line 4—G. Gary's line
_____ line 5—W. Jones' line
_____ line 6—B. Gray's line
_____ line 7—I. Brown's line
_____ line 8—J. Steel's line
_____ line 9—T. Cronin's line
_____ line 10—E. Mayo's line

2b. Rank in order of importance to you the following possible reasons for your first choice of upholstering line above (item 2a) by placing a *1* before the most important reason, a *2* before the next most important reason, and so forth until you have ranked all six reasons.

Rank   *Reasons for my first line choice above:*   *Check one*

_____ The work pace   (_____ fast _____ moderate to slow)
_____ The skill and craftsmanship re-
       quirements   (_____ high _____ moderate to low)
_____ The amount of worker cooperation with the foreman
_____ My knowledge of the styles, parts, and fabrics used on this line
_____ The variety of the work   (_____ lots _____ little)

2c. Now rank these reasons for your second choice of upholstering line above (item 2a).

Rank   *Reasons for my second choice of line:*   *Check one*

_____ The work pace   (_____ fast _____ moderate to slow)
_____ The skill and craftsmanship re-
       quirements   (_____ high _____ moderate to low)
_____ The amount of worker cooperation with the foreman
_____ The kind of guys who work on it
_____ My knowledge of the styles, parts and fabrics used on this line
_____ The variety of the work   (_____ lots _____ little)

2d. Now rank these reasons for your last choice of upholstering line above (item 2a).

Rank Reasons for my last line choice above: *Check one*

____ The work pace   (____ fast ____ moderate to slow)
____ The skill and craftsmanship re-
     quirements   (____ high ____ moderate to low)
____ The amount of worker cooperation with the foreman
____ The kind of guys who work on it
____ My knowledge of the styles, parts and fabrics used on this line
____ The variety of the work   (____ lots ____ little)

3a. Listed below are the names of the upholstering-line supervisors
in your plant. Some of them probably are better than others. Place a
1 before the person who you believe is the best supervisor, a *2* before
the second best, and so forth until you have ranked all the men from
1 through 8. Rank your own name along with the others.

Rank

____ J. Smith
____ G. Gary
____ W. Jones
____ B. Gray
____ I. Brown
____ J. Steel
____ T. Cronin
____ E. Mayo

3b. Now describe your *first* choice of foreman above (item 3a) by drawing a circle around the appropriate number on each of the following
scales.

(*a*) The way he treats his men   Easy-going 7 6 5 4 3 2 1 Strict

(*b*) His knowledge of his job and   Lots 7 6 5 4 3 2 1 Average or
     the work   little

(*c*) His ability to plan and organ-
     ize the work   Lots 7 6 5 4 3 2 1 Little

(*d*) His ability to get things for
     his men from management   Lots 7 6 5 4 3 2 1 Little

(*e*) His length of service   Long 7 6 5 4 3 2 1 Short

(*f*) His ability to get along with
    the union   Lots 7 6 5 4 3 2 1 Little

(*g*) His skill as an upholsterer   High 7 6 5 4 3 2 1 Low

(*h*) His personality   Pleasant 7 6 5 4 3 2 1 Unpleasant

3c. Now describe your *last* choice of foreman above (item 3a) by drawing a circle around the appropriate number on each of the following scales.

(*a*) The way he treats his men   Easy-going 7 6 5 4 3 2 1 Strict

(*b*) His knowledge of his job and
    the work   Lots 7 6 5 4 3 2 1 Average or
                              little

(*c*) His ability to plan and organ
    ize the work   Lots 7 6 5 4 3 2 1 Little

(*d*) His ability to get things for his
    men from management   Lots 7 6 5 4 3 2 1 Little

(*e*) His length of service   Long 7 6 5 4 3 2 1 Short

(*f*) His ability to get along with
    the union   Lots 7 6 5 4 3 2 1 Little

(*g*) His skill as an upholsterer   High 7 6 5 4 3 2 1 Low

(*h*) His personality   Pleasant 7 6 5 4 3 2 1 Unpleasant

4a. Pretend again that you are going to form a new line. Please print the name (first and last) of the upholsterer who is now working on your present upholstering line whom you would *least* like to have working under you on your new line.

Name: _____

4b. How would you describe the above-named man (item 4a)? (Circle the appropriate number on each of the following scales.)

(*a*) The amount of cooperation
    he gives supervisors   A lot 7 6 5 4 3 2 1 A little

(*b*) His speed at work   Very fast 7 6 5 4 3 2 1 Average to
                                 slow

(c) Your personal feelings   Like him 7 6 5 4 3 2 1 Don't like
                                     personally   him person-
                                                              ally

(d) The quality of his work-   Very good 7 6 5 4 3 2 1 Average to
     manship   poor

(e) Extent to which he gets   Very well 7 6 5 4 3 2 1 Not liked
     along with other workers   liked by other   by other
                                      workers   workers

(f) Amount of help he gives
     other workers when they
     get behind   A lot 7 6 5 4 3 2 1 Very little

(g) Ability to "take charge"
     when foreman is absent   A lot 7 6 5 4 3 2 1 Very little

(h) _____ Other?
     (write in)

5a. In answering this question, pretend that you are a *worker, not* the
foreman, on your upholstery line. If you had your choice of any *job*
on your line, which one would you choose? Show your choices by
placing a *1* next to your first choice, a *2* next to your second choice,
and so forth until you have *ranked* all the jobs in the order in which
you would choose them.

Rank   *Jobs*
_____ back-springer
_____ seat-maker
_____ arm-maker
_____ back-maker
_____ trimmer
_____ seat-springer

5b. If you were a worker, not a foreman, and wanted to make as much
money as possible (base rate plus incentive) without working too hard,
which of the following jobs on *your present* line would you try to
get? Place a *1* next to that job, a *2* next to the second best-paying job,
and continue until you have ranked all the jobs on their income possibilities from 1 through 6.

ies are allowed.

ank	*Jobs*
___	back-springer
___	seat-maker
___	arm-maker
___	back-maker
___	trimmer
___	seat-spirnger

Opinion Questionnaire
(Short Form of the California *F*-Scale)

Please indicate your extent of agreement or disagreement to these
items in the following manner: Write the corresponding number in
the left hand margin according to the following scale.

No. 1 if you *strongly* disagree with the item,
No. 2 if you disagree with the item,
No. 3 if you neither agree nor disagree with the item,
No. 4 if you agree with the item,
No. 5 if you *strongly* agree with the item.

There are no right or wrong answers for these statements; all we want
is your opinion.
[Thirteen items followed the above instructions.]

Opinion Questionnaire II

Instructions

On the pages to follow you will find a number of statements which
ask you about your beliefs and attitudes about a number of things.
After each statement there are six possible answers; your job is to
circle the answer which shows how you feel about the statement.

Example:

Competition does more harm than good.

Strongly   (Disagree)   Slightly   Slightly   Agree   Strong
disagree   disagree   agree   agree

Example:

There are many things in life which are a lot more important tha
succeeding in one's occupation.

Strongly   Disagree   Slightly   (Slightly)   Agree   Strong
disagree   disagree   agree   agree

Some of the questions are hard to answer but try to answer eve
item. Remember to answer the way *you* feel, not the way you thi
other people feel. There are no right answers. Just circle the answ
that shows how you personally feel about the statement.

All answers will be kept strictly *confidential,* and will not be se
by anyone else in your company.

[Thirty questions followed these instructions, all dealing with co
petition and cooperation.]

Foreman Booklet, Post-experimental

New York State School of Industrial and Labor Relations

A Contract College of the State University

Cornell University   Ithaca, New York 14850

June 25, 1964

To Northeast Upholsterers and Foremen:

We are about to ask you a few questions on a questionnaire. There are no "right" or "wrong" answers to these questions— they are all a matter of personal opinion for research purposes only.

Many of the questions are quite personal or private. For this reason we want to tell you again that nobody at Northeast (managers, foremen, fellow workers or union officials will ever see your answers. The only people who will see them will be some of my students at Cornell and me. Any reports to the company or union will be based on combined answers and percentages. No individual's name will be identified in any way.

Your name is on the outside of your envelope so that we can come back to see you in case we need to. This also will make it possible for us to link together certain information that we otherwise would not be able to do. Thus, we need your name for *research* purposes only.

Thank you again for all your assistance.

Cordially yours,
Ned Rosen
Assistant Professor

1a. Suppose you had your choice of supervising any one of the present upholstering lines as they are now set up. Place a *1* next to the line you would like to have most, a *2* next to your second choice, and so on, until you have ranked all eight lines.

Rank order of lines I'd like to supervise:

____ line 1—J. Steel's line
____ line 3—I. Brown's line
____ line 5—E. Mayo's line
____ line 6—T. Cronin's line
____ line 7—G. Gary's line
____ line 8—W. Jones' line
____ line 9—B. Gray's line
____ line 10—J. Smith's line

1b. **Rank** in order of importance to you the following possible reasons for your *first* choice of upholstering line above (item 1a) by placing a *1* before the most important reason, a *2* before the next most important reason, and so forth until you have ranked all six reasons.

Rank Reasons for my first line choice above: *Check one*

____ The work pace   (____ fast ____ moderate to slow)
____ The skill and craftsmanship re-
         quirements   (____ high ____ moderate to low)
____ The amount of worker cooperation with the foreman
____ The kind of guys who work on it
____ My knowledge of the styles, parts, and fabrics used on this line
____ The variety of the work   (____ lots ____ little)

1c. **Now** rank these reasons for your *last choice* of upholstering line above (item 1a).

Rank Reasons for my last line choice above: *Check one*

____ The work pace   (____ fast ____ moderate to slow)
____ The skill and craftsmanship re-
         quirements   (____ high ____ moderate to low)
____ The amount of worker cooperation with the foreman
____ The kind of guys who work on it
____ My knowledge of the styles, parts, and fabrics used on this line
____ The variety of the work   (____ lots ____ little)

2a. Listed below are the names of the upholstering-line supervisors in your plant. Some of them probably are better than others. Place a *1* before the person who you believe is the best supervisor, a *2* before the second best, and so forth until you have ranked all the men from 1 through 8. Rank your own name along with the others.

Rank

_____ J. Smith

_____ G. Gary

_____ W. Jones

_____ B. Gray

_____ I. Brown

_____ J. Steel

_____ T. Cronin

_____ E. Mayo

2b. Now describe your *first* choice of foreman above (item 2a) by drawing a circle around the appropriate number on each of the following scales.

(*a*) The way he treats his men Easy-going 7 6 5 4 3 2 1 Strict

(*b*) His knowledge of his job and the work Lots 7 6 5 4 3 2 1 Average or little

(*c*) His ability to plan and organize the work Lots 7 6 5 4 3 2 1 Little

(*d*) His ability to get things for his men from management Lots 7 6 5 4 3 2 1 Little

(*e*) His length of service Long 7 6 5 4 3 2 1 Short

(*f*) His ability to get along with the union Lots 7 6 5 4 3 2 1 Little

(*g*) His skill as an upholsterer High 7 6 5 4 3 2 1 Low

(*h*) His personality Pleasant 7 6 5 4 3 2 1 Unpleasant

2c. Now describe your *last* choice of foreman above (item 2a) by drawing a circle around the appropriate number on each of the following scales.

(a) The way he treats his men   Easy-going 7 6 5 4 3 2 1 Strict

(b) His knowledge of his job and   Lots 7 6 5 4 3 2 1 Average or
the work   little

(c) His ability to plan and organ-
ize the work   Lots 7 6 5 4 3 2 1 Little

(d) His ability to get things for his
men from management   Lots 7 6 5 4 3 2 1 Little

(e) His length of service   Long 7 6 5 4 3 2 1 Short

(f) His ability to get along with
the union   Lots 7 6 5 4 3 2 1 Little

(g) His skill as an upholsterer   High 7 6 5 4 3 2 1 Low

(h) His personality   Pleasant 7 6 5 4 3 2 1 Unpleasant

3a. Now describe the *personality* of your *first*-choice foreman (item 2a) by drawing a circle around the appropriate number on each of the following scales.

(a) Enthusiastic about his work   Always 7 6 5 4 3 2 1 Never

(b) Changes his mind   A lot 7 6 5 4 3 2 1 Seldom

(c) Moody-temperamental   Very 7 6 5 4 3 2 1 Not at all

(d) Hard to talk to   Very 7 6 5 4 3 2 1 Not at all

(e) Likes to remind his men of their
mistakes   Always 7 6 5 4 3 2 1 Never

(f) Flies off the handle   Often 7 6 5 4 3 2 1 Never

(g) Friendly   Always 7 6 5 4 3 2 1 Seldom

(h) Takes life too seriously   Always 7 6 5 4 3 2 1 Never

(i) Grouchy-grumpy   Always 7 6 5 4 3 2 1 Never

(j) Acts too quickly without think-
ing   Always 7 6 5 4 3 2 1 Never

(k) Energetic, lots of drive   Always 7 6 5 4 3 2 1 Never

(l) Talks too much   Always 7 6 5 4 3 2 1 Never

(m) Makes his men feel important   Always 7 6 5 4 3 2 1 Never

(n) Can be "pushed around"   Always 7 6 5 4 3 2 1 Never

(o) Good listener   Always 7 6 5 4 3 2 1 Never

(p) Has a "chip on his shoulder"   Usually 7 6 5 4 3 2 1 Never

(q) Handles emergencies   Very well 7 6 5 4 3 2 1 Poorly

(r) Shy   Very 7 6 5 4 3 2 1 Not at all

(s) Sticks to company rules   Always 7 6 5 4 3 2 1 Never

(t) Can take criticism   Usually 7 6 5 4 3 2 1 Never

(u) Puts his own problems ahead
     of his men's   Always 7 6 5 4 3 2 1 Never

(v) "Bossy"   Always 7 6 5 4 3 2 1 Never

(w) Uses foul language   Frequently 7 6 5 4 3 2 1 Never

(x) Gets upset   Frequently 7 6 5 4 3 2 1 Never

(y) Avoids problems that he should
     tackle   Frequently 7 6 5 4 3 2 1 Never

(z) "Looks for fights or trouble"   Always 7 6 5 4 3 2 1 Never

(aa) Is relaxed   Always 7 6 5 4 3 2 1 Never

(bb) Things have to be done *his* way   Always 7 6 5 4 3 2 1 Never

(cc) Polite   Always 7 6 5 4 3 2 1 Never

(dd) Acts like he is "better" than his
     men   Always 7 6 5 4 3 2 1 Never

(ee) Interested in his men   Always 7 6 5 4 3 2 1 Never

(ff) Likes to criticize   Always 7 6 5 4 3 2 1 Never

(gg) Shows off his upholstering skill   Frequently 7 6 5 4 3 2 1 Never

3b. Now describe the personality of your *last*-choice foreman (item 2a) by drawing a circle around the appropriate number on each of the following scales.

(*a*) Enthusiastic about his work   Always 7 6 5 4 3 2 1 Never

(*b*) Changes his mind   A lot 7 6 5 4 3 2 1 Seldom

(*c*) Moody-temperamental   Very 7 6 5 4 3 2 1 Not at all

(*d*) Hard to talk to   Very 7 6 5 4 3 2 1 Not at all

(*e*) Likes to remind his men of their
      mistakes   Always 7 6 5 4 3 2 1 Never

(*f*) Flies off the handle   Often 7 6 5 4 3 2 1 Never

(*g*) Friendly   Always 7 6 5 4 3 2 1 Seldom

(*h*) Takes life too seriously   Always 7 6 5 4 3 2 1 Never

(*i*) Grouchy-grumpy   Always 7 6 5 4 3 2 1 Never

(*j*) Acts too quickly without think-
      ing   Always 7 6 5 4 3 2 1 Never

(*k*) Energetic, lots of drive   Always 7 6 5 4 3 2 1 Never

(*l*) Talks too much   Always 7 6 5 4 3 2 1 Never

(*m*) Makes his men feel important   Always 7 6 5 4 3 2 1 Never

(*n*) Can be "pushed around"   Always 7 6 5 4 3 2 1 Never

(*o*) Good listener   Always 7 6 5 4 3 2 1 Never

(*p*) Has a "chip on his shoulder"   Usually 7 6 5 4 3 2 1 Never

(*q*) Handles emergencies   Very well 7 6 5 4 3 2 1 Poorly

(*r*) Shy   Very 7 6 5 4 3 2 1 Not at all

(*s*) Sticks to company rules   Always 7 6 5 4 3 2 1 Never

(*t*) Can take criticism   Usually 7 6 5 4 3 2 1 Never

(*u*) Puts his own problems ahead
      of his men's   Always 7 6 5 4 3 2 1 Never

(*v*) "Bossy"   Always 7 6 5 4 3 2 1 Never

(*w*) Uses foul language   Frequently 7 6 5 4 3 2 1 Never

(*x*) Gets upset   Frequently 7 6 5 4 3 2 1 Never

(*y*) Avoids problems that he should
  tackle   Frequently 7 6 5 4 3 2 1 Never

(*z*) "Looks for fights or trouble"   Always 7 6 5 4 3 2 1 Never

(*aa*) Is relaxed   Always 7 6 5 4 3 2 1 Never

(*bb*) Things have to be done *his* way   Always 7 6 5 4 3 2 1 Never

(*cc*) Polite   Always 7 6 5 4 3 2 1 Never

(*dd*) Acts like he is "better" than his
  men   Always 7 6 5 4 3 2 1 Never

(*ee*) Interested in his men   Always 7 6 5 4 3 2 1 Never

(*ff*) Likes to criticize   Always 7 6 5 4 3 2 1 Never

(*gg*) Shows off his upholstering skill   Frequently 7 6 5 4 3 2 1 Never

Letters Mailed to Workers' and Foremen's Homes Prior to Data Collection in Factory

New York State School of Industrial and Labor Relations

A Contract College of the State University

Cornell University   Ithaca, New York 14850

March 22, 1963

Dear Northeast Employee:

To meet the requirements for my master's degree I am writing a thesis about workers in the furniture industry. In order to gather first-hand information for my thesis, another student, Al Schwartzbaum, and I plan to visit your plant for approximately a week, beginning on April 2, 1963.

We have discussed our project with both Mr. R., the plant manager, Mr. A., your union president, and Mr. H., your chief steward. They have agreed to cooperate with our study.

Most of our time will be spent watching the work process on the upholstering lines. In addition, Mr. R. is willing to allow us to take one hour of one of your working days during our visit to have you personally answer some questions for me. I hope you will be willing to do this for me, since this information will be a vital part of my thesis. For this time (one hour) you will receive your average incentive earnings.

The information we obtain in this study will be held in strict confidence. It will be seen only by us at the New York State

School of Industrial and Labor Relations at Cornell University. This School, as you may know, is chartered to be of impartial service to both management and labor and no individual has ever had occasion to complain as a result of our past studies. Our major interest is in the general trends of people in your industry. In this sense our project is similar to such surveys as the Gallup Poll, which you may have had experience with in the past or read about in the newspapers. A general report of our findings, in which no one individual will be able to be identified, will be made available to both your company and your union, if it is so desired.

I am writing to you to seek your cooperation with our efforts. Thank you for your interest. We are looking forward to being with you early in April.

> Very truly yours,
> Walter Nord
> Graduate Assistant

New York State School of Industrial and Labor Relations

A Contract College of the State University

Cornell University   Ithaca, New York 14850

June 19, 1964

Dear Northeast Employee:

I am taking this opportunity to ask you to assist us, once again, in the conduct of research in your workplace. Most of you will remember the research conducted by Walt Nord and Al Schwartzbaum a little over one year ago. At this time, we wish to ask you some more questions regarding your opinions relevant to the work situation at Northeast. This time, however, our questionnaire is much shorter. We will need only ten minutes of your time sometime during the workday on June 25. We hope very much that you will be willing to help us at that time. Our presence in the plant has been cleared with both Mr. R. and Mr. F., your local union president.

As you have learned from your last experience with us, we mean it sincerely when we say that your answers to our research questions will be strictly confidential. Nobody in the company will see your individual answers to any of our questions. A report on our research study will be made both to the company and to your union through E. F.

The answers to the questions we are going to ask you are strictly a matter of personal opinion. This will not be a test.

I expect to accompany some of my graduate students to the plant on June 25 to conduct this research. I shall look forward very much to seeing you again at that time. Meanwhile, thank you in advance for your cooperation, which is extremely helpful to those of us who try to teach students about what really goes on in industry.

Cordially yours,
Ned A. Rosen
Assistant Professor

The Statistical Significance
of Group Productivity Changes

For each of the sixteen weeks following the experimental manipulation, a plus sign was entered in the following table every time a particular group exceeded its pre-experimental level and a minus sign every time it was below its pre-experimental level. The signs for each group then were summed from left to right. Thus, Group F showed an increase in fifteen out of sixteen weeks, Group G increased in eleven out of sixteen weeks, and so on for the remaining groups. The table then was analyzed for statistical significance through the use of Cochran's Q-method. This is a nonparametric statistical procedure designed for use with nominal data where measurements are correlated. (See Siegel [1956].) The obtained Q-value, 22.9, exceeds the .01 level critical value of Chi². Thus, the groups differed beyond chance expectations in their propensity to increase or decrease their performance levels following the foreman reassignments.

The primary data on which this analysis is based may be found in Appendix G.

Table F. Post-experimental productivity, expressed as greater than (+) or less than (−) pre-experimental twelve-week average, by week and intact work group, and Cochran's Q-analysis results*

Group†	Pre-experimental productivity (12-wk. $\bar{X}$)	Post-experimental week																Total of + signs	Post-experimental productivity (16-wk. $\bar{X}$)	16-week % increase or decrease
		1	2	3	4	5	6	7	8	9	10	11	12	13	14	15	16			
F	130	+	+	+	+	+	+	+	+	+	+	+	+	+	+	+	+	15	144	+10.8
G	136	+	−	+	−	−	−	+	−	+	+	+	+	+	−	+	+	11	141	+3.7
E	131	+	+	+	−	−	+	−	−	+	−	+	−	−	+	+	+	8	129	−1.5
H	140	+	+	−	+	−	−	−	−	−	+	+	−	−	−	+	+	7	140	0.0
C	156	+	+	+	+	+	+	+	+	+	+	+	+	+	+	−	−	14	165	+5.8
B	123	+	+	−	+	+	+	+	+	+	+	−	+	+	+	+	+	15	134	+8.9
D	140	+	+	+	−	−	−	+	+	−	−	−	−	+	+	+	+	7	138	−1.4

*Obtained Q exceeds the .01 level critical Chi². $Q = 22.9 >$ Chi²$_{crit}$, $k - 1$ df (16.8).

† Groups are ordered on the experimental variable; Group F received the most favorable foreman change and Group D the most unfavorable.

Group Productivity
after Experimental Change

Table G. Productivity (% of base rate) every two weeks after experimental change, by group, and pre-experimental twelve-week base period

Group*	Pre-experimental 12-week base period	1–2	3–4	5–6	7–8	9–10	11–12	13–14	15–16	16-wk. total
F	130	148	132	140	145	142	147	149	148	144
G	136	138	147	127	135	138	154	143	145	141
E	131	145	124	129	122	127	130	128	132	129
H	140	152	140	136	130	139	140	136	152	140
C	156	170	165	162	168	162	162	174	155	165
B	123	146	128	124	131	133	134	132	140	134
D	140	144	139	138	141	135	126	140	143	138

* Groups are ordered on the experimental findings. Group F received the most favorable foreman change, Group D the least.

Primary Data
on Workers' Descriptions
of Foremen's Personalities

Table H. Workers' $(N = 73)$* mean personality description differences of their first- and last-choice foremen, and *t*-tests on the differences, by scale

Rating-scale item	Mean difference †	*t* ‡
Moody-temperamental	−2.60	12.86
Hard to talk to	−2.87	11.91
Grouchy-grumpy	−2.58	11.78
Bossy	−2.47	11.28
Has a chip on his shoulder	−2.21	10.83
Friendly	2.41	10.57
Flies off handle	−2.51	10.45
Gets upset	−2.10	10.40
Acts too quickly without thinking	−2.01	10.31
Likes to criticize	−2.04	10.15
Handles emergencies	2.01	9.57
Likes to remind them of their mistakes	−1.99	9.26
Interested in his men	1.90	9.05
Changes his mind	−1.86	9.03
Makes his men feel important	1.81	8.62
Avoids problems that he should tackle	−1.77	8.55
Things have to be done his way	−1.60	8.51
Puts his own problems ahead of his men's	−1.71	8.47
Acts like he is better than his men	−1.92	8.35
Shows off his upholstering skills	−1.78	8.20
Is relaxed	1.67	7.99
Good listener	1.92	7.80
Can take criticism	1.73	7.69
Looks for fights or trouble	−1.41	7.34
Polite	1.29	6.35
Uses foul language	−1.07	6.22
Talks too much	−1.19	6.17

Table H. (Continued)

Rating-scale item	Mean difference†	$t^{\ddagger}$
Can be pushed around	−1.12	5.77
Takes life too seriously	−1.07	4.86
Enthusiastic about his work	1.01	4.02
Shy	−0.64	3.76
Energetic, lots of drive	0.38	2.26
Sticks to company rules	−0.18	0.89

* All workers participating in post-experimental research included, although ten were not involved in the experiment proper.

† *Positive differences* indicate respondent gives higher score to first-choice foreman and lower score to last-choice foreman in response to the item; thus showing approval of this characteristic in foreman. *Negative differences* indicate respondent gives higher score to last-choice foreman and lower score to first-choice foreman; thus showing disapproval of this characteristic in the foreman.

‡ Last scale item not significant. All other scale items significant beyond 0.05 level by both one- and two-tail test standards. (Critical values = 1.67 and 1.29 respectively. All *t*'s calculated using formula for correlated measures.)

Procedures Employed in Factor Analysis of Foreman-Personality Descriptions

The factor analysis was carried out at the Cornell Computing Center using the FACTESSO program available in the Center's program library. This program performs principal component analysis, factor analysis, and determines the communalities to be inserted in the matrix for the factor analysis. The factor analysis solution may be rotated according to either the raw varimax or the normal varimax criterion. The researcher decides the angle of rotation.

All provisions of the program were employed. The product-moment correlation coefficients (using difference scores as variables, see Chapter 4) were factored by the principal-components method, using unities in the diagonal of the correlation matrix. This resulted in a general factor accounting for 27 per cent of the variance, although eleven factors with eigenvalues over 1.00 were obtained, accounting for 75.3 per cent of the variance. However, the first five factors, all with eigenvalues greater than two, accounted for 54 per cent of the variance. In the subsequent factor analysis, in which fewer factors were extracted, a general factor accounting for 32 per cent of the obtained communality emerged in the unrotated solution. In this attempt, seven factors with eigenvalues over 1.00 were obtained in the characteristic roots matrix; the first five factors had loadings greater than 0.30 on more than three variables. The five factors were subjected to a normal varimax rotation (arcsin 0.25).

The communalities employed in the factor analysis and subsequent varimax rotation were calculated by the FACTESSO program; this program used the squared multiple-correlation coefficient as the first communality estimate and factor analyses were carried out with new estimates of communalities being obtained until the communalities converged (criteria 0.01) after the seventh iteration.

Four of the five factors appeared to have reasonable structures. However, factor four did not appear to have unique items. The entire procedure, heretofore described, was repeated for four factors. Again, a general factor appeared. However, normal varimax rotation (arcsin 0.25) produced the factor loadings shown in Table 13, Chapter 4.

Development and Reliability Analysis
of Money-Motivation Index

The money-motivation variable was measured a year before the foreman change by having each worker describe on a seven-point scale "the amount of money you can make" on his first-choice upholstering line and his last-choice line. Table J summarizes the t-test results, showing the extent to which each group's members discriminated perceptually on this scale between their most- and least-preferred work groups. (See Chapter 3 for methodological details and Appendix A for the questionnaire item.) The reader can see in Table J that some groups seemed to discriminate more on "amount of money you can make" than other groups did. Line C, for example, has a t of 2.47, while line E has one of only 1.06. Thus, line C appears to be the most money-oriented or motivated and line E the least. The groups were *ranked* on the basis of these t-test results; a large t being ranked 1 (highly money-motivated) and the smallest t being ranked 7. The same procedure was followed in analyzing the workers' post-experimental ratings on the same item. The pre- and post-experimental rankings were then analyzed by Spearman's Rho technique. The result was a stability reliability coefficient of .79. The pre-experimental measure was used as an indirect measure of energy mobilization in the systems-equilibrium analysis described in Chapter 5.

Table J. Pre-experimental money-motivation
index (*t*) and *N* for each group

t and *N*	Group						
	B	C	D	E	F	G	H
t	1.91*	2.47*	1.60*	1.06	2.07*	1.84*	1.58*
N	10	10	9	8	9	10	8

* Significant beyond .05 level, one-tail test, repeated measurement.

Bibliography

Argyle, M., *et al.* The measurement of supervisory methods. *Hum. Relat.*, 1957, 10, 295–313.

Argyris, C. Diagnosing defenses against the outsider. *J. soc. Issues*, 1952, 8 (3), 24–34.

Bass, B. M. *Leadership, psychology, and organizational behavior.* New York: Harper, 1960.

Block, J., and Block, Jeanne. An interpersonal experiment on reactions to authority. In McClelland, D. (ed.). *Studies in motivation.* New York: Appleton-Century-Crofts, 1955.

Brayfield, A. H., and Crockett, W. H. Employee attitudes and employee performance. *Psychol. Bull.*, 1955, 52, 396–424.

Burton, Virginia. *Mike Mulligan and his steam shovel.* Boston: Houghton-Mifflin, 1939.

Cantor, R. R., Jr. An experimental study of a human relations training program. *J. appl. Psychol.*, 1951, 35, 38–45.

Coch, L., and French, J. R., Jr. Overcoming resistance to change. *Hum. Relat.*, 1948, 1, 512–532.

Cook, D. L. The Hawthorne effect in educational research. *Phi Delta Kappan*, 1962, Dec., 116–122.

Dubin, R., *et al. Leadership and productivity.* San Francisco: Chandler Pub., 1965.

Dunnette, M., and Heneman, H. Influence of scale administrator on employee attitude responses. *J. appl. Psychol.*, 1956, 40, 73–77.

Feldman, H. *Problems in labor relations.* New York: Macmillan, 1937.

Fiedler, F. E. A contingency model of leadership effectiveness. In Berkowitz, L. (ed.). *Advances in experimental social psychology, 1.* New York: Academic Press, 1964.

Heslin, R., and Dunphy, D. Three dimensions of member satisfaction in small groups. *Hum. Relat.*, 1964, 17, 99–112.

Jackson, J. M. The effect of changing the leadership of small work groups. *Hum. Relat.*, 1953, 6, 25–44.

Kahn, R. L., and Katz, D. Leadership practises in relation to productivity and morale. In Cartwright, D., and Zander, A. (eds.). *Group dynamics.* (2nd ed.). New York: Harper and Row, 1960.

Katz, D., and Kahn, R. L. *The social psychology of organizations.* New York: Wiley, 1966.

Katzell, R. Contrasting systems of work organization. *Amer. Psychologist,* 1962, 17, 102–109.

Kendall, Patricia, and Lazersfeld, P. F. Problems of survey analysis. In Merton, R., and Lazersfeld, P. F. (eds.). *Continuities in social research.* Glencoe, Ill.: Free Press, 1950.

Klein, S. M., *et al.* Differences between identified and anonymous subjects in responding to an industrial opinion survey. *J. appl. Psychol.,* 1967, 51, 152–160.

Krech, D., *et al. Individual in society.* New York: McGraw-Hill, 1962.

Likert, R. *New patterns of management.* New York: McGraw-Hill, 1961.

McKeachie, W. J. Research on teaching at the college and university level. In Gage, N. (ed.). *Handbook of research on teaching.* Chicago: Rand-McNally, 1963.

Melbin, M. Organizational practice and individual behavior: Absenteeism among psychiatric aides. *Amer. soc. Rev.,* 1961, 26, 14–23.

Morse, Nancy, and Reimer, E. The experimental change of a major organizational variable. *J. abnorm. soc. Psychol.,* 1956, 52, 120–129.

Nord, W. R. A field experiment on Hawthorne effect and psychological demand characteristics. Unpub. M.S. thesis, New York State School of Industrial and Labor Relations, Cornell University, 1963.

Orne, M. The demand characteristics of an experimental design and their implications. In *The problem of experimenter bias.* Symposium presented at American Psychological Association, Cincinnati, 1959.

——. On the social psychology of the psychological experiment: With particular reference to demand characteristics and their implications. *Amer. Psychologist*, 1962, 17, 776–783.

Pelz, D. C. Leadership within a hierarchal organization. *J. soc. Issues*, 1951, 7 (3), 49–55.

——. The influence of anonymity on expressed attitudes. *Hum. Org.*, 1959, 18, 88–91.

Pryer, Margaret, *et al.* Group effectiveness and consistency of leadership. *Sociometry*, 1962, 25, 391–397.

Remmers, H. H. *Introduction to opinion and attitude measurement.* New York: Harper, 1954.

Richardson, F. L. W. *Talk, work and action.* Monograph of the Society for Applied Anthropology, no. 3. Ithaca, N.Y.: New York State School of Industrial and Labor Relations, Cornell University, 1961.

Roethlisberger, F. J., and Dickson, W. J. *Management and the worker.* Cambridge: Harvard University Press, 1947.

Rosen, N. A. Anonymity and attitude measurement. *Pub. opin. Quart.*, 1960, 24, 675–679.

——, and Sales, S. M. Behavior in a non-experiment: The effects of behavioral field research on the work performance of factory workers. *J. appl. Psychol.*, 1966, 50, 165–171.

Rosenthal, R. Experimenter attributes as determinants of subjects' responses. *J. proj. Techs.*, 1963, 27, 324–331.

Schachter, S., *et al.* Emotional disruption and productivity. *J. appl. Psychol.*, 1961, 45, 201–213.

Scott, W. R. Field work in a formal organization: Some dilemmas in the role of observer. *Hum. Org.*, 1963, 22, 162–168.

Seashore, S. E. *Group cohesiveness in the industrial work group.* Ann Arbor: Institute for Social Research, 1954.

Selltiz, Claire, *et al. Research methods in social relations.* New York: Holt, Rinehart and Winston, 1961.

Sherif, M. A. A study of some factors in perception. *Arch. Psychol.*, 1935, no. 185.

Stagner, R. Homeostasis as a unifying concept in personality theory. *Psychol. Rev.*, 1951, 58, 5–17.

Strauss, G., and Sayles, L. *Personnel: The human problems of management.* Englewood Cliffs, N.J.: Prentice-Hall, 1960.

Thibaut, J. W., and Kelley, H. H. *The social psychology of groups.* New York: Wiley, 1959.

Vidich, A., and Bensman, J. Validity of field data. In Adams, R. N., and Preiss, J. J. (eds.). *Human organization research.* Homewood, Ill.: Dorsey, 1960.

Viteles, M. S. *Motivation and morale in industry.* New York: Norton, 1953.

Vroom, V. H. Some personality determinants of the effects of participation. *J. abnorm. soc. Psychol.,* 1959, 59, 322–327.

——. *Work and motivation.* New York: Wiley, 1964.

——, and Mann, F. C. Leader authoritarianism and employee attitudes. *Personnel Psychol.,* 1960, 13, 125–140.

Whyte, W. F. *Money and motivation.* New York: Harper, 1955.

Winer, B. J. *Statistical principles in experimental design.* New York: McGraw-Hill, 1962.

Wolman, B. B. Impact of failure on group cohesiveness. *J. soc. Psychol.,* 1960, 51, 409–418.

Index